JG MONTGOMERY

HAUNTED AUSTRALIA

GHOSTS OF THE GREAT SOUTHERN LAND

Schiffer Publishing Ltd

4880 Lower Valley Road · Atglen, PA 19310

Other Schiffer Books by JG Montgomery

Haunted Britain: Supernatural Realms of the United Kingdom.
ISBN: 978-0-7643-5165-5

Other Schiffer Books on Related Subjects:

Ghosts in the Cemetery II: Farther Afield. Stuart Schneider.
ISBN: 978-0-7643-3590-7

Haunted Closets: True Tales of "The Boogeyman." Katie Boyd.
ISBN: 978-0-7643-3474-0

Tales From Beyond: Deadly Fortune, The Attic, Unbreakable. Written, directed, and produced by Kevin Herren and Jim O'Rear. Starring: Kyle Hebert, Mary Elizabeth McGlynn, Jim O'Rear, Robert Picardo, Daniel Roebuck, and Betsy Rue.
ISBN: 978-0-7643-4762-7

Grim Shadows Falling: Haunting Tales from Terrifying Places. Benjamin S. Jeffries.
ISBN: 978-0-7643-4708-5

Designed by Brenda McCallum
Cover design by Matt Goodman
Type set in MasonSans/Times

ISBN: 978-0-7643-5228-7
Printed in China

Published by Schiffer Publishing, Ltd.
4880 Lower Valley Road
Atglen, PA 19310
Phone: (610) 593-1777; Fax: (610) 593-2002
E-mail: Info@schifferbooks.com
Web: www.schifferbooks.com

For our complete selection of fine books on this and related subjects, please visit our website at www.schifferbooks.com. You may also write for a free catalog.

Schiffer Publishing's titles are available at special discounts for bulk purchases for sales promotions or premiums. Special editions, including personalized covers, corporate imprints, and excerpts, can be created in large quantities for special needs. For more information, contact the publisher.

We are always looking for people to write books on new and related subjects. If you have an idea for a book, please contact us at proposals@schifferbooks.com.

To my mother, Jill,
without whom none of this would have been possible.

contents

Epigraph

"She'll cross the moonlit road in haste
And vanish down the track;
Her long black hair hangs to her waist
And she is dressed in black;
Her face is white, a dull dead white
Her eyes are opened wide
She never looks to left or right,
Or turns to either side."

I didn't b'lieve in ghosts at all,
Tho' I was rather young,
But still I wished with all my heart
That Jack would hold his tongue.
The time and place, as you will say,
('Twas twelve o'clock almost)
Were both historically favourable,
for a ghost.

But have you seen the Second Bridge
Beneath the "Camel's Back"?
It fills a gap that broke the ridge
When convicts made the track;
And o'er the right old Hartley Vale
In homely beauty lies,
And o'er the left the mighty walls
Of Mount Victoria rise.

And there's a spot above the bridge,
Just where the track is steep,
From which poor Convict Govett rode
To christen Govett's Leap;
And here a teamster killed his wife—
For those old days were rough—
And here a dozen others had
Been murdered, right enough.

The lonely moon was over all
And she was shining well,
At angles from the sandstone wall
The shifting moonbeams fell.
In short, the shifting moonbeams beamed,
The air was still as death,
Save when the listening silence seemed
To speak beneath its breath.

The tangled bushes were not stirred
Because there was no wind,
But now and then I thought I heard
A startling noise behind.
Then Johnny Jones began to quake;
His face was like the dead.
"Don't look behind, for heaven's sake!
The ghost is there!" he said.

Extract from "The Ghost at the Second Bridge"
(Henry Lawson, 1891)

Thoughts on the Supernatural

Now I know what a ghost is. Unfinished business, that's what.
—Salman Rushdie, *The Satanic Verses*

This book is my fourth in a line of books I have written regarding the paranormal and supernatural. My first book on the subject, *A Case for Ghosts,* was published in 2012 and, although exploring a large number of Australian hauntings, also looked at numerous cases in the United Kingdom and the United States of America. As well, it tended to examine each case and put forward a rational explanation as to what had been reported, even though, in most cases a rational explanation was not forthcoming.

I wrote about a number of the sites I had visited and indeed, even stayed in haunted premises, and, in a few cases, experienced some strange phenomena, some of which I could explain and some I could not. Indeed, in my capacity as a cultural historian, I attempted to take the reader on a social, historical, and cultural journey of supernatural discovery where they (the reader) could examine and question what I heard, saw, and experienced.

In the book I looked at the ghosts of Australia's convict past at Port Arthur as well as spectral prime ministers in Canberra. I travelled to the wilds of Bodmin Moor and the Jamaica Inn in Cornwall as well as to the brooding serenity of Woodchester Mansion in leafy Gloucestershire. I sat in haunted pubs and walked the ancient battlegrounds of the English countryside in my quest to find out more. I talked to people who witnessed what they thought were ghosts, and I read through countless newspaper reports and books gathering more and more information so as to come to some sort of conclusion as to *what is a ghost*, something I think I am still discovering.

I examined other phenomenon relating to the subject such as psychics, mediums, out of body experiences, folklore, evolution, and religion, all being included to form a rich tapestry of experiences that appeared to lead to the conclusion that ghosts and ghostly encounters must be true, or at least, can conceivably be true.

From an early age I had a fascination with ghosts and all things supernatural, including UFOs, Bigfoot, the Loch Ness Monster, and other supernatural or paranormal subjects. As a child living in England, I visited numerous old castles and ruins, places that seemed to have a strange feeling, a feeling that one cannot quite explain or understand, and this, with my love of history is why ghosts now captivate me.

In England I was lucky enough to be able to wander pretty much anywhere I wanted to. My parents were of the opinion that I could look after myself and that I could find my own amusements. As such I found the countryside to be a playground with amazing things, such as old World War II airfields and bomb shelters, now abandoned and overgrown, disused train stations complete with platforms but no tracks, small frog ponds hidden in ancient green forests, and old abandoned houses. What did the pea soup fogs of the Lincolnshire countryside hide? What creatures lurked in the dark in the woods? Did Roman ghosts still tread wearily on old Roman roads that ran across the commons?

Later in life I attended an old boarding school in Victoria, Australia, which was reputed to be haunted by the ghost of a young schoolboy who died from fever in the early 1900s. At night, when it was deathly quiet, disembodied footsteps were often heard by the students, and faint organ music would sometimes float from the unattended chapel. Were these signs of ghosts? Or were they simply an overactive imagination, a result of suggestion?

And one could add, when I lived in the USA, I had the chance to visit the eerie and ominous cornfields of Gettysburg where the corn stalks bobbed in the soft summer breeze and whispered voices could be heard. Was this proof of an afterlife? Or again, was the wind simply playing tricks with my mind?

How do we explain these strange occurrences? How is it that so many people with no connection to each other and over such a length of time report such similar ghostly happenings? The Tower of London, the Flying Dutchman, the Spaniard's Inn, the White House or Monte Cristo? Surely all these witnesses cannot have invented the almost exact same story every time over a period of years and years? Or does this fact legitimise their experiences and prove that ghosts do exist?

Or is it something else? Are we predisposed to believe in ghosts, or even hardwired to see them? Are the imaginary friends of our childhood really imaginary, or are they in facts ghosts, entities that we as adults have somehow lost the ability to see? And if this is so, can we suggest that mediums and psychics still possess this ability to see and converse with spirits?

My second book on the subject delved further into the murky world of the supernatural and paranormal, including cryptozoology, demonology, witchcraft, mythology, and folklore, including fairies, giants, standing stones, and numerous strange phenomena reported over the years by countless thousands of witnesses.

It also contained a chapter on ghosts, specifically, English castles and sites, and in it I described an encounter I had in the Hellfire Caves of Buckinghamshire, an encounter that, to this day, I cannot explain. I also recounted a strange and slightly unnerving experience I had in the London Dungeons, again, something I simply cannot explain.

In addition, over the years I have also looked at personal experiences as well as compiled hundreds of reports of supernatural activity in the United Kingdom from the Tower of London to Glastonbury to Scottish Graveyards and Welsh hotels. It also looked at ghostly devil dogs and other animal ghosts plus some extremely strange encounters that one could suggest might just lie outside the real definition of a ghost, but nevertheless, almost seem to fit the pattern.

I am what one could describe as a sceptical believer in that, although I believe in ghosts and the supernatural, I like to think that there is a rational explanation for most occurrences. Many have commented that, after reading *Ghosts*, I am much more sceptical than they expected. This statement is true. When I started to write *Ghosts* I was convinced that pretty much all reported ghostly activity was in fact the result of genuine paranormal activity. However, over time and after delving deeper into the subject, I came to realise that most phenomena can be explained by simple means and that they are no more supernatural than the workings of a computer.

However, even if one is to discount ninety percent of sightings or reports of ghosts or ghostly phenomena, then we are left with the sobering fact that there are still literally thousands and thousands of reports that cannot be explained. This begs the question, what is it that we are really dealing with?

Whereas in my first book I took a philosophical approach to examining the phenomena from all angles, in this book I intend more to cover a wide variety of ghosts, apparitions, spirits, and hauntings without attempting to explain in detail what could be the cause of the happenings. Rather, I intend to present the stories, legends, and tales to the reader and allow them to make up their own minds. And if the reader wishes to do so, they may visit the places that I have written about and see for themselves what all the fuss is about.

As such, I hope that this book will shed just a little more light on the subject and, through it, allow for more research into the topic—and just as importantly, an open mind into the subject.

Of course, for most people, the word "ghost" conjures up images of moss-encrusted tombstones and white wispy figures that float around lonely castles and graveyards in England and other European places. However, as this book will show, Australia, while lacking castles and medieval graveyards, has a rich heritage of ghost stories and supernatural incidents that more than reflect the country's harsh convict past—and, if anything, forces us to reflect upon this history.

J G Montgomery
Canberra 2016

CHAPTER ONE

The Australian Capital Territory

Of National Institutions, Politics, and a Haunted Military Academy

As I trudge uphill towards Weetangera Cemetery I am reminded that it's been the coldest winter in Canberra for over forty years. Beneath my feet the grass is crisp and white and crunches, and my breath is evident from the clouds of condensation that appear with every breath. Above is a crystal clear sky filled with a myriad of sparkling stars.

I open an old rusted gate and pass beneath two towering pine trees that mark the entrance to the cemetery. Under the pines it is dark and quiet, and one feels a chill run up their spine. I switch on my torch and shine it around. All is silent and still. There is nothing here but the long dead bodies of pioneers and farmers.

As I step out of the shadow of the pines I notice that the moon is full and its eerie grey light shines down upon the handful of old headstones that have stood for a hundred or so years in this lonely rural paddock. I hear a noise and my heart skips a beat. Turning around, I shine the torch into the distance only to see a large kangaroo that is looking back at me with a slightly quizzical look. There has been precious little change to this cemetery in the past century, apart from a small wooden chapel that was demolished in the 1970s.

I have visited this quaint little cemetery on numerous occasions, both at night and during the day, but apart from some vague reports of some sort of unseen presence, there is little here to interest a serious ghost hunter. However, just recently I have been made aware of something strange apparently happening along the road that runs past the site.

According to reports, people have witnessed the ghostly figure of a tall, thin man in old-style clothes, sometimes in a hat, sometimes not, walking either along the road or across it, depending upon reports, who then completely vanishes. Of course, one could point out that this is simply a pedestrian, but the area where he is seen has no nearby houses and there is no reason why someone would walk across the road at this point.

Interestingly, a couple of my friends visited this cemetery a few years ago to take photographs and whilst there felt a sense of unease and trepidation as if something was watching them. Rather than hang around, they decided to leave and later relayed to me that they felt as if something was following them.

However, as interesting as this is, why would a quaint rural cemetery on the outskirts of suburbia be haunted? After all, why would a ghost be in a graveyard in the first place, as a graveyard or cemetery is simply a repository for the dead, and ghosts are traditionally supposed to haunt the places where they die?

The inhabitants of this old cemetery have now been dead and forgotten for over a hundred years. They were some of the first settlers in this area and their headstones are a tangible reminder of Canberra's recent rural past. Surely they are now at rest? But what of the tall, thin man that apparently stalks the nearby road?

A report in the local newspaper, the *Canberra Times*, of 17 May 2014, suggests that a woman by the name of Liz Stergiou first reported the apparition in early 2014, describing it as "an old slim tall man that appears with a haze." She also stated that she had "seen him twice just after the 90km/h sign when heading city-bound."

Local identity "Tim the Yowie Man" also noted in his weekly newspaper column that a Margaret McLeod reported that "last year I was driving home along William Hovell (Drive) at around 10:00 p.m., and just as I got towards the bend in the road with a stand of big trees on the left, I saw the figure of someone start to loom." She added that he "appeared to be in a big black coat with a hat and didn't appear old or slim." Concerned that whoever it was could be hit by a car, she rang the police who said they had received quite a number of similar calls.

So, is our ghostly apparition simply a late-night visitor to the cemetery? Perhaps a relative paying respects, or a night-time photographer, like my friends? Whatever the case, I am out of luck and apart from seeing another kangaroo, I see nothing of note and so decide to retreat back to the warmth of my car.

Tonight I may have failed in my attempt to catch a glimpse of the Weetangera ghost but tall ghosts in top hats are not unheard of. At Collector, just north of Canberra, the ghost of a man dressed in all black and wearing a top hat is said to occasionally appear. Interestingly, this apparition has also been seen walking along the shorelines of Lake George, as well as at Bungendore to Canberra's east, and even on the outskirts of Queanbeyan.

As a result, we must ask, is this ghostly figure one and same? Is it possible for a ghost to appear in many different places, or are they tied to a certain site—for instance, a graveyard, church, gaol, or whatever? Although beyond the scope of this book, I have found in previous research that yes, it is possible for a ghost to appear in numerous places as is evident by sightings of Anne Boleyn whose ghost has been reported at Hever Castle in Kent, Blickling Hall in Norfolk and the Tower of London where she was executed in 1536.

In addition, Sir Walter Raleigh, the English soldier, poet, courtier, and explorer who was well known for introducing tobacco into England has also been seen at the Tower of London, the Old Palace Yard at Westminster, and a church at Beddington. Another case of multiple sighting of a ghost is that of Dirk Turpin, the infamous English highwayman of the 1700s, who has been seen from the Spaniards Inn in London to Hampstead Heath, Epping Forest, and Hounslow Heath, the site of Heathrow Airport.

Given this, it does appear that ghosts can appear in a number of places rather than simply haunt a specific area, and so it is little wonder that people report the same thing. Having said this, how does one differentiate between tall, dark figures in hats late at night along lonely stretches of roads? Indeed, as the Collector ghost has been sighted at Bungendore, it would seem prudent to suggest that a famous photograph taken in 1949 at the Royal Hotel, which seemingly shows the upper torso and face of a man, could be the same entity. As the photo is in sepia tones, it is almost impossible to tell what colour the actual hat is, although one could conclude, as was the fashion of the times, that it was probably brown and, looking at the photograph, one gets the impression that it is of a different person than that described alongside the roads that lead to the small village.

As such, as much as we can say that ghosts appear to be able to move around, the Collector ghost and the Bungendore ghost are not the same, and, as interesting as the accounts are, I have not heard of any recent reports of either ghost. However, this is not to say that this region is devoid of ghosts; in fact, if anything, it would appear that the Canberra region can pretty much match anywhere in Australia for strange tales of spooks and apparitions.

Westbourne Woods lie roughly in the centre of Canberra and surround the Royal Canberra golf course. They are, like most things in Canberra, only a recent addition to the landscape being planted some 100 years previous. And yet there are tales of ghostly figures appearing in the dark and tangled undergrowth; indeed, legend tells of the ghost of an Aboriginal boy who haunts this place as well as the governor-general's residence, which also borders the woods.

As well, nestled quietly in these woods is the Yarralumla Brickworks, one of the earliest construction projects in Canberra and built to produce bricks for many of Canberra's early buildings. Opened in 1913, it remained in operation until 1976 and is now closed to the public due to safety concerns. At night it sits silently and ominously in between the pine trees, a sad and neglected reminder of our recent past, now decaying away due to a lack of political will or enthusiasm for built heritage. It is a very spooky place and stories abound of ghostly figures moving in the shadows and between the lonely and derelict buildings.

But is this place really haunted, or do we as humans simply have a fear of the dark and the unknown that manifests itself in a belief that something is out there in the dark, something unexplainable, something of a supernatural or paranormal origin? The old brickworks have been abandoned for a long time and the wind whistles around the neglected buildings sounding like the shrieks of souls lost or stuck in hell. At times it is easy to believe a place is haunted, even if it isn't a majestic medieval stone building in England or Wales.

Having said that, All Saints Church, in the sleepy suburbs of inner Canberra, is a quaint limestone building and seems very much in the tradition of medieval churches. Built in the 1860s it was originally the Rookwood Cemetery funeral train station in Sydney although it fell into disrepair in the 1920s and was then transported to Canberra, stone by stone, in 1957.

And, being a former cemetery station, it is reputed to be haunted.

I have visited the church on numerous occasions and, except for late at night when the suburbs are quiet and the street lights struggle to illuminate the surrounding houses and roads, it doesn't really appear haunted. True, I have never been in the building alone at night but the question still remains, who or what haunts this delightful building? And if it really is haunted, then where do the ghosts come from?

Are the reported spirits of this building a recent phenomenon from its days as a peaceful Anglican church? Or are they ghosts from the old Rookwood cemetery who have been unwillingly transported from their previous hauntings to Canberra?

Given that there is a school of thought that ghosts and apparitions are some sort of built up residual energy over time, then we must suspect that the ghosts of All Saints Church are the latter, that is, a collective energy that has somehow been transported from Rookwood in Sydney to this new site in Canberra. Of course, this suggests that ghosts are not permanent and can move about. Is it possible that, odd as it seems, ghosts can be a part of the building or building fabric itself? That they are connected not to a certain place, but a certain building?

Of course, we can never know although this does help explain a theory that suggests that ghosts may be recordings of past events made by the physical environment. This hypothesis about residual hauntings has since been called the stone tape theory and in many ways, makes a lot of sense.

Put simply, the theory notes that often ghosts or apparitions behave like recordings in that they repeat their actions time and time again over a long period of time without ever deviating away from the original sighting. In addition, the ghost shows no acknowledgment of its surroundings, environment, or even people around it and at times appears to be in a completely different building or environment to the one that currently exists. For example, they walk through walls or appear only from the waist up, suggesting that many years ago the building may have had a different configuration.

In essence the stone tape theory puts forward the idea that, just like a magnetic recording tape, stones can somehow store information that at some time in the future can be replayed and viewed by a witness. This means that when we replay a music tape, we hear music, and when we replay a stone, we see an event being repeated from history, in that a place can somehow record certain snippets of history and replay them at a later date under certain atmospheric conditions.

Of course, we have no idea how this happens, or even if this is what is happening and, as such, is open to interpretation. For one, we have no idea how to turn the recording on or off. Secondly, not all ghosts or hauntings happen in this way, which suggests that this is only one sort of ghost and that there may be others who act in different ways. Thirdly, we really have no idea if a stone can record events that have occurred throughout history, and if they could, then why record only a certain sliver of this history?

Sometimes a person will enter an abandoned building or even a room and feel as if there is some sort of unexplained ambience or feeling to the place. Quite often we find that these buildings have been associated with large gatherings of people in an emotional state, for instance, a wake, a funeral, a wedding, or something similar. If these areas have been used for a specific purpose for decades, then is it not possible that the emotions expressed can somehow be absorbed by the actual building itself and, over time, gather more energy until it becomes strong enough to be able to be felt by visitors, and in some cases, manifest itself as some sort of conglomeration of energy, emotions, and feelings and thoughts. And if so, would this be what we consider to be a ghost in the traditional sense?

Of course, there does appear to be many different types of ghosts and this is something we will look at further, however, at this stage, we are talking about All Saints Church and the stone tape theory of ghosts.

Can it be that the souls of the dead, from many years ago, and from another place, have somehow become trapped within the stone of All Saints Church? And if so, where else in Canberra can we find evidence of this sort of haunting?

The Air Disaster Memorial, behind Mount Ainslie, is also reputed to be haunted. Stories abound of cars losing power and failing to start, torch lights failing, whispered voices, ghostly airmen and nurses, strange human-shaped shadows that lurk in the trees, and most oddly, cars rolling uphill of their own accord.

The memorial itself sits in a pine plantation on the eastern edge of Canberra, and even during the day it is rather unnerving and spooky. Surrounded by thick vegetation, the memorial is simply a large rock sitting on a round bed of gravel. Attached to the rock is a plaque dedicated to the dead.

In August 1940, just after the start of the Second World War, a Royal Australian Air Force Lockheed Hudson bomber stalled and crashed into the mountain killing three cabinet ministers, the chief of the general staff, and another six RAAF crew members. Emergency crews were on the scene within minutes, but there was nothing anyone could do and all were presumed killed instantly.

One of the stories associated with this site is that, if your car stops on the cattle grid near the memorial, a ghostly nurse, who was supposedly present after the aircraft crash, will coming running from the forest and try to get into the car as if to rescue the passengers. The legend even goes as far as suggesting that she has smashed windows to get into the car, believing them to be part of the Hudson crash. Having said this, no nurse ever died in the rescue attempt, and, as far as I can ascertain, no World War II nurse has ever died on Mount Ainslie.

Of course, if we are to follow the stone tape theory of hauntings, then it is possible that there was a nurse involved in the rescue attempt, and the whole thing was so traumatic that somehow she left some emotional remnant of herself at the site, and somehow this now manifests itself as a ghostly figure.

Another story suggests that a young girl was once found dead under a nearby cattle grid and she can sometimes be seen lying on her back, her pitiful eyes staring up at startled witnesses. Of course, there are no reports of any girls being found dead under cattle grids, so it is doubtful that she even existed, thus the whole story is urban legend rather than supernatural.

Still, one must wonder about the ten men killed in that fiery inferno in 1940. Could it be possible that the reports of supernatural and odd events at the site are a direct result of these tragic deaths so many years ago? Do the spirits of these men haunt the pine forests and lonely dirt roads that lead to the memorial and give rise to the stories associated with the place—stories of whispering voices, disembodied footsteps, strange lights that fly around the memorial, photos that contain numerous orbs, ghostly sightings of men in old style flight overalls, screaming voices, and even apparitions that appear to follow tour groups?

And yet, probably the most disturbing of these stories is that of the twenty-year-old Keren Rowland, who was murdered in 1971 and whose decomposing body was later found close to the memorial itself. According to reports, her ghost has been seen standing on the edge of a clearing, a brown sepia image that people have described accurately as her, even down to such details as having her hair pulled back, something she rarely did, but had done so on the day of her death.

But Canberra is an interesting place and the Air Disaster Memorial is not alone in supernatural or ghostly occurrences. In fact, it seems that Canberra has a great deal more paranormal occurrences than one would suspect from such a modern city.

The Hotel Kurrajong is a delightful heritage listed hotel in the comfortable suburb of Barton. It is close to Parliament House and the national institutions within the Parliamentary Triangle precinct. Built between 1925 and 1927 as a hostel for public servants, it was designed as an example of the Garden Pavilion style in keeping with Walter Burley Griffin's garden city concept for the capital.

Apart from that it was the residence of Ben Chifley, the Australian prime minister from 1945 until 1949 and the place of his death from a fatal heart attack at age sixty-four in 1951. Today, guests often report seeing the ghostly figure of a man in a grey suit either looking or pointing towards the old Parliament House. Others have reported cold spots that seem to randomly move around the very room he died in.

Could it be that Chifley's ghost is unable to let go of the past? Did he die a broken man with unfinished business and unfulfilled dreams? Did he believe so passionately in his calling that his ghost now haunts room 205 hoping for one last chance to lead?

Only a short journey from the Kurrajong is the equally delightful Hyatt Hotel, another Canberra landmark building and one with its own tales of ghostly happenings.

The Hyatt is an exceptional example of Australian art deco architecture and was built between 1922 and 1925 in the now lake-side suburb of Yarralumla. It was built to house politicians when the Federal Parliament moved to Canberra from Melbourne in 1927, and, by the 1950s it was the centre of the capital's social life. Today it remains one of the city's most prestigious addresses, and like the Kurrajong, it is a magnificent white building with a red tiled roof and was also frequented by politicians and prime ministers alike. Indeed, Prime Minister James Scullin and his wife resided at the hotel during parliamentary sessions. However, unlike the Kurrajong, the Hyatt is not known for its ghostly prime ministers; instead, it has a range of spectral inhabitants that would make an English castle jealous.

Guests and staff members, current and past, have reported rooms where strange things happen, such as taps turning themselves on and off, feelings of being watched by an unknown presence, and ghostly footsteps. Others have reported seeing the apparition of a young girl with wavy dark brown hair and a long elegant dress who stands alone in a corridor before vanishing into thin air. It is rumoured that she is a young girl who died in the late 1920s after drowning or being suffocated by her parents.

In addition, in 1997, a staff member was shocked to find a complete apparition after going to investigate the sounds of partying in the hotel's deserted ballroom at 2:00 a.m., while in the Oak Room, during refurbishment, painters often complained about paint tins being tipped over, lights mysteriously turning themselves on and off, and chandeliers violently shaking. Indeed, one contractor even claimed that he heard a voice telling him to leave the room and not continue with the work. Even today staff claim to hear whispering and faint laughter in the room, especially when setting up for a function.

As well, in the old boiler room, now converted to a wine cellar, staff have reported being surprised by the apparition of a young girl in a red dress who runs past them. It has been suggested that she is the ghost of a caretaker's daughter and was scalded to death.

But if a grand old art deco hotel with decades of human interaction can be haunted, what about smaller, much more insignificant structures? Indeed, what about farm outbuildings?

Kambah Woolshed is another physical link back to Canberra's past. It sits quietly in suburbia, only a few hundred metres from a major road with a car park, BBQs, and crunchy red gravel paths. Many years ago it was a shearing shed with corrugated iron walls and roof and roughly hewn beams, but these days the walls are long gone and it is simply a suburban picnic site.

It does not appear haunted in any way although I keep hearing reports of ghostly screams and howls and the occasional frightening shadow.

Although the woolshed was part of a working sheep station up until 1971, it has been suggested that it once also housed convicts and that executions took place within its walls. Not surprisingly, I can find no evidence of convicts being imprisoned in the building, although I don't doubt that some may have worked there. As for the executions, this is simply a fabrication, and sadly, I find it hard to believe that this quiet little tin shed is haunted by anything more than the odd stray dog or cat.

Still, if one is to visit the building at night they could find it a little unnerving. The car park is deserted and the noise from cars on the nearby major road are muffled and somehow far away. As you walk up to the dark building your feet crunch quietly in the soft gravel and the wind makes an eerie noise in the exposed beams. Is it possible that I have underestimated this place? Is it possible that the spirit of a shearer still haunts the old structure? Looking around, I can imagine the place in its heyday, bustling with tough, lean, hard drinking shearers in singlets, swearing and sweating as they shear. But these men are not ghosts; they are history. Which begs the question: are ghosts simply history? Or is history somehow inextricably tied up in ghosts and the supernatural? And if this place is not haunted, then surely there must be somewhere else that I can examine?

Not far to the south of the woolshed is Lanyon homestead, a delightful mid-1800s homestead with superb gardens, courtyards, and out buildings, and sitting serenely in the shadow of the majestic Brindabella ranges. Originally settled by James Wright in the 1830s, it grew rapidly, employing up to thirty convicts at one stage, and by the late-1880s, it carried over 25,000 sheep, a huge amount even today.

It is a museum today and is managed by the Australian Capital Territory government and the National Trust and holds the culturally significant Sidney Nolan Gallery, which opened to the public in 1975. In 2003, it was seriously threatened by the huge bushfires that ripped through the region; however, it was saved by a single fire-truck at the time. It is, without doubt, a wonderful place, and I spent many a long hour there while studying at university towards qualifications in cultural heritage management.

However, even with such a rich history, is it haunted? Do unknown entities sweep noiselessly down its elegant corridors? Do the immaculate pebbled yards crunch with disembodied footsteps?

Sadly, when I approached staff at the homestead and asked about ghosts and supernatural activity within the place I was given a terse and abrupt answer in the negative. Apparently, according to them, it is all made up by a disgruntled staff member and is completely and utterly untrue. Who knew that governments were into suppressing stories of the supernatural that may or may not occur on their premises?

And yet, for all these denials, I seem to receive quite a few reports of ghostly activities at the homestead. Indeed it has been suggested to me by none other than Tim the Yowie Man, among others, that there is considerable poltergeist-like activity in the stately house, mainly it seems in the dining room. In fact, apart from stories of items mysteriously moving or even disappearing, Tim states that he witnessed some activity with his own eye, that is, cutlery moving by its own accord.

Just south of the homestead is the Lanyon cemetery where it is believed that the body of William Wright was buried, weighed down with large stones to protect the body from being dug up and torn to pieces by dingos. William was the brother of James Wright, who settled at Lanyon in 1833; and Jane Cunningham, who tragically died from a ruptured appendix at the age of twenty, is also buried here. However, typhoid was also suspected and she was hastily buried at night under candlelight with her clothes later being burned so as to ensure no one else was infected.

Is it possible that the ghost of young Jane Cunningham walks the quiet, deserted corridors of her former home? And does she wonder why she was never afforded a full burial? After all, it is said that ghosts are often the spirits of disturbed souls or of lives cut short in their prime.

But questions about Lanyon aside, let us travel north of Lake Burley Griffin to another building of roughly the same age, and indeed, just as impressive and interesting in its own way. And of course, it is also reputed to be haunted.

Duntroon is the heart of Australia's military culture and heritage. Built in 1833 as a residence for the Campbell family, it was established in 1911 as the Royal Military College and is situated on attractive grounds at the foot of Mount Pleasant near Lake Burley Griffen. The grounds themselves have numerous historically significant buildings, including the officer's mess, known as Duntroon House, which is an imposing stone building.

And it is this building that interests us as local folklore has long spoken about a ghost that is reputed to haunt the building and gardens surrounding the house.

Born in 1857, Sophia Susanna Campbell was the daughter of George and Marianne Campbell and later died a mysterious death at the age of twenty-seven after a fall from the upper window of Duntroon House in which she suffered massive injuries and apoplexy. Apparently it took her a day to die, and she was later buried in a grave marked by a marble cross in the family plot.

It is her ghost that is reputed to haunt the room from where she fell, or was thrown, to her death, as well as the rose gardens that grow on the well-manicured gardens next to the house.

Over time witnesses have described a young woman with a sad look dressed in a long light blue dress walking the gardens. Others have reported seeing her walking along the top floor of the officer's mess, again, a lonely and forlorn figure. Indeed there are reports of the bed in her room appearing to be slept in when no one has stayed in the room. Other eerie happenings in the room are windows that bang, doors that shut of their own accord, and massive temperature drops. In addition, a young officer cadet once reported that he had encountered a young woman in an older-style blue dress in the hedge maze at Duntroon and that she had literally vanished before his eyes.

It has been suggested that Sophia was pregnant to the gardener and had been later rejected by him, leading to her jumping from the window to her death. However, even though there is the grave of a baby next to hers, there is little evidence to support this theory. Another rumour suggests that she was murdered by her very own family for seeing a man whom her father objected to. However, once again, this is false as her father died four years previous to her.

At one stage, a spirit medium was contacted to get to the bottom of the mysterious Sophia Campbell death, and she came to the opinion that Sophia did not commit suicide and was in fact pushed from the top floor by persons unknown. However, once again, this cannot be substantiated, so we must reconcile ourselves to the fact that Sophia Campbell fell from a window and died and for some reason unknown to us; her restless spirit now haunts the rooms and gardens of her former home.

Interestingly, there is another story of a ghostly presence at Duntroon, this time that of a young soldier by the name of Casey. Apparently Casey was a staff cadet who on the very last day of term managed to lock himself in a broom closet and, given that everyone was excited to be leaving and going home for a break, was sadly overlooked and he died, entombed in the cupboard. His decomposing body was apparently found when staff returned and noticed a bad smell, and from that day his shadowy form has been seen stalking the corridors on graduation day. Indeed, so strong is the rumour about Casey that, as he will never graduate, to appease his spirit, a place is set for him at every graduation dinner and his skeleton is present at each graduation ball.

Sadly though, the story is spoilt by the facts. In the early twentieth century cadets were taught basic anatomy and horsemanship, and to demonstrate this they had a human skeleton and a horse skeleton. When these courses were later discontinued, the cadets adopted these skeletons as mascots. As such, Casey is one of these skeletons. It would seem that the story of Casey was invented to go with the tradition. Having said this, no one is quite sure where Casey's skeleton actually came from, which raises its own set of questions.

But back to Sophia Campbell and, fascinatingly, there is a story that concerns the existence of a diary owned by her, which is supposedly hidden somewhere in Duntroon House. This diary is reputed to detail all the facts surrounding her death, and that one day it will be found and the truth revealed. Annoyingly, but really not surprising, the spirit medium failed to pick up the whereabouts of the diary. But then again, it is probably just a story and, so, whatever the case, the ghost of Sophia Campbell is now common knowledge in Canberra folklore circles, much like our next story, which also pertains to a young girl who met an early and untimely end.

Built in the early 1860s, Blundells Cottage is a small rubble and brick structure nestled in Commonwealth Park next to Lake Burley Griffin and reflects the history of Australia's white settlement through the establishment of large stations that laid the foundations for rural socio-economic growth. It is now a house museum and was also a part of the Campbell dynasty and, as such, a part of Duntroon estate.

The cottage itself sits quietly under Yellow Box, White Cedar, and Pencil Pines and seems a world away from the cares and worries of today's modern day Canberra. In every sense, it is a relic from our past, a past that is often seen through sentimental eyes.

Walking down to the cottage one is struck by the beauty of its present position overlooking Lake Burley Griffin. But it was not always like this, remembering that the lake itself is an artificial construct of the 1960s and being the centrepiece of Walter Burley Griffin's capital city, was not always there. Instead, the cottage sat above the shallow river valley surrounded by open fields and was, as previously mentioned, a part of the Duntroon Estate.

As I stand there gazing at this wonderful little piece of built history I find myself asking, how can this quaint little cottage be haunted? After all, with its English cottage garden and white picket fences it looks more like a prop from a film about rural England than a haunted house.

And yet, tragically, in 1892, Flora Susanna Blundell, whilst wearing a white crinoline dress, was seriously burnt when the dress touched a hot iron, immediately engulfing her in flames. She died not long after from her horrific injuries, and today one can visit her grave in the Queanbeyan Riverside Cemetery. As such, stories of her ghost haunting the old house have some basis in history.

Staff that man the little house museum talk about odd things that happen in the cottage, including items being mysteriously moved overnight to unexplained feelings of being watched and, even more unnerving, the smell of burning human flesh, all put down to the ghost of Flora. Strangely, it has been suggested to me that only people wearing a necklace can feel the presence of Flora's ghost as it is believed that she was wearing a necklace, maybe a favourite one, when she died.

Odd as these stories may seem, it is hard to dismiss them given that the guides that work at the cottage are volunteers who generally come from university educated cultural heritage backgrounds. Apart from that, while on a visit one cold July night with a local ghost tour, two members of the group claimed to be able to smell something burning as we stood on the cold wooden veranda at the front of the house. Even more surprising was when my partner Kirsten claimed that she could smell something as well. Of course, she later dismissed this as the smell of wood smoke from fireplaces in suburban homes, even though there are no residential dwellings in the immediate vicinity, and it was a dead still night.

Whatever the case, the visit was interesting, even if suggestion and the atmosphere may have played a large part in anyone experiencing anything slightly untoward. Having said that, my next point of call is not somewhere you'd normally associate with ghosts, being that it is only a bit over a decade old and is one of the most futuristic looking buildings in Australia.

Opened in 2001, the National Museum of Australia's 1997 origin is shrouded by the tragedy of the Katie Bender, a young girl who was killed by flying debris from the demolition of the Royal Canberra Hospital on which the museum now sits. Today her death is marked by a small memorial on the foreshore of the lake where she met her untimely and unnecessary death. However, this is not what we are interested in as the National Museum throws up some interesting questions regarding ghosts and hauntings.

I have visited the National Museum of Australia on numerous occasions and even, at one stage early in its construction, worked on some of the exhibition material, cataloguing a collection of old sepia-toned photos that showed Sydney before the Harbour Bridge was built.

When one enters the National Museum they are immediately taken by the massive and cavernous entry foyer that is usually filled with tourists and school groups all milling around with excited or bored looks on their faces. I wander past the milling crowd and head towards the Circa Theatrette where people have reported a presence that feels as if it is watching them. Apparently, so spooked are some staff that they have been caught on security camera furtively glancing over their shoulder as they rapidly exit the room.

Moving on I come to an exhibition that appears to be a tree house. This display consists of a rough wooden replica of a child's tree house that is overhung by a large ghost gum. There is a set of steps that lead up to the tree house and a small balcony where one can stop and view the exhibit. Bizarrely, there have been reports by visitors and staff alike of small ghostly heads that have been seen floating above the railing on the balcony. And even more bizarrely, the witnesses have stated that they are not even sure that the heads are human.

I don't linger at the tree house for long and head farther into the gallery where I come to a lift in the Gallery of First Australians, which I have been told security guards don't like taking after hours as it stops for no reason, and when it does, children's laughter can be heard coming from the floor just above the lift entrance. Security cameras, however, always show a lack of children, or anyone, when played back, even at the very time when the guards report the laughter.

When one considers the newness of the museum one is confronted by an odd question. How is it that such a modern building with little or no real history or past, and certainly no violence, be haunted? Where do these ghosts come from? Have they somehow been transported here in the material that lays behind the glass museum cases? Are they somehow attached to the actual historical items?

We spoke earlier of how the old Royal Canberra Hospital was destroyed to make way for the museum. Is it possible that the spirits of the hospital have somehow transcended the bricks and mortar of the previous building and now find themselves in the new building? And if so, how do they react with their new environment?

Oddly, they appear to be interacting with the present and not with the past, which begs the question, are they intelligent ghosts? Are they the ghosts of children who died in the old Royal Canberra Hospital when it existed on the site? Could it be that these spirits have somehow moved through time and now exist within the present while actually being ghosts from the past? And if so, then why and how?

Whatever the case, it is the next ghostly sighting in the museum that really intrigues me and makes me question all my previous beliefs about ghosts and the supernatural as, like the tree house heads, this ghost appears not only intelligent and able to interact with present day people, but also appears to be from the past whilst following present day building layouts and structures. Put simply, this ghost walks the corridors of the museum as it stands today, and not as it was when it was a hospital—which completely rules out the stone tape theory and suggests that some hauntings have some intelligence to them.

Staff and visitors in the museum have on numerous occasions reported being startled by the ghost of a nursing sister. Indeed, one staff member I spoke to recalled a story whereby she was asked by a couple of visitors about a woman in an old-style nurse's uniform who seemed to be part of a reenactment. The staff member replied that no, they did not have any reenactments in the museum at that time.

The spectral nursing sister is somewhat surprisingly seen all over the museum but is generally witnessed along a first-floor corridor that holds the Upper Nation or Snapshots Gallery. The corridor itself is open and roughly thirty metres in length and seven or eight metres wide with a railing that overlooks other displays on one side, and a row of glass cabinets on the other.

While visiting the museum I was told by a staff member that they had once begun their rounds at the end of the day to check that no one was left in the museum and, after checking the previous galleries, then checked on the empty Snapshots Gallery corridor. Thinking his job was finished, the guard turned to leave when he got the biggest shock of his life. While looking into a glass display case he saw the distinct reflection of the figure of a woman in a nurse's uniform standing directly behind him. Understandably frightened he spun around, but there was no one there.

In another strange encounter a person standing at one end of the corridor reported that they plainly saw the ghostly nurse enter the corridor from a doorway at the other end, before walking along the corridor and straight through a small group of other visitors, before disappearing. Interestingly, it was reported that no one else saw the spectral nurse, and the people whom she'd walked through apparently felt, heard, and saw nothing.

Staff at the museum who have witnessed her ghostly presence have suggested that she is possibly a head nursing sister as she apparently does not like to be criticised or thought of as a common nurse. In fact, Tim the Yowie Man, who used to take visitors on nightly ghost trips through the museum, at one stage said something disparaging about the ghostly nurse at which point a loud screeching, grinding noise was heard coming from the next gallery at the end of the corridor. When investigated, the gallery was found to be empty, the loud screeching noise apparently coming from an interactive display item that requires a person to move it to make the sound. Indeed, so convinced are staff of the ghostly nursing sister that they speak of her in hushed tones.

But the ghostly nurse and floating heads are not all that this modern building contains. In another area of the museum staff have been terrified by the apparition of a young boy in 1940s or 1950s garb who pops out from behind displays and sometimes follows people before vanishing. Again, like the ghostly nurse, in this case we appear to be dealing with the ghost of a person from a past not connected to the museum but the demolished hospital, and so it is hard to understand how they can interact intelligently with the new building.

Whatever the case, I continue my quest and presently come to a large locked door in the lower Gallery of First Australians, which holds the Open Collections, objects from across Australia that show the great diversity of Indigenous material culture. Finding a guard, I am able to get the door unlocked and, after flicking on the lights, I enter the room. Inside is an incredible array of Aboriginal artefacts from many decades, and indeed, centuries past.

The room itself is long and thin with a large glass-fronted display cabinet on both sides and a floor-to-ceiling cabinet that runs down the centre of the room. Entering the room you feel a sort of presence, not in a frightening way, but a presence all the same, as if the objects themselves are trying to talk to you. I am later told that some people find this presence too much and either refuse to enter the room or rapidly leave claiming to feel sick.

However, on this day I do not feel ill, nor do I feel threatened in any way. As such I wander past the exhibits for a while until I decide to turn off the light to see if this has any effect upon the "feeling" in the room.

With the lights off the displays now take on a slightly menacing air, and reflections and shadows look like human shapes moving amongst the displays. At one stage I suddenly feel a chill and the hairs on the back of my neck stand up, and the staff member I am with tells me, quite matter-of-factly, that this area is one of the spots that lots of people seem to mention. Strangely, it feels colder in this area than anywhere else in the gallery.

However, cold spot or not, this is a museum and they are air-conditioned. For all I know there is a duct somewhere above me that blew onto the back of my neck creating the feeling that I was experiencing a cold spot, something often associated with ghosts. And of course, the cabinets, artefacts, and shelves tend to throw up some unusual shadows ,which when viewed by someone walking along in the dark could account for many sightings of ghosts in museums or like places.

Elsewhere in the building is the Dance Gallery where the spirit of a person has been heard saying in a loud male voice the Aboriginal word "nardoo" (an Aboriginal name for a small water plant). This gallery contains a collection of Stone Age tools discovered when the museum foundations were being excavated and are possibly 20,000 years old. Could it be that this ghostly voice is connected to these Stone Age tools? Is it possible that this site was once of such importance to the original inhabitants of the area that a part of them has remained?

Other strange experiences at the museum include the ghostly figure of an old woman who has been seen having a bath in the old Medical Superintendent's Cottage which is now the National Museum Centre for Historical Research. This figure has been reported on numerous occasions, and, more baffling, there is no bath in the room that she is seen, which makes one wonder whether ghosts can influence their surroundings, as in, can their historical surroundings be a part of an apparition? In this case it would appear to be so. And more so, if one were to report a ghostly figure, surely it would not be an old woman having a bath in a room devoid of a bath.

Other manifestations include poltergeist activity, especially in the Friend's Lounge, where chairs have been found stacked on top of each other in odd ways, as well as books and items going missing and being found days later. There is also the report of a young blonde woman in a blue dress who appears near a display where the actual blue dress is exhibited. Strangely, it is thought that this ghostly woman is actually wearing the blue dress from the display, and that she did not die anywhere near the museum site yet was so attached to the dress in life that she now returns in death to wear the beloved garment.

Oddly, for such a modern building, the museum appears to be as haunted as any building in Australia, and why this is, I have no idea but to suggest that the building may somehow contribute to these strange experiences in that its very layout is designed to heighten experiences and emotions for visitors. Could it be that the building design itself is responsible for these sightings? Is it possible that somehow the walls and corridors have been accidentally laid out in a way that the visitor cannot help but misinterpret things they see?

Likewise, is it possible that this building amplifies whatever spirits that may have existed on the site previous to the museum, and as such they apparently exist in the present day format of the museum and not as a stone tape historical replay of years ago when the site was a hospital? In addition, museums are places full of artefacts and items that once belonged to people. Could these items somehow hold on to some sort of residual energy that later manifests itself, in ways unknown to us, as a ghost?

I find it difficult to answer the questions that the National Museum of Australia has thrown up. It appears to have ghosts from a previous building that now interact with the present day design of the building, a phenomena not usually witnessed in most supernatural accounts and hard to explain except to say that these ghosts appear to not be of the stone tape variety but are somehow intelligent and able to interact with their current environment.

Whatever the case, the museum is an interesting study, but, as it seems so different from numerous other reported haunted places, we shall move on to some much older and much more likely sites.

Not far from the National Museum is graceful and gentile Government House at Yarralumla. The official residence of the governor-general, it is set in fifty-four hectares of green, rolling parkland, designed and planted by horticulturist Charles Weston. The grounds include expansive lawns and extensive plantations of trees, which provide sweeping vistas towards Black Mountain to the north and the Brindabella Ranges to the south. The house itself consists of a central brick structure, which was erected by Frederick Campbell in 1890–1891 on the remains of an old 1830s homestead. This was then renovated and expanded in 1899 and again during the 1920s. Further additions were made in the 1930s and 1940s. It is also rendered and painted cream with green roof tiles and is a truly beautiful building to behold.

However, as lovely as the house and gardens are, it is an unusual story of a diamond and the ghost of an Aboriginal person that interests us.

The Yarralumla ghost is a well published story, although its veracity is somewhat clouded. Well before being acquired by the federal government in 1913, the site was a grazing property, and it is reputed that, just before the last private owner, Frederick Campbell, left, a document was discovered that reported the details of an Aboriginal ghost on the grounds of the now stately building.

Apparently, a visitor to the house was being shown around a stone vault in the garden that contained the remains of a previous owner, a Colonel Gibbes, when he discovered an old dust-covered manuscript. It would seem that the letter was unsigned. It read:

> In 1826, a large diamond was stolen from James Cobbity on an obscure station in Queensland. The theft was traced to one of the convicts who had run away, probably to New South Wales. The convict was captured in 1858, but the diamond could not be traced; neither would the convict (name unknown) give any information, in spite of frequent floggings.
>
> During 1842, he left a statement to a groom and a map of the hiding place of the hidden diamond. The groom, for a minor offence, was sent

to Berrima Gaol. He was clever with horses and one day, when left to his duties, cleverly plaited a rope of straw and then escaped by throwing it over the wall, where it caught an iron bar. Passing it over, he swung himself down and escaped. He and his family lived out west for several years, according to Rev. James Hassall who, seeing him living honestly, did not think it necessary to inform against him. I have no reason to think he tried to sell the diamond. Probably the ownership of a thing so valuable would bring suspicion and lead to rearrest.

After his death his son took possession of the jewel and, with a trusty blackfellow, set off for Sydney. After leaving Cooma for Queanbeyan, they met with, it was after ascertained, a bushranging gang. The blackfellow and his companion were separated, and finally the former was captured and searched, to no avail, for he had swallowed the jewel.

The gang in anger shot him. He was buried in a piece of land belonging to Colonel Gibbes, and later Mr. Campbell. I believe the diamond to be among his bones. It is of great value. My hand is enfeebled with age, or I should describe the troubles through which I have passed. My life has been wasted, my money expended, I die almost destitute, and in sight of my goal.

I believe the grave to be under the large deodar tree. Buried by blacks, it would be in a round hole. Believe and receive a fortune. Scoff and leave the jewel in its hiding place.

Written near Yarralumla, 1881

Contemporary sources suggest that Campbell accepted the authenticity of the document due to the references to Gibbes and himself and to the large deodar tree. Surprisingly, there still exists a huge and long-lived deodar (Himalayan cedar) in the grounds of Government House and fortunately, no one has ever thought to dig it up.

However, as previously mentioned, the veracity of this particular ghost is subject to doubt. It is said that, on moonlit nights, the ghost of the Aboriginal man can be seen digging around the roots of the deodar tree. However, there are no firsthand reports of this apparition, although Bill Whittle, a security guard at Government House from 1939 until 1962, published a small and rather obscure book of witty anecdotes about the house, the grounds, and the inhabitants in 1984. In one chapter he describes how a woman turned up at the front gate one day in 1942 asking if she could have a look over what she claimed was her previous home. Apparently the wife of the incumbent governor-general agreed and, with Whittle assigned to minding the woman's children, she visited the house. According to Whittle, she signed her name as a Mrs. Little although it was later revealed that she was in fact the former Kate Campbell, daughter of Frederick Campbell.

Upon her departure Whittle asked Mrs. Little if she knew anything about the legend of the ghost and the diamond. The woman apparently told him that, aided by a school friend staying at Yarralumla during the school holidays, they had written the letter on heavy parchment paper taken from her father's study

and had simply made up the story before disguising it with dust and cobwebs to make it appear old before placing it in the vault as a practical joke.

And so, sadly, it seems that the story of the diamond and the Aboriginal ghost is nothing more than a flight of fancy from a couple of mischievous young schoolgirls. Or is it?

Later research showed Frederick Campbell did have a daughter named Kate; however, her married name was Newman, and not Little. And while the visitor's book for 1942 does show the signature of a "Mrs. Little," it doesn't show a "Mrs. Newman." Having said that, another former security guard, a Mr. Bert Sheedy, also claimed to have met the woman on the day that she visited and had also been told about the hoaxed ghost. However, Sheedy claims that it was in 1952, not 1942.

Just to confuse the issue more, a letter to the editor of the *Sydney Morning Herald*, published in August 1945, seemed to confirm both Whittle's and Sheedy's stories and read, in part:

In the past few years I have occasionally read allusions to a story of a diamond under the old deodar tree beside Yarralumla House. Hitherto I have ventured no public comment but when, on reading [another book) mentioning the story, bringing in my mother's name, I felt an urge to give the facts as I know them.

The letter was signed by a "Kate Newman" and seems to put the Yarralumla ghost stories to rest. Having said this, there is another report of a ghost at the governor-general's residence and whereas the previous tale can be discarded as legend, this one is not so easily dismissed.

In February 1963, while preparing for a Royal visit, Sir Murray Tyrrell, private secretary to a number of governors-general from 1947 to 1973, was walking towards his cottage in the grounds when an agitated official approached him and asked if he had seen a strange person entering the front door of Government House. Sir Murray replied in the negative and suggested that, with the security being increased, no one could have possibly entered. However, the official was insistent so Tyrrell decided to check.

As he entered the front door he was surprised to see a strange figure slowly climbing the stairs from the foyer to the first floor. Perturbed and somewhat perplexed, Tyrrell shouted out, but the figure took no notice. He then decided to take matters into his own hands and ran up the stairs in pursuit of the figure only to find that when he reached the first floor landing, the figure had apparently vanished into thin air.

Carefully searching each and every room Tyrrell could find no trace of the figure and so he called one of the security guards who were patrolling the grounds with guard dogs, explaining exactly what he had seen. The security man and his dogs then started to ascend the staircase in search of the apparent intruder when the dog suddenly refused to go any further, even baring its teeth at its handler when coaxed to go upstairs.

Tyrrell apparently stood by his account until his death and could never offer a rational explanation for the events of that day. Given that there is an old and unconfirmed story of a man either dying or being murdered in the original homestead that once stood on the grounds, is it possible that Tyrrell and the dog had come across this spirit? Maybe the ghost of Yarralumla is not simply the result of a letter forged by two schoolgirls while on holiday?

Whatever the case, if the governor-general's residence is somewhat devoid of ghosts, then we need not search far to find another place of some relative antiquity that suits the bill, and indeed, is also tied up in the intricate politics of Canberra. This is the veritable old Parliament House that sits serenely at the base of Capital Hill on manicured lawns in the middle of the parliamentary triangle, the heart of Walter Burley Griffin's open vista design for Canberra, including Lake Burley Griffin, Anzac Parade, the Australian War Memorial and Mount Ainslie.

The building was officially opened in May 1927 as neither a temporary or permanent base (the building was deemed as provisional) for the Commonwealth Parliament after its relocation from Melbourne to Canberra. It was the house of the Parliament of Australia from 1927 to 1988 and now houses the Museum of Australian Democracy.

And apparently it is haunted, with security guards reporting that they have had their walkie-talkies ripped off their belts and thrown across rooms while doing night shifts to seeing a ghostly pair of legs wandering through the courtyards and windows that open and close by themselves. Although no one is sure who is responsible for these seemingly paranormal occurrences, it is believed that a clerk-of-the-courts died in the building many years ago, and he could be behind the haunting. Apart from this, many guards have been reported as refusing to do night shifts in the building.

Interestingly, during the celebrations surrounding the opening of what is now Old Parliament House in May 1927, Flying Officer Francis Ewen, while flying a single seat SE-5 fighter aircraft, crashed on Rottenbury Rise, the site of today's National Library. The aircraft ploughed into the ground 600 metres from the legislative building, landing on its nose and port wing before turning over amid a cloud of dust. Ewen died from his injuries that evening without recovering consciousness and was buried two days later in St. Johns churchyard. No explanation could be found for what caused the accident and, maybe not surprisingly, in the basement of the National Library, many have reported seeing the ghostly image of an aviator.

But ghosts in public buildings are seemingly not that uncommon in the nation's capital. At the John Gorton Building, a stone's throw from Old Parliament House, cleaners of the fifth floor have complained of feelings of being watched and heavy toilet doors opening by themselves, while in 1951, a newspaper report suggested that the Department of Health building was haunted as two cleaners who worked in the office claimed that "a ghost is roaming the corridors of the building." One cleaner said that he had spoken to the ghost and it had "just disappeared," and that it "looked like a woman dressed in a long flowing robe with a cardigan wrapped around her. The outline, very vague and misty, just vanished when I said goodnight to it." A second cleaner said that the ghost had been seen in various rooms and offices and had vanished when approached.

But if cleaners reporting ghostly encounters in public service buildings seem somewhat strange, then what of the next couple of stories that occurred in another well-known public building, the National Film and Sound Archive?

The National Film and Sound Archives is a splendid neoclassical building in the old Canberra suburb of Acton and from 1931 until 1984 was the home of the Australian Institute of Anatomy. It once had a morgue in the basement where autopsies were performed and even held a vast collection of human skulls. As a result, it seems not that surprising that there are numerous reports of supernatural-like events in the building, including movement sensors in the basement that are regularly triggered even with no one present, electronic counters on the front door that often show that people have entered or exited the building after closing time when the front door is locked, and, according to Tim the Yowie Man, "quite a few people get pinned up against the wall by an unknown force in the basement."

Indeed, I managed to interview a man who works in air-conditioning and heating and was once working in the basement of the National Film and Sound Archive when he said that he felt "as if someone was standing behind me and watching me; I mean right behind me." Spinning around he found he was alone in the room and so, nervously, went back to work until, again, he felt as if he was being watched. As it was nearing lunchtime, he decided to step out, although as he walked from the basement he said that he could "feel something following me; it wasn't enough just to freak me out by watching me, it was now following me! I bolted!"

As far as I know he hasn't set foot in the building again. However, this is not the story we are seeking at this stage as, just after 6:00 p.m. on a winter's day a number of years ago, Professor Jeff Brownrigg walked down the stairs from his office towards the building's foyer. Reaching the foyer he was astonished to find over a hundred people milling around as if for some official function. As he stood there wondering what was going on and why he had not be informed of the event, a tall man in period costume with a bowler hat, winged collar, and walrus-style moustache blocked his way for a moment, and in this moment Brownrigg noticed that everyone in the room seemed to be bathed in sepia-like light or tone.

He took a step back and shook his head and blinked only to find that this incredible scene seemed to vanish, leaving him alone and perplexed. Of course, one could suggest that Brownrigg simply had some sort of auditory and visual hallucination, yet, as he was soon to find out, others who had worked in the building also reported seeing the tall man with the walrus moustache.

Brownrigg followed up his strange sighting and soon learned of other ghostly occurrences in the building, including a report of a glass dish being apparently thrown across a room by an invisible force and the sightings of a ghostly woman in an upstairs gallery. As well he became aware of reports of the ghost of a young girl known as the Pyjama Girl who was murdered near Albury on the New South Wales Victorian border and whose body was held in the basement morgue for some time after her death.

Brownrigg is a professor in cultural heritage at the University of Canberra and is a man well versed in anthropology, archaeology, and history, and, if the story had been told by someone of less standing, it may have easily been laughed off as delusional. However, he has always stood by what he saw and to this day is at a loss to explain it, not an uncommon thing as we will see at our next public institution.

The Australian War Memorial in Campbell is a most impressive and solemn building that sits upon a small rise at the end of the sweeping Anzac Parade with a clear line of sight to both Old and New Parliament House. Opened in 1941, it is widely regarded as one of the most significant memorials of its type in the world and consists of three major parts: the Commemorative Area, including the Hall of Memory with the Tomb of the Unknown Australian Soldier, the Memorial's galleries, the museum, and the Research Centre. It also has an outside sculpture garden and many relics of war scattered around its grounds, including a Japanese miniature submarine that was involved in the shelling of Sydney in 1942 and the barrel from the Amiens Gun, an enormous railroad gun captured from the Germans during World War I.

Officially opened on 11 November 1941 by the then-Governor-General Lord Gowrie, a former soldier and Victoria Cross holder, it holds a deep and significant meaning to Australians from all walks of life. However, as poignant and thought provoking as it is, we are searching for more than just memories as it appears to be very much haunted.

The Hall of Valour at the Australian War Memorial honours Australians who have received the Victoria Cross as well as those who have directly received the George Cross, and the exploits of these courageous individuals are recognised by this display. It is also the site of an extremely perplexing, but rather heart-warming tale from the 1980s when an elderly Queensland man, reportedly from Gympie, visited the place. As a World War II veteran, the man visited the place on numerous occasions, almost as a pilgrimage. However, on this day, after wandering around and viewing the displays and military memorabilia, including the life-like dioramas for which the Memorial is known for, he suddenly felt dizzy and faint.

He later recalled that he was quite distressed and stated, "I hadn't had any lunch. I guess that's why I got crook. I felt myself falling, then a strong arm grabbed my left elbow and another caught me round the waist. It was a young soldier in a World War II AIF uniform. He was smiling and said 'whoa there'.

The next thing I remember is sitting on a bench with two attendants fussing over me. I looked around for the soldier to thank him but he was gone. I said it was lucky the soldier had caught me and the attendants gave me very odd looks. There was no soldier, they said; they had seen me stumble to the bench by myself. I've gone over that event in my mind dozens of times since and I know what I felt and saw."

Staff have also reported that this section of the memorial often has a certain "feel" to it and that many of them actively avoid the place after hours, not because they believe it is evil or anything like that, but more so because of the eerie feeling that someone or something is also there amongst the displays. Is it possible that, like the Australian National Museum, the artefacts themselves somehow contribute to the manifestation of a ghost? Is the spirit of a young soldier somehow inextricably linked to the items on display?

I guess we'll never know; however, this leads us to another story, this time in the Hall of Memory where people have also reported seeing a soldier dressed in World War II clothes. Is it possible that this is the same ghost as the one who has been seen in the Hall of Valour? And if so, what is his purpose? After all, the soldier most certainly didn't die in the building, rather, he died halfway around the world while fighting in France. Could it be that the ghost of the Unknown Soldier who is buried at the Memorial somehow returned with his remains to this most poignant of places? And now does he haunt the lonely corridors of the memorial? And if so, why? Surely his spirit should haunt the green overgrown battlefields of First World War France and not these hallowed halls?

Canberra is a new city, a modern city, a city that looks forward to a future of prosperity and growth. However, in its scramble to move forward it sometimes appears to forget the past, and the next story is just that, a reminder, like Blundell's Cottage, of where the city has come from.

Edward Kendall Crace was a pastoralist who owned extensive lands around the Canberra region from the 1870s until his death. He arrived in Australia in 1865 on the *Duncan Dunbar*, a clipper that was shipwrecked off the coast of Brazil on 7 October 1865, while en route to Sydney. In 1871, he married Kate Marion, who had also been on the *Duncan Dunbar*, and together they had six daughters and two sons.

Life in the new colony for Crace was good. He was prosperous and his future looked bright, indeed, by the 1870s he had acquired 30,000 acres. That is, until one fateful night in 1892 when he and his coachman attempted to cross the flooded Ginninderra Creek. Confronted by a raging torrent of flooding water, the two men were swept away with their bodies being later found some 500 metres downstream tangled up in debris.

The crossing where Crace and his footman drowned no longer exists, but a pedestrian footbridge over the creek sits very close to the place where they found the bodies. Many people walking or jogging at night have claimed to have witnessed a wispy but strangely glowing figure standing by the edge of the creek. Some people have walked past and then looked back only to notice that the figure has disappeared. Some people have even seen the shape from their car when driving home late at night. Others have reported the figure of a man in a large hat and overcoat standing under or next to the bridge. Bizarrely, others have suggested that they have witnessed a ghostly female figure wearing late 1800s garb.

Crace's ghost, if it is indeed Crace, has been reported numerous times and with the area becoming more popular with walkers and joggers, one would think that the reports should continue. I have also walked this lonely part of the creek many times yet, sadly, have not yet managed to get a glimpse of the apparition.

Whatever the case, if there are doubts as to the authenticity of the Ginninderra Creek ghost, there is little doubt about the reports from just across the border in New South Wales, especially in places such as Queanbeyan and Lake George as well as farther afield.

CHAPTER TWO

ΠEW SOUTH WALES

OF GAOLS, SPECTRAL COΠVICTS,
AΠD HAUΠTED HIGHLAΠDS

Lake George is an eerie place. Situated just north of Canberra, the twenty-five kilometre long and ten kilometre wide lake is now mostly dry, although there are patches of shallow water on its southern end. It is an unusual place, and over the years has built up an enviable reputation for ghosts, hauntings, UFOs, and strange phenomena.

When full the lake is an immense stretch of shallow water that reaches beyond the horizon. Some 27,000 years ago it flowed into the nearby Yass River until the escarpment rose and blocked its surface link leaving it without any major rivers or streams to replenish the waters. Although it covers a huge area, the lake is very shallow and so, with evaporation, dries out extremely quickly, in some cases within days.

Another interesting aspect of the lake is the tendency for strong winds to actually blow the water back upon itself meaning that the water can congregate in the centre with the shorelines dry. Or even more bizarre, the lake can be dry on one side and have waves washing against its shoreline on the other side because of the shallowness and wind.

In the local Indigenous language, the lake is called Werriwa. Originally spelt *Weereewa* in the journals of the explorers who noted the name, it literally means "bad water." Whether or not this describes the quality of the water, which can be stagnant for decades, or something more sinister is not known. However, it is known that the lake itself was a special place for local Aboriginal clans in that it quite possibly had a women's secret place somewhere on its western shores.

Over the years the lake has seen its fair share of deaths, including five cadets from the Royal Military College Duntroon, who drowned in July 1956 whilst yachting on the lake. This event, plus numerous deaths from car accidents on the highway that skirts the lake's western edge have given rise to a number of ghost stories. One of these is that of a phantom hitchhiker.

The phantom hitchhiker tale is one of the most well-known camp fire stories ever told and it tends to follow the same sort of narrative every time, albeit, with slight variations: man driving car picks up a usually young woman hitchhiker late at night. Hitchhiker seems slightly odd but quiet and pleasant enough. Driver doesn't stop car but later looks around and notices hitchhiker has

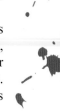

disappeared. He stops at next town and is told that hitchhiker is the ghost of someone killed on the highway in some tragic fashion, usually murdered and buried in an unknown grave. Or else they drop the hitchhiker off at a place only to find out later that the place is where they used to live before they were murdered or tragically died.

And so it is with our Lake George ghost, except that there are no records of any young girl being murdered and, even though I have driven that road countless times at night, I have never seen anything odd, not even a *real* hitchhiker. And so this I am afraid, no matter how many times it is earnestly retold, appears to be an urban myth, that is, except for the following, which was mentioned on a local Canberra website in recent years:

"My brother tells me of this time he was driving past Lake George and saw this random guy, emotionless standing by the road, but apparently when my brother turned his head to see the guy again he wasn't there. He rang the car behind him [they were travelling together] and they said they saw him too. He was explaining this to our mother and she reiterated this story of a friend of hers. Apparently, this bloke driving around the same corner as my brother saw another bloke standing beside the road waving to slow him down. He slowed down and saw the results of a nasty crash. Which he could have plunged straight into had he not slowed down. Anyway, the bloke picked up a paper the next day and got the shock of his life when he saw a photo of that same person who was waving to slow him down listed as killed instantly in that car crash" (www.the-riotact.com).

Ghostly hitchhiker or not? Who is to say, however, this lonely stretch of road also contains another spooky apparition, the so-called Collector ghost, who has been described as a man dressed in all black and a top hat and who is said to have appeared occasionally since the 1930s near the town of Collector, just north of Canberra. Interestingly, this ghost has also been seen walking along the shorelines of Lake George, at Bungendore, and as far afield as the outskirts of Queanbeyan, just on Canberra's eastern border.

Collector itself has an old pub that dates back to the 1860s and was the scene of a terrible murder in which Constable Samuel Nelson lost his life. Formerly Kimberley's Public House, the pub is now known as the Bushranger Hotel and for very good reason as, on 26 January 1865, bushrangers Ben Hall, John Gilbert, and John Dunn made their way into the town after spending the morning robbing people on a road south of Goulburn. Aware that the bushrangers were in the area, two constables were dispatched from Collector to find and apprehend them, leaving Samuel Nelson in the town on his own.

After taking a number of hostages, Hall and Gilbert stole items from the hotel; however, Nelson soon learned of their deeds and set off to confront the bushrangers. Although accounts of the events are somewhat contentious, it seems that as Nelson headed down a grassy slope towards the hotel, Dunn shot him in the stomach with a shotgun and, as he lay on the ground, shot him again, this time in the face. The gang then rifled through the dead constable's belongings and escaped.

With the bushrangers gone, Nelson's body was taken into the hotel, and he was later buried in the local cemetery. Dunn managed to evade capture until Boxing Day 1965, and he was later hanged at Darlinghurst gaol in March 1866.

Now known as the Bushranger Hotel, the place retains an old world colonial feel and oozes charm with its narrow passages, rickety stairs, and open fireplaces. And given its age and history, it is not surprising that it can be quite eerie at times as it is said to be haunted by the ghost of a previous publican, among others. Glasses on the bar have been seen to move on their own and sometimes are found neatly stacked. White wispy figures have also been reported, especially on the first landing of the stairs, and patrons often report disembodied footsteps and the feeling of ghostly fingers being run through their hair. In the upstairs dormitory people have reported seeing a child's handprint on the mirrors of the antique furniture, and in one of the other bedrooms a dark figure is said to reside. Cameras and other electrical equipment often fail when being used upstairs and, indeed, my video camera, which had functioned perfectly all day, suddenly stopped working when I was videoing the upstairs room, only to start working again later that night when I left the village. Is it possible that Constable Nelson's tragic figure still walks these creaky old corridors? After all, a stone memorial to Nelson sits quietly next to the pub to this day.

But Collector aside, just east of Canberra lies the small rural town of Bungendore, an historic village dating back to the early 1800s with many well-preserved examples of colonial Australian architecture. It boasts cool climate wines, a charming old-world railway station, galleries, gift shops, and is in close proximity to Lake George. Add to this boutique coffee and cake shops, antique dealers, and other handicraft sort of cottage industries, and this small town, only minutes from Canberra, is a delight for day trippers or holiday makers. However, for all its charm, we are only interested in an intriguing photograph, taken in 1949 at the Royal Hotel—a photograph that appears to show a ghost.

The Royal Hotel is old by Australian standards. Built in 1882, the colonial style two-story building is still remarkably unchanged from those early days of settlement in the region. One can easily picture men in hats on carriages dropping in for a quick drink and a bite to eat on hot, dusty summer days. Like most old Australian pubs it has a bar downstairs with basic accommodation, including upstairs shared bathrooms.

The photograph, taken in 1949 by a local journalist, does not appear to be faked, nor does it appear to be a quirk of light or a combination of light and shadow, although this can never be written off. However, on closer inspection one is hard pressed to come to this conclusion.

The photo appears to show an indistinct but somehow recognisable face and upper torso. He is wearing a hat, what appears to be a white shirt, and possibly a tie. As the photo is in sepia tones it is almost impossible to conclude that the hat is black, but it most certainly could be a darkish colour, possible brown as was the style at that time in Australian history.

Given the proximity of Bungendore to Lake George and therefore Collector, it would not be out of the question to suggest that maybe they are one and the same. In addition, the Bungendore ghost and the Collector ghost both appear roughly around the same time, that being the period from the 1930s up until the late 1950s, with some sporadic reports having been filed up to the present day. And, as we have seen, it is not unusual for a ghost to be reported in more than one place.

However, having said this, there is no way that we can adequately compare the two, and so at this stage, these ghostly presences will have to remain as separate identities. But these old-time ghosts are apparently not that rare in this region; indeed, at Bredbo, south of Canberra it is believed that the ghost of the "Man from Snowy River" haunts the local pub.

Although many Victorians believe that the "Man from Snowy River" was John (Jack) Riley, a legendary horseman who migrated from Ireland to Australia as a thirteen-year-old in 1851, WF "Bill" Refshauge, author of *Searching for the Man from Snowy River* claims that Charles Lachlan McKeahnie, a rider from Adaminaby is the real "Man from Snowy River" and who, in 1885, at just seventeen years of age, chased a runaway stallion across the wild country that is now the Kosciuszko National Park. And it said that McKeahnie's ghost now haunts the pub in which he died, ironically after a horse-riding incident.

Apparently McKeahnie's horse skidded on green timber on a newly made bridge, and he fell off, hitting his head. He was then taken to the nearby Bredbo Inn where he died two days later. Tim the Yowie Man, in his book *In the Spirit of Banjo,* recalled waking suddenly at 3:00 a.m. to the sound of "a jingling of keys . . . moving up and down the corridor," and when he went to investigate found no one there. Then, after settling down, he apparently heard the jingle sounding like it was rushing "straight past the door." Puzzled, in the morning when he asked the pub owner about the noise, he was surprised to find that the owner had no idea what it was, although the pub owner's wife confessed that she had witnessed a couple of unexplained happenings, including doors opening by themselves.

Not far from Bredbo is the Cooma, the main town of the Monaro region with a name believed to be derived from an Aboriginal word *Coombah*, meaning "big lake" or "open country." First surveyed in 1840 and proclaimed a municipality in 1879, it was a vital link to the Snowy Mountains Scheme, indeed, becoming the headquarters for workers and administration for the project. It is a cold, dry, and somewhat desolate place.

Recently a friend of mine told me of a strange encounter she had at a small abandoned church graveyard just on the outskirts of the town. While taking her dog for a walk she decided, out of interest, to visit the graveyard one afternoon and, although feeling a little uneasy upon entering the site, nonetheless found it interesting with graves reaching back into the late 1800s. Then she related, "I felt as if something was standing in front of me, watching me," although when she looked up there was nothing to see. Feeling uncomfortable, she noticed that her dog was staring ahead, its body stiff and its hackles raised. The dog then started growling as if there was a person standing directly in front of it. This was enough for my friend, and she turned around and left the graveyard rapidly, explaining that she "felt something was following me" and that she "hoped it didn't follow me home."

Of course, visiting an old graveyard on your own in a lonely windswept place like Cooma is likely to make you feel slightly uneasy. In such places the mind goes into overdrive, and we are open to the suggestion that something may just haunt the old gravestones. And yet, for all of this, what was it that made the dog aggressive and protective? Could it have been a rabbit or a fox or some other small animal? Possibly, and yet, as she said, the dog "appeared to be looking directly in front of it as if someone, quite tall, was standing there."

Suggestion or hyper-arousal? Either way, the fact that my friend said she felt uneasy and that she was being watched, coupled with the fact that the dog seemed to detect something invisible, tends to suggest that something supernatural or paranormal may have occurred.

This episode, however, is nothing like another report I have read and, although not exactly in Cooma, is in relation to a late 1800s coach house just south of the town. Apparently a Canberra couple, Carlos and Heidi, seeking accommodation for the night, turned up at the old place, and, with the rain beating down incessantly, decided that it was the perfect place to spend the night.

After a suitable dinner, the couple retired to their room, which was adorned with a huge four-poster bed and comfortable furnishing. Soon they were asleep; however, after about an hour, Heidi began to stir in her sleep and mumble. Then, to the alarm of her partner, she suddenly sat bolt upright and began to speak in a voice unfamiliar to Carlos.

"T'was not I who put the noose about his neck," she said in a high-pitched, ringing voice before falling back to sleep.

Worried, Carlos woke her, and as they lay there in the dark they slowly became aware of scrapings and noises from outside their room, as if the furniture was being moved around. Before long they also heard footsteps, which were impossible as the owners of the inn lived in an adjacent cottage, not the inn itself.

After a while the noises stopped and the terrified couple managed to get some fitful sleep. In the morning, while discussing the strange events of the previous night, the hostess interrupted and asked if they had seen the ghost? She then continued explaining that, over a century ago the owner of the inn had murdered his wife in a fit of rage by pushing her down the stairs and that visitors often complained that the ghostly resident quite often appeared to guests as well as the residents, making noises and rattling kettles and pans in the kitchen.

In addition, she explained that maids often felt that someone was following them, especially on the stairs and had taken to holding on to the banister, just in case they too were pushed. As well, violent arguments could often be heard coming from one of the rooms, although when checked, was always empty.

This room has always been believed to be the most haunted in the building and another report from the place suggests that people rarely enjoy a full night's sleep in this room. Indeed, another story involves the visit of a young Sydney couple and their five-year-old daughter. They had been asleep for a while when the husband awoke to see a young girl, who he believed to be his daughter, standing in the doorway of his room staring at him.

The husband wearily told the girl to go back to bed, but she remained unmoved. Perplexed, he sat up and asked the girl once again; however, again she did not move. At this stage the wife, now roused from her slumber by the noise, looked at the little girl and a feeling of dread came over her as she realised that this was not her daughter.

With this, the ghostly figure simply vanished and the couple leapt from their bed and rushed next door where they found their daughter sleeping soundly, obviously completely unaware of what had just happened. Not surprisingly, they left in a rush the next morning.

As previously mentioned, the Monaro Plains are a cold, windswept and lonely place and shrouded in the ghostly lore of ancient bushmen and pioneers. As such, what can we make of our next stop, the Victorian mansion just outside Bombala called Burnima?

Built in 1896 for grazier Mr. Henry Tollemache Edwards by Frederick Young, incidentally the builder of Yarralumla, the governor-general's residence in Canberra, it is situated five miles from Bombala on the picturesque Bombala River.

The homestead itself is a two-storied Victorian Gothic style mansion and includes thirty-two rooms plus servant's quarters and outbuildings. It also has a wonderful garden, set out with trees, pines, conifers, spruces, cedars from every part of the world, and a hedge surrounds the tennis court separating the period stables from the formal garden.

Importantly, the mansion is a complete example of a working Victorian homestead and one distinctly gets the odd feeling that, upon entering the grounds, one is stepping back in time. Of course, being in such an isolated spot, this feeling is somewhat magnified, and the opulence of the main building and the tranquility of the gardens place you in an era now long gone.

Henry Tollemache Edwards was born at Parramatta in 1837, the second son of a Captain Edwards of the 17th Infantry Regiment, which was stationed there at the time. He was privately educated and associated with pastoral matters all his life. According to all reports, he was a fine judge of cattle. He died on 19 November 1915, at the ripe old age of eighty-one.

Bombala was one of the major contenders for the nation's capital and, although losing out in the end to Canberra, it is intriguing to think that, if Bombala was chosen, the Burnima Homestead would have ended up as the governor-general's residence.

But as interesting as this is, it is also a place of dark secrets and murder, and it is little wonder that it is reputed to be haunted and, as Tim the Yowie Man is at pains to point out, it is possibly more haunted than another homestead, Monte Cristo, which we shall look at later in this chapter.

Owned by Steve Rickett, who bought the sprawling Victoria Gothic mansion in 2002, it has ten bedrooms, a sitting room, formal dining room, study, reception room, billiards room, and servants' quarters, all set in four hectares of sprawling Victorian-era influenced gardens. And among these gardens is a large fish pond, which apparently was a favourite spot for Henry's eldest daughter, Miss Edith Edwards, who lived at Burnima up until her death in 1952.

Miss Edith's love of the fish pond and its fish seems to have carried on to the present day as her spirit lingers on with a number of sightings of her apparition. This includes a bulldozer driver who recently was waiting to meet Rickett for a landscaping job and spotted "a lady wearing a long white gown walking to the old fish pond, only for her to vanish before his very eyes."

Rickett himself admits that he too strolls around the gardens and pond area hoping to catch a glimpse of the elusive Miss Edith but thus far has been unsuccessful. Having said this, it is not just the grounds that seem haunted in this majestic building, for the house itself is said to contain a number of spirits, including the ghost of a young girl who, one night in 2006, appeared at the side of Rickett's bed. As he recalled, "I turned over towards the noise only to see a girl standing right along my bed. I screamed at it, kicked the doona at it and it vanished."

Ricketts explains that Burnima possesses a number of gruesome mysteries, including the sudden disappearance of a young servant girl who was thought to have become pregnant by Edwards. He adds, "The well in the southern garden was apparently filled in the very day she vanished"and suggests that "her body is most likely still buried at the bottom of the well."

Not surprising, in a house of such age, the spirits of Miss Edith and the young girl aren't the only ghosts prowling the building and grounds as other strange phenomena include phantom phone calls, unexplained hammerings, and knockings—and even a wardrobe that moves by itself. And yet, for all its supernatural happenings, Rickett is quite at ease with the fact that he may live in a haunted house, noting that he is "used to all the ghostly goings-on now as it's been happening for quite some time and no one has been hurt." Having said this, he also admits that he "never watches any thriller television shows or movies as it heightens the senses."

But if Burnima is just an atmospheric mansion in the middle of nowhere, then what of our next destination, the unnerving and intimidating Monte Cristo in Junee?

Monte Cristo is an historic two-story Georgian style house near Junee in New South Wales. Built in 1884, it was originally the home of Christopher Crawley and his family. And, if contemporary reports are to be believed, it would appear that they, and others, may still haunt the buildings with residents and visitors reporting strange lights, unseen forces, ghostly voices, phantom footsteps of a woman, disembodied faces at windows, floating figures in white, and opening and closing doors. In all it is believed that seven separate ghosts haunt the house and its surrounds.

According to paranormal researchers, the most prolific of ghosts at Monte Cristo is Mrs. Crawley herself, which is not that surprising given that after her husband died bizarrely from an infected boil on his neck caused by wearing starched collars, she only left the house twice in the next twenty-three years. She is seen predominantly in the house drawing room and chapel, the rooms she spent much of her time in after her husband's death. She is usually seen dressed in black and sometimes carrying a silver tray.

Interestingly, although the ghost of Mrs. Crawley sounds very much like a stone tape theory haunting, people have reported that she has ordered them out of the room, thus showing intelligence, something that seems to be lacking in a lot of ghostly encounters.

Besides the spirit of Mrs. Crawley, an unknown woman in period dress is often seen walking along the veranda and, although it has never been confirmed, it is thought that she may be the ghost of a maid who fell to her death off a balcony onto some stone steps.

The upper story of the house has witnessed much death, such as a woman reputed to have died in childbirth as well as the tragic death of the Crawley's baby daughter who slipped from her nanny's arms and down the stairs, subsequently dying from her injuries. Given the reputation of the house, the maid claimed that something pushed the baby from her grasp.

The upper regions of the house are known for the sound of disembodied footsteps on wooden floorboards even though the floors now are carpeted or linoed. As well, in the drawing room, vases and objects are often found to have been moved from their original position.

It is not just the house that appears haunted, but the surrounding gardens as well, including the stables where the ghost of a stable boy called Morris, who died after his boss set his bedding on fire believing him to be lazy and not sick, is said to haunt. Sadly, Morris was too sick to escape the fire and was burnt to death.

In addition, a mentally retarded man by the name of Harold, the son of a housekeeper, was said to have been locked in shackles in the caretaker's cottage for forty years. When his mother died he was sent away to an asylum where he died soon after. Is it possible that the energy of this tortured and anguished man could have been absorbed by the very cottage itself and now replays like a scene from a tragic historical movie to visitors to this place?

But not all Monte Cristo deaths are from the distant past. In 1951, a psychotic youth shot dead the then caretaker Jackie Simpson after watching the movie *Psycho* three times, and it is said that Simpson's ghost can be seen wandering the grounds.

As with other haunted sites, we must ask why it is that certain places, like Monte Cristo, seem to be more haunted than others, almost as if the place itself either attracts or retains unearthly spirits? Lots of people die in lots of places, so why is it that some seem to hold on to spirits more so than others? Is it something to do with the architecture or design? Or maybe the land it is built upon? Whatever the case, our next site is another that for some reason seems to have attracted and held spirits for many years.

Cooma Cottage is a National Trust property on the banks of the Yass River just outside Yass. It is in the heart of the rich sheep-grazing country of New South Wales and attracted numerous pioneers in the early 1820s and 1830s. The original colonial house forms part of the earliest complex of dwellings and stables on the site and was built by pastoralist Cornelius O'Brien.

The property is most noted as the home of Australian born explorer Hamilton Hume, who was born in 1797 and died in 1873. It has been suggested that Hume fell in love with the site when camping there in 1824, on his marathon overland journey to Port Phillip Bay in Victoria with William Hovell, another of Australia's great explorers. In 1839, Hume purchased the cottage and 100 acres and over the next twenty or so years extended the original building, including Palladian style wings and a Greek revival portico. In the 1890s, it was apparently converted into a private hospital for consumption patients. It is also considered to be haunted.

Staff and visitors complain of occurrences, such as doors being locked without a key, lights turning themselves on and off, beds appearing crumpled and as if they have been slept on, and whispered voices when no one is around. Others have insisted that they have felt a ghostly hand touch them on the shoulder, and some claim to have heard a woman's footsteps follow them around various sections of the cottage. A few people have also claimed to have seen the image of a lady or a girl in a white dress; however, who she is nobody knows, although it is suspected that she is the ghost of a girl by the name of Emma who, from reports, died in the hospice. It is also said that if one is to listen carefully enough, then you might hear a sound that has reputedly terrified staff and visitors: the sound of a baby crying—Emma's deceased eighteen-month-old child crying out for her also deceased mother.

A local website (www.the-riotact.com) that publishes articles about Canberra and district had an interesting post regarding Cooma Cottage and its alleged hauntings. Whereas most people discounted the thought that ghosts even exist, one comment caught my eye as I have heard others comment in a similar fashion. The comment began with a disclaimer of sorts:

> No matter how hard I try, as a sceptic, there are sometimes (sic) incidents that offer no clear explanation. You know that goosebumpy, hair standing up kind of reaction that happens? Sometimes, it's just a cold wind or a noise that catches you off-guard. Other times, not.

This was followed by:

> I don't believe in lots of things, but whilst visiting Cooma Cottage, I entered the ladies drawing room. The rest of the place was really interesting, but in the drawing room, a sense of fear set in; didn't see or hear anything, just didn't like the room and left; pronto.

My visit to Cooma Cottage was sadly uneventful. It was a beautiful spring day and I just happened to be driving back from Yass to Canberra when I decided to stop and have a look at the place. It is without doubt a superb home with stunning views across rolling green pastures all the way down to the Yass River. Admittedly, I wouldn't want to stay in the cellar on my own overnight, but this is simply the result of suggestion in that something may happen. The building does, however, have a certain feeling to it, not a bad feeling like an old gaol, but some sort of indescribable "vibe." Whether or not this is due to the empty corridors and rooms or the age of the place is unknown, but whatever the case, it is a place that one should endeavour to visit, if only to experience a vital part of Australia's historical past.

Moving on from Cooma Cottage and heading roughly north on the aptly named Hume Highway, we soon come across Goulburn, Australia's first inland city. Founded in the early 1800s, the city contains numerous buildings that reflect its heritage past, including a magnificent cathedral, imposing schools, stately homes, and quaint cottages. Not only does the city possess abundant heritage architecture, but it also has a prison, a giant concrete merino ram, and what appears to be a lighthouse, albeit, a war memorial that sits on a hill overlooking the city. It also has a mental asylum and an abandoned orphanage.

It is late afternoon and a cool breeze is blowing from the south as I stop the car and step out. The sun sits low in the sky, and pieces of paper and other rubbish are caught in the breeze, which pushes them around the deserted car park at St. Johns Orphanage. The place feels cold and deserted, as if the very life of the building has been sucked out and replaced with a void.

Opened in March 1912, by the Reverend Gallagher Bishop of Goulburn, St. Johns Orphanage now stands abandoned, a lonely reminder of a past probably best forgotten. Run by the Sisters of Mercy until closing in 1978, the building was designed to house up to 100 boys although, at its peak during the Second World War, that figure reached as high as 250. In all, over 2,500 boys attended the orphanage over its 66 years of operation. Interestingly, only a very small number were orphans with most coming from poor or "broken" families.

The front entrance to the building is an imposing red-bricked, three-story structure topped by a stark white marble cross with an alcove just beneath containing the statue of a woman in robes, possibly Mary, the mother of Jesus. On either side of the entrance the building has two wings that stretch out from the centre. These contain rooms on the lower level plus a covered walkway, while the top level has a glassed in veranda, or at least, would have in its heyday, as now it appears that almost every piece of glass in the building has been broken. To the back, another wing juts out, much the same as the other two.

It is a proud old building that sadly sits neglected and abandoned in what appears to be a disused paddock surrounded by shrubs and trees just off the main road that used to be the old highway. Even during the day it fills one with a sense of dread, so I can only imagine how much this is amplified at night.

At night the building's demeanour seems to change from bad to worse. The brick entrance façade seems to jut out aggressively at the visitor as if warning people not to enter, and the dilapidated white wooden balconies on either side of the entrance seem to hold dark shadows that appear like fleeting human figures. It is a place of misery and despair, and the overall feeling coming from the building is menacing.

Many believe it to be haunted by the spirits of the children who once lived there, and there have been reports of the sounds of children playing from within the building. Sadly, my attempt to gain permission to spend a night in the old building was rejected, although, in hindsight this is probably a good thing as I am not exactly sure if I could have spent a night alone in such a place.

Although in a rundown state, it is believed that the building will be refurbished and turned into apartments or flats. And if this eventuates, will the building find a new lease of life? Will the tormented spirits that seemingly haunt this place be placated and move on? We have previously seen that, at the National Museum of Australia, the ghosts of the past care little for the present, so will the same happen here? It is an intriguing thought and one I hope to follow up on in a decade or so.

These days one can take a Goulburn ghost tour that includes a visit to the orphanage where one can walk along the deserted, lonely corridors and contemplate the tough lives that previous residents must have endured. And it is a sobering thought that it only closed down in 1978. Sadly, at the time of writing, the orphanage was subject to a fire, believed to be arson, and its current state will be unknown until the damage has been assessed by engineers. At the time of this printing, it remains a burnt-out ruin. Hopefully, the damage will not be too tragic, and the place can be restored—after all, it is an important part of our history, of Goulburn's history, and ultimately, Australia's history. However, fire or not, this is not the only ghostly place in this old inland city.

Kinghorne Street, which runs roughly east-west through the centre of Goulburn, is believed to be the location of the first recorded hanging in Goulburn and, according to Louise, a guide for a local ghost tour, "It involved two men convicted of murdering a third man in 1830. Once hung, their corpses remained in place as a grisly reminder to others. Some months later, Governor Bourke was visiting Goulburn and took exception to the display, ordering that the bodies be removed."

Is it possible that the tormented souls of these men still lurk in the shadows of this federation-style street? Did their violent death at the hands off an unknown hangman sentence them to a life after death more horrible than if they had simply ceased to exist?

Not far from Kinghorne Street is the Saint Saviour's Cemetery, the final resting place of many of the city's early pioneers, indeed, it is possible that explorer William Hovell could be one of those interred, although there is some doubt as to the truth of this. Having said that, it is believed to be haunted by a number of apparitions that appear as shrouds of mist or dark shadows that move across the rough grassy ground in between headstones and graves.

A short drive or walk from the cemetery brings the visitor to Riversdale, an early colonial house that is now classified by the Heritage Council as a property of historical significance. Initially opened as a coaching inn, it was built about 1840, although some of the outbuildings are much older. These days one can take a tour of the house and flowering gardens; however, it too is said to be haunted, possibly by the ghost of a traveller who drowned in the river in the 1840s, although, oddly, when I asked a guide about this alleged haunting, she replied tersely in the negative. As such I dropped the subject and decided to explore what I could by myself, but I have to admit, except for an eerie feeling in some rooms, I saw or heard nothing out of the normal.

And from Australia's first inland city we will travel north along the Hume Highway towards the gentile Southern Highlands, roughly situated halfway between Canberra and Sydney and a stunning rural retreat for those who can afford to live here. Centred around the major towns of Mittagong, Bowral, Moss Vale, Bundanoon, and Robertson, it sits between 500 metres and 900 metres above sea level on the Great Dividing Range and, like other regions along this plateau, is known for its cool temperate climate, which promotes lush vegetation growth.

And, if you believe the locals at the Bundanoon Royal Hotel, it is also the location of what appears to be a ghostly girl of about ten years of age who is known as Mary.

Built in 1922, the hotel was, like many hotels and guest lodges in the Southern Highlands, built to capture the ever-increasing tourism from Sydney, attracted by the cool mountain air, rollicking English-like landscape, spring waters, and bushwalks. Indeed, at one stage Bundanoon was described as possibly Australia's first resort and at one stage had around forty guesthouses.

When arriving at the hotel the visitor is greeted by an impressive mock Tudor façade that overhangs the main entrance. Inside one is pleasantly surprised by the friendly ambience of the place with its old world furnishings and décor. It boasts over fifty rooms plus a public bar, dining room, private lounge, tennis court, swimming pool, and cosy open wood fires in the winter. It also has a full-sized billiards table, and it is here that the ghost is mainly seen, although she has been seen and photographed all over the hotel.

In 2012, one intrepid ghost investigator reported seeing her ghost in a reflection in one of the upstairs rooms and described her to be wearing a long mourning gown, circa early 1900s with her hair in a bun at the nape of her neck.

In a visit to the hotel in 2014, I spoke to a barman who told me of watching chip packets simply fly off the counter one night, and, when he called another staff member to also witness it, they saw a glass slide across the bar untouched by human hands. As well, the barman told me of doors that open by their own means and guests at the hotel commenting that they had seen a strange little girl in the upstairs corridors or in the billiard room and that she looked sad.

Sadly, I have never witnessed the ghostly Mary in all my visits to the hotel, although I have heard rumours that there is also the ghost of a young boy who has been seen in some of the upstairs rooms. At time of writing I cannot confirm this, but I do intend to follow it up at a later stage.

But moving on from the lovely little township of Bundanoon we soon come across Berrima, a romantic and historic village literally teeming with colonial heritage and charm from its solid and imposing sandstone buildings, historic courthouse, and gaol, not to mention Australia's oldest licenced pub, the Surveyor General Inn, which was established in 1834. Indeed, at the height of the town's popularity, there where fourteen hotels either in, or around, the town in the 1840s.

The name Berrima is believed to derive from an Aboriginal word meaning either "southward" or "black swan" and was once occupied by the Dharawal Aborigines until they were driven off or killed by the 1870s. The village, which was once a major town, is on the Old Hume Highway, although the building of a new highway directly between Canberra and Sydney saw it cut off from passing traffic, which probably contributed to it remaining a quaint historical town. Previously the railway had also bypassed the town in favour of other Southern Highland towns such as Bowral, Bundanoon, and Moss Vale, and due to this no new houses were built for a hundred years. Its historical and cultural significance has been retained and now, as a country retreat for wealthy Sydneysiders, its future remains bright and assured.

Whatever the case, this little town is reputed to be one of the most haunted places in New South Wales, if not the whole of Australia.

The Berrima Courthouse was designed by the New South Wales government architect Mortimer Lewis, who was appointed by Governor Bourke in 1835 and was also responsible for courthouses at Goulburn, Bathurst, Berrima, and

Hartley, as well as gaols at Maitland, Bathurst, and Goulburn. Lewis resigned in 1849, but well and truly left his mark on the new colony, including the Berrima Gaol, which we will look at in due course.

The courthouse itself is built in a Roman style and was constructed between 1836 and 1838 from sandstone and features four Doric columns supporting a classical pediment. Strictly speaking, the building is stylistically classified as Georgian, but, whatever the case, one cannot but be impressed by the imposing façade and gravitas that seems to emanate from its sturdy walls. At night it reminds the visitor of another world, possibly of Greek antiquity.

The first trial by jury in the new colony of New South Wales was heard in the courthouse, although, in 1850, the district court moved to Goulburn, south of Berrima. Minor courts continued at Berrima until 1873, and a number of notable trials were held, including that of John Lynch, who was hanged for the murder of at least nine people, and of Lucretia Dunkley and her lover Martin Beech, who were both hanged in 1843 for the murder of Dunkley's husband. These days one can visit the building that is now a museum and relive the trial through audio commentary and realistic manikins. Lucretia Dunkley remains the only woman to be hanged at Berrima Gaol and, along with the ghost of a long dead judge, among others, her spirit is said to haunt the corridors and rooms of the historic old building.

Ghost hunter Judy Kemme and psychic June Cleeland of Southern Highlands Ghost Hunts and Investigations are well versed in the supernatural stories of the courthouse with Kemme suggesting that she has "heard doors slamming, voices," and that one will "probably feel the presence as you go in."

Cleeland is equally enthusiastic, stating that "this is one of the most haunted places I've been in." And to be fair, the place does have a certain feel to it, almost menacing, especially at night or when one finds themselves unexpectedly alone in one of its rooms. In the courtroom itself is a display of manikins that unnervingly seem to move every time you turn away from them, but, as I tell myself, this is simply suggestion; manikins cannot move by themselves, can they? And yet, I am reminded of a story from some of my previous ghost hunting trips in England where, in the London Dungeon, manikins have been known to move as if possessed. Knowing this, I endeavour to stay away from them, just in case.

The women's holding cell is where the ghost of Lucretia is said to be most active. It is a small room and has a feeling of dread, very much the same feeling I got when visiting Port Arthur many years ago where I entered one of the cells in the model prison. It is a feeling of doom, of panic, of not wanting to be where you are but for no apparent reason. If Lucretia's ghost is here, I am not sure if I want to see her or not, and, to be perfectly honest, if I do, I think I'll simply panic and run.

Tonight, however, I am lucky—or unlucky depending on your point of view. No ghosts appear in front of me and I am somewhat relieved. And yet, this is not the only ghostly visitor to these rooms and corridors; occasionally people complain of being poked in the back or grabbed by unearthly, invisible hands, and others have reported crying and whimpering from behind locked doors. As well, others have reported seeing the figure of a man in the judge's chambers.

But the courthouse isn't the only haunted building in this wonderful little town as next door is the gaol, also designed by Mortimer Lewis and equally as impressive. Berrima Gaol was built between 1836 and 1839, mainly by convicts in leg-irons to imprison the bushrangers who preyed on the travellers between Goulburn to Sydney and only closed as recently as 2011 when the New South Wales government undertook a restructuring of its correction facilities. In its last years as an operational gaol it was an all female low-to-medium security prison although in its past, it was known as a brutal and savage place where prisoners spent most of their days in cells, and the only light was through a small grate set in the door.

In addition, prisoners were not allowed to speak to anyone for the first nine months of their sentence; those who broke this rule were gagged with a harness of leather and wood or put into solitary confinement cells that measured eight feet by five feet. Some prisoners were said to have spent a year living in these conditions and bushranger Dick Marston described it as "enough to drive any man mad that had been used to a free life. Day after day, night after night, the same and the same."

In fact, so cruel and heartless were the conditions at the gaol that, in 1877, a royal commission was held into brutality at Berrima. Not surprisingly given the times, none of the recommendations were implemented.

During World War I, the gaol was used as a German prisoner internment camp with most of the 329 internees being enemy aliens from shipping companies. There were also captured German officers from Rabaul as well as officers from the light cruiser SMS Emden. After the war, it fell into disuse, although it reopened in 1949 as a medium-security prison.

And it was here that Lucretia Dunkley was hanged and, although no one is quite sure where her remains are buried, many people have reported seeing her agonised spirit either in the gaol or walking the streets of the town. Interestingly, as her head was removed for scientific purposes, she is sometimes seen headless in a grove of pine trees close to the gaol itself, whereas the spirit in the courthouse is not described as headless. Is it possible that the ghostly woman in the courthouse is not in fact Lucretia Dunkley but someone else?

Dunkley was not the only person to suffer within the walls of this building. Nor was she the only to be hanged as Martin Beech, her lover, and Jack Lynch also met this grisly end. Lynch was hanged for the murder of eleven people, including a couple with two children. As a result, it is little wonder that people describe the interior of the gaol as cold and depressing and report strange noises and voices as well as visions of dark, shadowy shapes that scurry across corridors to strange lights that dance in the corners of cells. Unfortunately, I have not had the chance to visit the gaol, so I cannot confirm reports of ghostly visitations and disembodied voices.

As we continue on our ghostly journey, we soon find Picton, another quaint town south of Sydney and also reputed to be Australia's most haunted town—indeed, so much so that it once held well known ghost tours up until 2011, until an over-zealous council forced the venture to close, leaving a generation of ghost hunters to wonder what they had missed out on.

Picton itself is only eighty kilometres from Sydney and in the heart of the Wollondilly Shire. Originally named Stonequarry, it was changed to Picton in 1841 by Sir Thomas Picton, obviously a man with an enormous ego and no sense of self-deprecation. Originally founded in 1822, it is similar to most Southern Highland towns in that it is the home of many historic and culturally significant buildings, including two types of bridges not found easily anymore elsewhere in the state, a timber-framed trestle bridge called Victoria Bridge opened in 1897, and the Picton Railway Viaduct, a stone viaduct opened in 1863. As well, the town holds the George IV Inn, reputed to have been constructed in 1839 and considered to be one of the oldest hotel buildings in Australia. The cellar contains remnants of convict shackles, a legacy of when prisoners being transported from Sydney to Berrima prison would be held in Picton overnight.

Whereas the viaduct is still in use by the railways, the same cannot be said for the disused railway tunnel on Redbank Range, which was used to store mustard gas during World War II. And it is here that residents and visitors claim to have experienced supernatural activity in the form of full body apparitions, as well as strange lights and noises.

The tunnel itself is 592 feet in length and was used between 1867 and 1919, serving as a corridor for trains to and from Melbourne until a new line was built that passed around the hills. Although the closure of the tunnel seems straightforward, some believe that the real reason for its closure was due to the numerous suicides by local residents who would throw themselves in front of the train. However, like most rural legends, it is most probably untrue, although, as with most legends, there is usually a grain of truth to it all.

As a result it is said that many spirits wander the abandoned tunnel. Witnesses have reported seeing lights and shadows, feeling gusts of wind and being touched by unseen hands. As well, there is a rumour that a girl was once raped and murdered in the tunnel, and her sad ghost sometimes used to appear with tour groups as they explored the tunnel's dark depths. In addition, the ghost of a girl who hung herself at the entrance of the tunnel has also been reported.

Emily Bollard, who was fifty when she was killed by an oncoming train in 1916, is just one of many spirits who are said to haunt the tunnel. Witnesses have consistently reported her walking in the tunnel wearing a white dress, although she disappears when approached. This reminds me somewhat of an encounter I had in the Hellfire Caves in Buckinghamshire in 2010 where, much to my surprise, I came across what I can only describe as a ghost or spiritual entity and, as such, very unexplainable, so much so that even today I question what happened and what I had seen.

While walking down a length of the cave that led to a junction that split to the left and right, I came across a short, thin, apparently middle-aged woman in old clothes. She was standing against the wall at the end of the corridor and did not appear to notice me approach in the semi-darkness. When I reached her I said hello, but she didn't move, just stood there with her head slightly bowed.

As she didn't acknowledge me or move, I simply slid past her into the next part of the cave when it occurred to me that something seemed not quite right, although what I mean by this I cannot explain. As a result, I turned around and to my surprise found that she had disappeared. And not only disappeared from the spot where she was standing only seconds ago but there was also no sign of her in the corridor from which I'd come, the only place she could have gone. Put simply, she appeared to have disappeared.

Is it possible I literally said hello to a ghost? And if so, then who was it? Hellfire Caves are reputed to be haunted by a number of entities, including a young girl by the name of Sukie. And yet, this was no young and forlorn girl. Maybe it was simply a shy tourist, albeit, one who seemed to possess the ability of vanishing into thin air.

Over time, as I thought more about this encounter, it occurred to me that the woman was somewhat see through, like a hologram projected in front of the stone wall. Today I cannot be sure whether what I saw was a real person or some sort of apparition. Maybe over time I have convinced myself that something was amiss due to the underlying eeriness of the place, but then again, maybe not.

Having said that, Emily Boland is not the only spiritual visitor in the charming historic town of Picton. St. Mark's Church, which was started in 1850 and finished in 1856, due to the workers leaving to find their fortunes on the goldfields, has a typical country graveyard with moss-encrusted tombstones leaning on strange angles and weather-swept headstones that have slowly eroded over time. It is a lovely, peaceful place during the daylight hours, although it is reported that many visitors have seen the ghosts of children in old-fashioned clothes walking through the tombstones. Others have reported children's laughter, as if they were playing. Local legend suggests that the two children are David Shaw and Blanche Moon, who died sixty years apart, Blanche being crushed to death in 1886 when a pile of sleepers that she and a number of children were playing on slipped, and David, the son of a minister, who died from polio in 1946. Is it possible that in death the two have been united across the years?

A photo taken in 2010 by Renee English from the New South Wales town of Port Macquarie while on a ghost tour appears to show exactly that: two children playing between the tombstones. She later stated that, "We were standing at the bank looking into the Cemetery. I was just snapping away and making jokes about the whole thing and asking when the ghosts were going to come out."

She also added that "I know that when I took that photo there was no one else in the cemetery. The only people we saw were a family of four about ten minutes later, but those kids were clinging to their parents the whole time. When we uploaded our photos and saw the children all the hairs on my arm stood up and I just went cold all over."

Pointedly, English, previously a sceptic added, "I wasn't a believer in ghosts, but now I'm intrigued."

But ghosts in tunnels and strange photographs of children who should not exist are not the only attractions for the ghost hunter in this colonial town. The Imperial Hotel, which was built in the 1860s, was originally called the Terminus due to its locality across from the local railway station from 1863 until 1867. It was then taken over by Colonel John Hay Goodlet, who transformed it into a hospice for the sick and infirm, having earlier lost his sister to tuberculosis. However, by 1884, the building became too small for its purpose and it reverted to its original role as a country pub. In the 1830s it had another name change, this time to the Imperial, which it retains to this day.

A recent bistro manager, a Mr. Karl Klein, skeptical as he was, could not explain a number of strange occurrences he witnessed in 2008. He later described how, while one day doing some paperwork at the end of the day, "I jumped and turned around because I felt someone looking over my shoulder, but nobody was there."

Another time Klein was working in the bottleshop when he looked up at a balcony to see "a white curtain move and thought somebody was opening the door because we have no curtains. Again, there was nobody up there."

Klein soon came to the belief that the old hotel was haunted by patients who had died during the building's stint as an infirmary, as in the late 1800s the stricken patients were brought there on the train and then through a tunnel that connected Picton station to the hotel's underground cellar. This way the sick could not contaminate anyone else.

Intrigued by this, he employed a spirit medium to visit the hotel who apparently walked halfway across the top floor and then fled, later stating that, "They're all over the place up there and on the balcony, and they're all wearing white!"

Other staff members, including Klein's wife and daughter, also reported strange phenomena, ranging from their hair being pulled to doors inexplicably closing themselves. A chef also reported being scratched on the head by an unseen hand.

But if Picton is as haunted as it is reported, what will we find as we move north, closer to Sydney and its wealth of convict and colonial history?

The highway from Canberra to Sydney is unremarkable except when it passes through Pheasant's Nest, where one can peer down into the deep river gorges that crisscross this area of the Great Dividing Range. Travelling through this country is now a simple task, but one simply cannot imagine how difficult it must have been for early settlers and explorers to make their way across these mountains.

Before long we notice houses and suburbs and an increase in the traffic. We are now on the outskirts of Sydney and coming in Campbelltown, a historic satellite city some 50 kilometres from the Sydney CBD and named after Elizabeth Campbell, the wife of former governor of New South Wales, Lachlan Macquarie.

Campbelltown has a rich and varied history. Prior to European settlement it was occupied by the Tharawal people. The colonial administration at the time was keen to establish cattle herds on the land, but John Macarthur took a liking to the prime grazing land with the view of establishing sheep in the colony. Not a man to be taken lightly, he convinced the government to grant him 5,000 acres just south of the Nepean River in 1805. Over the following years a number of other grants were also made to farmers between Camden and nearby Liverpool.

Tensions between the local Aboriginals and settlers developed and soon led to skirmishes and a number of deaths on each side. To alleviate this, Governor Macquarie decided to create a permanent settlement in the hope that it would lead to order in the area, and so Campbell-Town, as it was then called, came into existence in 1820.

At first development of the town was slow given that it was a reasonable distance from Sydney and had been subject to unrest. However, it was during this period that Campbelltown's most famous incident occurred when, in 1826, local farmer Frederick Fisher disappeared, and, according to legend, his ghost later appeared sitting on a fence rail over a creek just south of the town, pointing forlornly at a site where his body was later found to be buried.

Frederick George James Fisher was thirty-five years old and originally came to Australia from England as a convict in 1816. Soon after his arrival, he earned his ticket of leave, which meant that, as a convict, he could earn for himself in order to purchase land and thus settle. Fisher worked hard and soon purchased thirty acres of land in Campbelltown near Bow Bowing Creek. He soon prospered and bought more land in nearby Appin, Cabramatta, and Nepean.

Fisher had a friend, also an ex-convict with a ticket of leave, named George Worrall. George rented land next to Fisher's but had fallen on hard times and, according to the legend, envied his now prosperous neighbour. However, in time Fisher also experienced financial hardship and fell into debt, and he signed over all his property to Worrall so as not to lose it. Fisher then spent six months in gaol.

On release, Fisher headed back to Campbelltown to reclaim his land, but in June 1826 he disappeared. Suspicion inevitably fell on his close friend Worrall who had been seen walking around Sydney in a pair of Fisher's pants. When quizzed, Worrall claimed that Fisher had given him all his property and left for England.

In time, Fisher's battered body was found, and Worrall was convicted of his murder and later executed. The story of Fredrick Fisher appeared to be over.

However, in March or July 1836, depending upon sources, an article called "Fishers Ghost—A Legend of Campbelltown" was published in a monthly periodical. The article claimed that a well-known local farmer by the name of Hurley (or Farley) was out walking one night when he suddenly saw what appeared to be a man sitting on a post and rail fence. Thinking nothing unusual Hurley continued walking towards the figure until, to his horror, he realized he was looking at a ghost bathed in an eerie light.

The ghost apparently had blood dripping from a wound to the head and, with a moan, pointed to a spot in the creek flowing behind Fisher's property. At this point, Mr. Hurley, as would most I suspect, passed out and upon coming back to consciousness, found that the ghost had gone. He later told a magistrate, and Fisher's body was found exactly where the ghost had pointed. In his death Fisher had somehow alerted the authorities as to where he was laying!

Sadly, as romantic and interesting this story is, the facts conclusively point to Worrall murdering Fisher for personal gain. There is no mention of a ghost, only court transcripts. Fisher's ghost, for all its celebrated telling, is simply a story. The site where Frederick Fisher's body was originally found is along what remains of the banks of the Fishers Creek, now a playground and drain site where residents of Campbelltown play and picnic.

And so, what are we to believe? Australia's most celebrated ghost story is a fraud. A tale made up by an anonymous writer simply to titillate readers of the periodical. Most probably the magazine itself wrote the article to boost sales in the area, given the remoteness of the location and the lack of news that would have filtered through to the residents in those times.

Fisher's ghost is a perfect example of ghost folklore that can be found not only in Australia but all over the world. The pattern of these stories is always the same: man gets murdered, man comes back as a ghost and points out his killer or his final resting place, thus ensuring that justice has been served.

It is easy to see how and why these sorts of stories were written. Tough, hardworking, hard drinking, and hard swearing men lived a dangerous and uneasy life in colonial Australia. The land was foreign and unforgiving, Aboriginal people could often be hostile, and your neighbour could be an ex-convict, a violent one at that. Although a semblance of civility outwardly appeared, a dark, seedy underbelly lurked just below the surface.

Stories such as Fisher's ghost would have soothed people in the knowledge that, in the end, justice would be served and those who sinned would meet the bitter rewards of their deeds.

And yet, even allowing for folklore stories there are other stories that do not follow this tact. These are odd tales that seem to not give us an answer but leave us wondering whether or not they are true, or if they have some sort of message from the grave. Whether these stories are true or not sometimes can seem irrelevant as they intimate that people have a fear of the unknown and more so, need to know what happens when they die.

Even though Fisher's ghost is most probably only a legend, the local theatre, where George Worrall's house once stood, is alleged to have its very own theatre ghost by the name of Ginger. Whether Ginger is real or not I have no idea and, in any case, Fisher's ghost is so much more interesting.

Having said that, some believe the ghost of the theatre is actually Fisher, as George Worrall, who was executed for the murder of Fred Fisher, rented the land on which the buildings stands. Fisher was also living in Mr. Worrell's house at the time of his murder.

Although there are stories of Fisher's ghost popping up all over the place, it is believed that he is most active at the southern end of Queen Street, where he once had his farm and where he was murdered. The Town Hall Theatre is said to be the most regular haunting with many theatre group members recounting stories of flickering lights, eerie footsteps and misty figures walking on stage during rehearsals. Indeed, in 1991, the then-theatre group president, Barbara Handley, told a local newspaper that she had encountered the ghost and that it was "like somebody brushed up against you—it's the weirdest feeling."

Another theatre group president, a Mr. Neil Hatchman recalled, in 1995, that he was "working there a lot at night by myself, taking away rubbish around the back, when the lights went off." Not alarmed, as it was an old building, he found a light switch and turned the lights back on, only to see the shadowy figure of a man moving across the stage. Hatchman called for him to stop, but the figure ignored him and disappeared into a nearby room. Now somewhat worried, Hatchman picked up a lump of wood and entered the room only to find it empty.

A musical director by the name of Mary Phillips also recalled that she was directing a musical when the lights went out in the orchestra pit. Apparently no one was anywhere near the light switch, and Phillips, in exasperation, cried out, "For God's sake Fred, turn the lights back on," which to her surprise, happened.

Whether this ghost is indeed the spirit of Frederick Fisher is debatable, but whatever the case, it seems that his legend will never die. Having said that, Campbelltown has a wealth of historic buildings from St. Peter's Church of England to the Campbelltown Police Station and the old Post Office, all listed under the Register of the National Estate, so it is no wonder that rumours of ghosts abound.

Not far from Campbelltown is another historic New South Wales town, this time Camden, and, like Campbelltown, it too has its own tales of the supernatural, this time in the form of a haunted house that now sits on the Camden Golf Course.

Studley Park House has long been regarded as one of Camden's most haunted buildings and was constructed in 1889 by William Payne for his bride. However, Payne soon ran into debt and as a result sold it to Francis Buckle, an architect who then redesigned the house and used it as a weekend retreat. Buckle then later sold it to a Dr. Henry Oliver, the headmaster of the Camden Grammar School in 1902. A few decades later, it was transformed into an art deco playground for Arthur Adolphus Gregory, the sales manager of Twentieth Century Fox, and, during World War II, became the Eastern Command Training School for the army. At its height it had over 280 students and staff. It is certainly a place with an impressive history.

Walking up to the building one cannot be anything but impressed by the size of the mansion with its traditional Victorian windowpanes and high pointed rooftop. In a way it reminds me of Woodchester Mansion in Gloucestershire. And like Studley Park, Woodchester also had a history of grand ideals and debt and now stands uninhabited.

On October 15, 1909, fourteen-year-old student Ray Blackstone and five of his fellow boarders decided to go for a swim in a nearby dam. Although having being warned about the dangers of swimming in the dam, the boys ignored the warning and, while attempting to swim across it, Blackstone drowned. His body was recovered by senior students and was reputed to have been stored in the cellar of the mansion while awaiting burial.

As one would expect with such a tragedy, rumour now surrounds the death of the child and whether or not it is his ghost that haunts the opulent corridors and rooms of the stately mansion. However, if the ghost of Ray Blackstone *does* haunt the place, then it appears he is not on his own as there have been numerous reports of people hearing voices in the roof space and even a lady looking out of a window at night when the place is deserted.

Three decades after Blackstone's death, thirteen-year-old Noel Gregory, the son of Arthur Adolphus Gregory, died from appendicitis. These days it is believed that the two dead boys can be heard and seen playing together.

As well, a young girl called Amelia, complete with white stockings and curly hair, has been seen, and local legend has it that a man was once entombed in the walls of the mansion. The local fire brigade has also encountered some strange phenomena, stating that they have been called out to investigate alarms only to find that the fire alarm was switched off.

And yet these reports all seem to fade into insignificance when contractors repairing the roof in 2010 discovered a hangman's noose dangling from inside the house's steeple. Although it is not known whether or not it was ever used, it is suspected that more than one suicide has happened in the building.

In 2001, four contestants from the television program *Scream Test* spent time isolated in the dormitory, cellar, theatre, and tower. One of the contestants, who reported hearing voices, was too frightened to continue, and another said he'd heard a baby crying from a corner of the room.

Studley Park, for all its fearsome reputation is far from the only haunted building in Camden. Not far from the town is Gledswood Homestead, built in 1829 and set among sixty-four hectares of lush gardens, magnificent colonial buildings, and a winery. It is reputed to be haunted by numerous ghosts, including spectral dogs that roam the property's pet cemetery at night. And equally, Menangle House, built by George Taber in 1834 using convict labour, is also reputed to be haunted as we will see are many of the sites in our next stop, Sydney, the gateway to Australia.

Sydney, as everyone knows, is the capital of New South Wales and the most populous city in Australia. Located on one of the world's largest natural harbours, and sprawling west towards the Blue Mountains, it is considered one of the most multicultural cities in the world. And with a bloody convict past running back to the late 1700s, it is little wonder that it has reputation of being haunted; however, with such a big area and so much to examine, where does one start?

Of course, Sydney does have numerous well-known haunted places, from the old former quarantine station at North Head to the Rockwood Cemetery and even the New South Wales parliament building. However, although we will look at this later, at this time we shall concentrate on one of the oldest parts of Sydney: the Rocks.

When the First Fleet landed in 1788, they were confronted with a harsh, arid land with scrubby bush and grasslands. Today, Sydney is a modern, brash, and exciting metropolis with every modern convenience one could think of; however, back in those early days it wasn't even clear how the new penal colony would survive. The British didn't bring enough crop seed or stock to sustain the population of 1,300 convicts, crew, and soldiers, and they soon found, to their despair, that farming the dry, infertile soils was nearly impossible.

The first permanent settlements were built between Sydney Cove and Dawes Point, which is now a park under the benevolent gaze of the imposing and impressive Sydney Harbour Bridge and became known colloquially as the Rocks after the sandstone that was readily available for construction of houses and other buildings.

The Rocks is an historic urban district on the city centre located on the southern shore of Sydney Harbour. It sits adjacent to Circular Quay on Sydney Cove, the site of Australia's first European settlement and became established shortly after the colony's formation in 1788. With buildings generally made from local sandstone, the area had a reputation for lawlessness and was often frequented by sailors, criminals, and prostitutes.

In 1891, it was rumoured that there was an opium den in the area and that Chinese residents of the Rocks were using opium to drug young women and take advantage of them. Opium dens were then considered to be much worse places than sly grog shops and brothels, and even when investigations proved nothing, the combination of gambling, crime, prostitution, drugs, and violence that occurred here in the late 1800s all helped to form the popular opinion that the place was a den of iniquity.

Indeed, during the nineteenth century, it was a brave or foolish person who wandered down the alleyways of the Rocks at night. The area was seen as a place where "slang and vulgarity were mixed in lavish quantities, where harlots and riffraff, ex-convicts, and the scum of all the oceans collected."

In 1900, bubonic plague broke out in the area, killing many, and the state government resumed the area intending to demolish the now-squalid buildings. However, with the outbreak of the First World War, this plan was put on hold until the 1920s when several hundred buildings were demolished. The outbreak of the Second World War again provided some respite to the area although several hundred buildings were demolished to make way for the Sydney Harbour Bridge.

During the 1970s, the state government again planned to remove the decrepit old buildings, but a push by environmental and heritage groups and unions saw this plan discarded. These days the area, although still holding a large number of housing commission properties, is considered gentrified and extremely expensive due to its prime location.

But where do we start with such a rich history of violence and crime? Do we simply walk these old streets and marvel at the buildings or do we find somewhere likely to be haunted, for instance, an old hotel or pub, like the Russell Hotel?

The Russell Hotel is one of the oldest buildings in the Rocks and, like most buildings in the area, is constructed from sandstone. Being in the Rocks, the building has seen the worst of human interaction, such as murders, crime, plague, and death. As a result it is not surprising to hear that it is considered haunted with several ghostly visitors being reported to staff members, including an old seaman dressed in colonial clothing, who is often seen in Room 8 standing very still and simply staring at the guests who understandably, feel threatened by this otherworldly presence.

Many people have reported feeling cold spots in the room while others have had the horrifying sight of the seaman standing at the end of their beds. Sometimes he is seen strolling down the hotel's corridors before simply vanishing.

Other ghosts at the hotel include a number of women, assumed to be prostitutes and some other sailors, and in recent years, with the onset of major renovations, it appears that they have become more active than usual. Is it possible that the ghosts of the past are annoyed that their hotel is being changed? And even more so, what will happen to these spirits if the place is completely gutted and renovated?

Of course, given the history of the area, hotel ghosts are not the only denizens of the dark that haunt these time weary nooks and crannies and cobblestone alleys as, in February 2000, during excavation for the development of the Parbury Apartments, the remains of a stone cottage were discovered. Subsequent investigation revealed that the cottage's owners were ex-convicts Hugh Noble, who was born 1794, and Thomas Street, who was born four years earlier.

Noble purchased the site around 1820 and soon after began work on the cottage. In 1831, he moved on and sold the cottage to Street, who added the kitchen and basement in 1835. However, by the late 1860s, the cottage had been abandoned and partly demolished, and, in the 1870s, it was built over, sealing it away from the public eye seemingly forever.

However, with the excavations in 2000, the site was once again open to the air, and today visitors can descend a metal staircase and see the remains of the cottage, including an old kitchen trough and chimney. As well, one may also see a ghostly woman dressed in black veil and dress, believed to be named Amelia and reputed to have died a slow and lingering death in the cottage during its heyday. People also report that they have felt her presence and that she has touched them or pulled their hair.

Parbury is not alone in its dark, supernatural past. If one is to walk along Harrington Road, past the pubs and restaurants full of young city workers drinking and laughing after a day in the office, they will come across a nondescript white-walled house nestled behind a small courtyard. This is Reynolds' Cottages and is believed to be the second oldest building still standing in the Rocks and was recently the premises of the Gumnut Café.

The property, which comprises numbers 28, 30, and 32 Harrington Street, remained in the ownership of the Reynolds family until 1870 and continued to be occupied by a number of residents until the early 1900s. In 1901, the Sydney Harbour Trust assumed responsibility of the property following the outbreak of the plague. However, the site remained as a residence until the mid 1970s, by which time the Sydney Cove Redevelopment Authority took over responsibility. It is, without doubt, a very significant piece of Sydney's and, indeed, Australia's history.

The Gumnut Café was at number 28 and is the site of a number of strange occurrences that can only be described as supernatural. People have complained of cold spots and feelings of being watched, and although the place has an overall happy ambience during the day, it is said to change once the sun sinks in the western sky and the streets become dark and foreboding. Customers at the café have reported seeing a young girl in an old-fashioned dress sitting on the stairs nursing a doll. It's believed the little girl is the daughter of the Reynolds family. Although no one is quite sure how she died, one must remember that Sydney in the 1830s was a poverty-stricken and disease-ridden place, so early childhood death was not uncommon.

The Rocks is a place where one can listen to stories of murder, drunken sailors, prostitutes, and even dead Harbour Bridge workers, who still haunt the scene of their death, while at night, when the gnarled old trunks of the city's fig trees glow ghostly white in the dim street lights and the occasional bat flutters by, one can believe that the ghosts of this place truly exist.

Kenneth Slessor, the poet, journalist, and war correspondent, who was particularly notable for his contribution to modernist influences into Australian poetry once wrote:

Ghosts' trousers, like the dangle of hung men,
in pawn-shop windows, bumping knee by knee,
but none inside to suffer or condemn;

Slessor's William Street is about another age—not of today nor of the convict past but of pre-Second World War Sydney, a place recovering from the depression years and dragging itself into the modern age. And whereas Slessor is talking about Kings Cross, his words ring true for much of old Sydney, a vivid painting of a landscape on a wet and rainy night when the roads are covered by the reflection of the bright neon lights. And yet, as much as Slessor describes it as a beautiful place, the undertone to his prose is that we are talking about an ugly, desperate place where crime and poverty go hand in hand with riches and modernity.

Moving on from the Gumnut Café, the visitor soon comes across the historic the Hero of Waterloo, now a well-known landmark on the Sydney landscape and once home to Thomas Kirkman and his wife Anne. Named after the Duke of Wellington, the old pub celebrated its 170th birthday in 2013 and could lay claim to being the oldest continually licensed pub on the same premises in the whole of Australia, having been serving since 1845.

The Hero of Waterloo stands on the southwest corner of Lower Fort Street and Windmill Street in Millers Point and is a three-story, sandstone building with cellars and a hipped iron roof. Importantly, it has retained most of its original form, which makes it an excellent example of 1840s pub architecture. It has been claimed that, due to gauge marks on the sandstone bricks, that it may have once been used as a barracks for soldiers, but this has never been fully established. In addition, there are stories of secret tunnels leading from the pub's basement to nearby wharves and that these tunnels were used to press-gang drunken patrons onto ships looking for extra crew.

Whether or not this is true is sort of irrelevant given that the pub is the sort of place where such stories could be true. What is well known, however, is that the place is haunted by the ghost of Anne Kirkman, a woman believed to have been pushed down the pub's stairs in 1849.

Anne, despite her apparent untimely death, is thought to be quite benevolent and, although frightening for guests and staff alike, has never really caused anyone any harm. Ivan Nelson, the publican from 1988 until 2013, when asked about her ghost and others in the pub, commented that, "It's scary when it starts, but you can feel that they're happy. There's a happy, jovial mood in the place."

Having said that, the Waterloo apparently has a darker side as told by an old barman who stated that, while showing a couple of Americans around, "As one of them was leaving the lock-up, one of them suddenly jolted to a halt. Something had grabbed him and pulled him back by the hood of his jacket, and the cross pendant he was wearing was turned around as well."

Apart from this, it appears the pub is frequented by a poltergeist who likes to move chairs around in some of the upstairs rooms, and, in 2013, Nelson and his wife were regularly awoken in the middle of the night by piano music coming from the main bar area. In each case, as he descended the stairs from the upstairs apartment, the music stopped, and, upon entering the bar area, he would find the lid of the piano left open. Whether the ghost of Anne is responsible for the music is unknown, but upon reflection, maybe her ghost is quite content.

But if the ghost of Anne Kirkman is apparently content, then the following are anything but.

Rozelle Hospital is in the grounds of Callan Park, an area on the shores of Iron Cove in the Sydney suburb of Lilyfield. Formerly an insane asylum, it was built in 1878; it was renamed Callan Park Mental Hospital in 1915. Currently, the buildings are unoccupied but are not scheduled for demolition, and the surrounding parklands are open to public use.

Louisa Lawson, the mother of poet Henry Lawson, was once an inmate at the hospital, as was JF (Jules) Archibald, the editor and publisher of *The Bulletin*, who published much of Henry Lawson's work.

However, it is not this that we are interested in, as the former mental asylum is believed to be haunted, especially the old Ward 18 where people have reported ghostly screaming and unnerving moaning. In addition, the apparitions of a girl and an older woman have been seen.

A previous groundkeeper, who once worked at the hospital, also reported strange noises, voices, and screaming coming from the chapel, as well odd things happening in the gardens. What these odd things were is not known, but one look at the hospital is enough to suggest that it is a place where ghosts and spirits could be active.

A paranormal investigations group based in Sydney, while investigating the site in 2011, reported a number of strange events, including a long streak of blue light that shot up from the ground near a tree in the garden and then disappeared, metallic noises as if metal bars were being shaken, and, more frightening, one of the members being pushed off his feet by unseen hands, causing him to fall and injure his knees. At another stage, two members reported hearing strange noises and footsteps coming from a shower block and that a strange "black shadow" was seen and captured on video camera. Later examination of the film and area proved that no one had been anywhere near the camera nor was it possible that anyone could have sneaked in.

Today, the place is quite dilapidated with broken windows, unkempt gardens, and graffitied walls. In places ivy has grown up veranda supports and into the roof cavity, and missing tiles are evident on its red tiled roof giving it an unloved and unwanted demeanour. Whether or not the complex is restored is still unknown at this time, but one hopes that this fading glory of the past century, indeed, past *couple* of centuries, will once again come to life, and its superb brickwork and spacious grounds once again ring out with the voices of the living.

But whereas Callen Park sits abandoned and unloved waiting for its fate, the Abbey in Johnston Street in the suburb of Annandale is far from unloved and abandoned. And like the former mental hospital at Rozelle, it too is haunted.

The Abbey sits high upon a ridge in a line of grand nineteenth-century homes known as the Witches Houses in Annandale. And whereas their name is said to come from their tall spires shaped somewhat like witches hats, it's easier to imagine, such is their countenance, that these buildings harbour dark untold secrets or maybe places where witches may dwell before flying out on grim, dark nights.

The Abbey was built by John Young, a builder who was born in Kent in 1827 and later died in Annandale in 1907 and who had migrated from England to Australia in 1855. With his business thriving, he bought land in what is now the suburb of Annandale where he had visions of creating a suburb to rival exclusive harbour-side suburbs like Darling Point. As a result, he built a group of eight homes along a ridge near Rozelle Bay, the Abbey being one of these grand buildings and described as an "imaginative, romantic house loosely modelled on a Scottish manor."

Designed in a variation of the Victorian free Gothic style and incorporating timber architraves, stencil work, hand-painted panels, a Gothic vault, and a tower with gargoyles, the house was not only innovative but quite extraordinary. Young, who later became mayor of Sydney, was also a Freemason and so decorated the place with Masonic symbols. The building, including stables, a chapel, guesthouse, and servants' quarters, was completed in 1882.

In the early 1920s, the house was subdivided and converted to flats, and, in 1959, it was bought by Lancelot Davis for his son. The Davis family continued to occupy the Abbey for the next fifty years, and, after Dr. Davis died in 2008, the contents of the house were auctioned off. In 2009, it was purchased by a Michael Hogan, who began the long process of restoring the house to its former glory. And while he seems unperturbed at the rumours of secret tunnels, Masonic rituals and ghosts, he stated that he "looked forward to determining the facts and fantasies associated with the Abbey."

However, as much as Hogan seems unfussed at the rumours, others beg to differ and suggest that this magnificent and stately stone residence is the home of various ghosts, including a mysterious lady in white, who is said to haunt the tower. Indeed, no less than Lancelot's son Gervase claims the house is haunted stating that he has felt various presences from time to time and seen a lady in white. As well, he and his wife who lived there, used to become aware of supernatural happenings when their cat became agitated. Indeed his wife Estee suggested that, "If you live here you need a cat to warn you. Cats are sensitive to that kind of thing; that's how I know someone has come in."

As well as this, the couple reported doors that opened on their own and windows that did the same. Visitors also mentioned seeing dark, shadowy figures in the long, ornate hallways, and ghost hunters in the 1970s also reported strange phenomena.

Francesca Davis, the doctor's stepdaughter from his first marriage who was raised in the house with her brother Gervase and five other siblings, stated that, "Everyone has a ghost story to tell. The seven children all know it is haunted by ghosts, especially the Lady in White. The basement and the main bedroom are notorious for ghosts."

Francesca also told a local newspaper in the early 1970s that a taxi driver once told her that his sister was murdered at the Abbey in 1912 when the building was thought to have been used as a boarding house and private school. Whether or not this is the "White Lady" is unknown but Francesca believed it to be so, telling the *Daily News* that, "Once, I was in the music room and her ladylike footsteps came in the front hall, up the steps, and into the room, which went cold. I couldn't get out fast enough."

Kat, another sister, had a chilling experience in the same area of the house with an entity she called "The Joker," a strange and malevolent creature that she explained "was like a court jester, or a little joker from a pack of cards."

According to her, she would encounter the tiny, grotesque visitor in a small room just off the master bedroom whenever her parents were out. She recalls that, "This court jester used to sit at the end of my bed, taunting me, and I'd race down the stairs. You can't tell me you can sleepwalk down those stairs; you'd break your neck! I'd be awake and he'd be running after me; he'd be taunting me. It would start at the end of my bed, you know, hassling with my feet. Grandmother would try pacifying me when I got downstairs, but I'd be hysterical because that bloody thing would be behind me; he'd be behind me until I got to that bottom stair, just laughing at me."

To this day she is at a loss to explain what the creature was and why it tormented her.

Estee, who married Gervase in May 2009, also had an unnerving experience when, according to her, she was walking down the stairs when she felt a presence behind her. Upon reaching the landing at the bottom of the stairs, she found the sensation too powerful to ignore and so spoke out saying, "Look, enough! I'm not scared of you." At this stage she then turned and found herself confronted by the dark apparition of a tall male figure who didn't retreat from the verbal attack. As Estee backed away from the figure she felt herself slammed, chest-first, into the edge of the doorway. Surprisingly, considering the predicament she found herself in, she claims she wasn't frightened and later stated, "I just thought, okay, remain calm; just walk out and be nice."

Whether the current owner has encountered any of these entities is unknown as of the writing of this book, but if he has, then it has remained a secret, and given the strange events in the house, one can be forgiven for not speaking out; after all, how does one explain a tiny, abusive court jester-like creature that sits on the end of your bed taunting you?

Then again, maybe it was all simply a bad dream, somewhat like medieval reports of incubus and succubus whereby people in the Middle Ages believed that demons preyed on sleeping people and had sexual intercourse with them. While they had sex they drained the victim of energy to sustain themselves much like a fictional vampire does with blood. Repeated visitations by these demons were said to result in serious health problems or even death.

This experience has numerous names, including Old Hag Syndrome, which comes from the fact that many people report seeing an old shabbily dressed, and quite frightening old woman in their bedroom, who then sits on their chest and proceeds to strangle them. In severe cases people also report being bitten. Indeed, the Old Hag was even described by Shakespeare in *Romeo and Juliet*. However, in this case, Kat described it as chasing her down the stairs until she reached the bottom landing, something not reported in contemporary incubus and succubus attacks.

Whatever the case, it seems the Abbey has many more secrets than we are led to believe, and who knows what the future will hold? More stories or ghostly women, large dark men, and grotesque goblin-like creatures? We can only wait and see.

Interestingly, Annandale has another haunted location, this time an overgrown pathway that runs alongside a light rail viaduct and commonly known as "the street with no name." Less than five kilometres from the Sydney central business district (CBD), the overgrown pathway holds many disturbing and dark secrets and has become somewhat of an urban legend now ensconced in the folklore of this still youthful city.

The pathway itself is near Johnstons Creek and the arches of a railway viaduct near Jubilee Park and has developed an evil reputation with locals claiming there is something inexplicably malevolent about the viaduct and surrounding park, predominantly at night. Some say an eerie presence can be felt, others tell tales of unusual behaviour displayed by small children and dogs when visiting the area, while others speak of hearing strange, disembodied voices and encountering dark shadowy figures that appear to simply melt away into the gloom.

Whatever the case, the area does have a particularly violent and tragic history. In the late 1960s the body of an elderly man was found the day after he was seen walking along the railway viaduct, and, in January 1966, a railway worker by the name of Jock, who had gone to rescue an injured possum, was killed by a train when it loomed unawares out of the fog. A day after this tragic event the line was closed to rail traffic, although it has since been reopened for light-rail. Locals often report that on some nights, especially when foggy, Jock can be heard walking the tracks searching for the injured animal.

Then, in 1968, the mutilated body of a three-year-old boy was found half hidden in the undergrowth not far from the railway viaduct. This atrocious murder has never been solved. In 1976, the body of a twelve-year-old boy was found with serious head injuries apparently inflicted by a large rock. Then, seven months later, in almost exactly the same spot, another twelve-year-old boy was found dead, this time from multiple stab wounds to his chest, stomach, and legs. In 1977, a man was arrested and charged with these murders, and today people still shudder when they recall these events. Locals say that the ghosts of the two murdered boys still haunt the areas where they were killed, their spirits now orbs of light that float unnervingly in front of witnesses.

In 1976, a girl's body was found dumped in the park, and police investigations indicated that she may have been killed as a part of a satanic ritual. One would think that with the amount of tragic events happening in such a small area that the place had seen enough; yet, in 2000, a homeless man by the name of Reg Malvin, ignoring repeated warnings not to sleep there, was found clubbed to death in the grandstand of nearby Jubilee Park. It is rumoured that sections of the grandstand's timber floor had to be replaced to remove any trace of the blood stains. Only two years later the body of an Asian man was found floating in nearby Rozelle Bay. Both murders remain unsolved.

Numerous storage rooms now lie beneath the viaduct, having been created by bricking in the arches. These storage rooms have been dubbed "the tombs" by Mark Brynes, who used one of the rooms as a photographic studio, even though the body of one of the murdered boys was found right outside the place. Brynes himself has reported hearing ghostly footsteps outside the studio, and visitors have complained of feelings of nausea, headaches, feelings of being watched or followed, along with reports of unpleasant odours, bright lights, unexplained cold spots, and breezes. One visitor even complained of experiencing stabbing pains just below his ribs and lower back, even though unaware of the grisly history of the place.

Not surprisingly, given the gruesome reputation of the site, "the street with no name" draws large numbers of paranormal and supernatural investigators, many of whom also complain of anxiety, panicky feelings, the sensation of being watched, hearing footsteps, and experiencing strange odours.

Having said this, with its dreadful and gory past, it is no wonder that the place feels sinister. Add to the fact that it is overgrown, abandoned, and out of the way and you have the perfect recipe for a haunted place.

Of course, no book about Australian ghosts could pass without examining the North Head Quarantine Station, a series of heritage listed buildings on the north side of Sydney Harbour at North Head, near Manly.

Operating from 1832 to 1984, the quarantine station was established so that anyone arriving in the colony or country who might have an infectious disease would be kept in quarantine until it was considered safe to release them. Generally, arrivals would be held in quarantine for an average of forty days although some were held longer and some for shorter periods of time. Of course, with all human recollection, experiences of quarantine varied. Some passengers experienced a first-class resort and made friends and contacts for their new lives while for others it was a frightening experience of disempowerment, disease, and death. And for those of the latter class, death while in quarantine was a distinct possibility.

The station is now the site of a hotel, conference centre, and restaurant complex known as the Q Station and is a part of the Sydney Harbour National Park. And, with a history as such, it is supposedly haunted by the ghosts of former staff and patients, with many supernatural occurrences reported across the site.

At its peak, the station could see anything up to eight boats moored off Quarantine Beach, and with such an influx of people, the station often ran out of accommodation, forcing residents to camp out on the surrounding hill in unsanitary conditions. Those who were strong enough or well enough were often ordered to clear surrounding bushland as well as construct extra structures, such as residential buildings. Indeed, the station was at its busiest during the bubonic plague of 1900 and influenza epidemic of 1918–'19 when it handled up to 1,500 people a day.

After long voyages, many immigrants died while at the station. Indeed, in 1837, the Lady McNaughton arrived in Sydney Harbor with a crew and passengers stricken with typhus. It is believed that over fifty passengers died en route, and, as a result, the Quarantine Station proved to be no sanctuary. Thirteen more died soon after arrival in conditions that were described as "truly appalling with a sense of misery, wretchedness, and disease present everywhere."

No one is quite sure how many people actually died while being held at the station, although it is estimated to be more than 500. What *is* known, however, is that there existed three separate cemeteries and, according to the site's resident medium, there are at least fifty lost souls wandering the hospital, the dining halls, the shower block, and the morgue.

The Quarantine Station has, not surprisingly, been labelled as one of Australia's most haunted places. Visitors have reported seeing the ghosts of both immigrants and hospital staff, feeling cold spots, and being tapped on the shoulder when no one was anywhere near them. Mysterious lights have been seen in unoccupied hospital wards and nurses on night shift over the years would report the sighting of a ghostly Chinese man with long ponytails wandering through the wards and across verandas.

A small ghost child with thick blonde plaits is said to be a common resident ghost, and it is not unknown for her to join a tour group or grab a person's hand or tug at their sleeve. A psychic, who had never heard the stories of the young girl, once commented that she saw a forlorn-looking girl passing though the tour group looking up at the faces of all the women as if searching for someone. Some people have also spotted her hiding behind bushes and, at times, have reported that she spoke to them before disappearing.

A man working at the station once wrote that, as he was leaving one of the buildings in his car at sunset, a face suddenly appeared in front of his windscreen. Later he stated that he "tried to rationalize the situation" but, upon reflection, simply gave up and put it down to a sighting of a ghost.

In 2009, I had a similar sort of experience in the Hellfire Caves in Buckinghamshire in England. Indeed, so strange was this encounter that it took me months to realise what had happened and that possibly, just possibly, I had seen and spoken to a ghost. My experience there still has me scratching my head as to what I may, or may not have seen and experienced, or may have misinterpreted. Put simply, while walking down a length of the cave that led to a junction that split to the left and right, I came across a short, thin, apparently middle-aged woman in old clothes. She was standing against the wall at the end of the corridor and did not appear to notice me approach in the semi-darkness. When I reached her, I said hello, but she didn't move, just stood there with her head slightly bowed in a strange, almost unexplainable way.

As she didn't acknowledge me or move, I simply slid past her into the next part of the cave when it occurred to me that she seemed somewhat grey or misty, or not properly there, if you can understand what I mean. I turned around, and to my surprise she had disappeared—and not only from the spot where she was standing only seconds ago, but there was also no sign of her in the corridor from which I'd come, the only place she could have gone. She had disappeared into thin air.

But my story aside, the station has many, many more supernatural tales, including one by a staff member who used to reside in the isolation wards who often reported seeing a white figure walk past her window along the veranda. As well, at nights she would regularly see a man out of the corner of her eye dressed in what she described as an old-fashioned sailor's uniform. When she turned her head to get a better look he would simply disappear.

In addition, a caretaker at the station regularly complained of lights in one of the offices switching on and off for no apparent reason and would say that he often felt as if someone was in his office with him. According to reports, the wiring in the building was fixed, but this did little to stop the strange occurrences from happening. Apart from that, people have described hearing the ghostly noises of people disembarking from ships, and mysteriously the wharf has burnt down three times.

In 1992, a television crew was filming for a children's program in one of the cemeteries on a wet and windy night when the production manager turned away to find three figures standing above the cemetery on the hill behind her: a man, a woman, and a child, all wearing clothes similar to old-fashioned collared nightshirts. She waved at them and looked away for a moment only to find that, when she looked back, they had disappeared.

Of all the places in the Quarantine Station, the old shower block is considered one of the most haunted and some have described it as evil. A number of psychics have felt that some sort of sexual abuse took place in one of the corners of the building and many visitors to the building have reported feeling a presence lunging at them or hearing screams or whimpering coming from that specific corner.

In December 1992, it was reported that a hen's night went for a tour of the station, which included the shower block. When they entered, one of the showers apparently turned itself on, which was enough to scare the women from the building. After they had regained their composure, two of them were dared to go back in to turn the shower off and they did. However, once inside, a loud banging sound came from the other end of the showers that sounded as if someone was kicking the corrugated iron. Not surprising, the women once again fled.

In the old wards a ghostly matron supposedly still does her rounds and somewhat like the ghostly matron often encountered in the National Museum in Canberra, does not take kindly to any critical comments about the bathrooms. One man, during a night tour, noticed that the bath had dirt in it and commented about its filthy state and how the ghostly matron was obviously not doing her job. Immediately upon saying this he felt ill and had to rapidly exit the building where he was violently sick on the grass.

Later, the same man, as he was walking up a hill with the tour group to another part of the station, stated that he heard heavy breathing close behind him. Thinking it was another member of the group he commented, "Yeah it's pretty heavy going isn't it?" However, when he turned to see who it was labouring so hard up the hill he was surprised and somewhat frightened to see that no one was within ten metres of him. Later, all he could think of was that the old matron had followed him from the wards up the hill.

Meanwhile, the mortuary, which is truly a chilling place, has seen its own frightening dealings, such as a woman on a ghost tour who, when asked why she looked so pale answered that she'd seen a man on the slab and that he looked at her and spoke saying, "Look what they've done to me! Look what they've done to me!" before exposing an incision that ran from his throat to his navel. Apparently no one else in the room experienced this.

Sadly, a fire in 2001 destroyed a number of the buildings known for their paranormal activity, one of them being the original station's hospital building where witnesses had previously reported seeing the apparitions of former patients laying in the old hospital beds as well as walking the wards. However, if the Stone Tape theory of hauntings is correct, then these ghosts will not have disappeared but instead will simply exist within their current environment.

STONE TAPE THEORY

At this stage, I should give a brief description of the Stone Tape theory to those who are unaware of it. In 1961, Thomas Lethbridge, in his book *Ghost and Ghoul*, put forward the theory that ghosts may be recordings of past events made by the physical environment. This hypothesis about residual hauntings has since been called the Stone Tape theory. It basically states that ghosts in a historical context are somehow a recording of the past that is replayed in the present by some unknown means but believed to be the very fabric of the building that the ghost itself exists in.

In my book of 2012, *A Case for Ghosts*, I wrote the following: "In essence, the theory noted that often ghosts or apparitions behave like recordings in that they repeat their actions time and time again over a long period of time without ever deviating away from the original sighting. The ghost shows no knowledge or even acknowledgement of its surroundings, environment or even people around it. Indeed, sometimes they appear to be in a completely different building to the one that now exists, for example, they walk through walls or appear only from the waist up." And that "the Stone Tape theory puts forward the idea that, just like a magnetic recording tape, stones can hold magnetically stored information. Thus, when we replay a music tape we hear music, and when we replay a stone, we see an event being replayed from history. This theory also applies to buildings and other sites. Simply put, the theory states that a place can somehow record certain snippets of history and replay them at a later date."

What we are seeing in this case is people witnessing history repeating itself. And so it appears with most of the ghostly encounters at the Quarantine Station.

Whether the old North Head Quarantine Station is actually haunted or not is debatable. I would say that the evidence suggests that it is; however, sceptics could argue against this. Could it be people are simply hypersensitive to the fact that the place could be haunted and, therefore, misinterpret what they are seeing, feeling, and hearing? Whatever the case, I would not even contemplate spending a night alone in some of the old structures, even though I have spent quite a deal of time, including nights, in haunted buildings.

This brings me to our next haunted place, no longer in Sydney but in Newcastle, just north of the New South Wales capital and Australia's second-oldest city. Constructed in 1909, the house was the home of the Porter family and was continuously occupied by the family over a period of ninety years. Sisters Ella and Hazel, both spinsters, lived in the house their entire lives and many visitors and paranormal investigators visiting the house have claimed to have seen ghosts. In addition, volunteer staff at the house, which has been described as being "frozen in time" and is now maintained by the National Trust of Australia (NSW), claim that furniture often moves around, seemingly all by itself.

In one case a volunteer was dusting some of the artifacts when she felt "a presence enter the room" and, upon turning to greet the person, was shocked to see "what appeared to be an old lady in a white dress with what looked like slippers on her feet." Needless to say she didn't stay around and fled the building.

But this isn't the only place in Newcastle where ghosts can be found. The Civic Theatre on Hunter Street is also said to be haunted with the best known even having a name: Joe. However, who Joe actually is, no one knows.

Apparently, one night while sitting alone in the theatre, former Newcastle deputy lord mayor Frank Rigby was pondering how to get funding to refurbish the now-rundown establishment when to his surprise a man sat down next to him, introduced himself, and started talking. Rigby told the man that there was not enough money in the budget to cover the cost of refurbishing the orchestra pit to which the ghostly man smiled and told him not to worry about it as everything would turn out all right.

Not long after, in 1989, Newcastle was struck by an earthquake. The shock measured 5.6 on the Richter scale and was, at the time, one of Australia's most serious natural disasters, killing thirteen people and injuring more than 160. The damage was estimated at over $4 billion Australian dollars, and the effects were felt over an area of around 200,000 square kilometres. However, amongst this devastation, the Civic Theatre was miraculously spared, except for one place, the orchestra pit which was damaged beyond repair. Insurance covered the cost of fixing the problem and the theatre soon had a new and better pit.

Apart from this, Richard Laws, the theatre's long-standing house manager, once had his own strange tale. After hours, staff would sometimes turn all the lights off in the auditorium and dare each other to try to walk from the front to the back without bumping into seats or pillars. Laws, feeling up to the challenge, decided to try zigzagging across the stalls until, as he recalls, "Suddenly I struck a barrier—as if someone was sitting there alone in the dark. Someone's legs were blocking me. A moment later I could get through."

Had Laws bumped into the benevolent Joe, sitting silently in the dark, or had he just met another of the theatre's resident ghosts?

But if the ghosts of Miss Porters House and the Civic Theatre are benevolent and, in case of the latter, apparently very helpful, then what of other hauntings around the city? The old Newcastle Police Station in Hunter Street, which operated from 1861 until 1982, is reportedly haunted by a ghostly child called

Mary and who, it is claimed, walks the corridors of the gaol looking for her parents. As well, it is claimed that the ghost of an unknown police officer has also been seen on rare occasions, while at the nearby Newcastle Court House on Church Street jurors have reported feeling as though they were being watched from the upstairs public gallery during trials. Indeed, some have been so unnerved by the experience that they have claimed that it has upset their concentration. Apart from this, jurors often complain of rattling doors and cold spots throughout the building. One juror even described a ghost in a pillbox hat and gloves sitting in the gallery with her hands folded in her lap while she sat through a trial.

However, as interesting as all these are, it is Maitland Gaol and its long, turbulent history that really takes our attention. Built between 1844 and 1848, the gaol is a grim reminder of a harsh colonial past with its brutal history of rape, murder, suicide, and incarceration. The imposing sandstone compound may now be quiet, but it was once home to some of the country's most feared criminals and was the place of sixteen legal executions. As for other deaths, this figure is unknown, and as such, the silent halls now echo with an eerie loneliness that reaches deep into your soul, as if daring you to call out to the ghosts of those who once lived here.

Although built in the mid-1800s, it remained in service until 1998 and was the longest running gaol in Australian history. Now a museum, it has become a popular tourist attraction, especially for those seeking the supernatural and paranormal.

Floggings were common in the early years of the gaol, and executions were open to public viewing until 1861—and, from contemporary reports, they were usually well attended. Hangings took place near the main gates and in a back corner of the gaol, and in all, sixteen men were executed, all for murder or rape. The last man to be executed was a Charles Hines in May 1897 for raping his stepdaughter, although he proclaimed his innocence to the very end.

But the gaol did not solely cater to men as women often found themselves behind the thick sandstone walls and, if they had children, then they too were housed in the gaol for the duration of the sentence. As one would expect, conditions in the gaol were incredibly harsh as it was originally built to hold just 150 prisoners even though at times almost 300 languished behind the walls. Indeed, many ghost investigators cite this mental torment and anguish as a reason for the site's supernatural phenomena as it is embedded in the walls, in some cases, a lifetime of pain for the innocent children.

But it is not all ancient history as in 1980 an informant was found dead, his throat cut so viciously that his head swung back on his shoulders. Apparently his body was hidden with a sheet of plastic painted the same colour as the floor.

The gaol now runs regular ghost tours, sometimes led by ex-wardens or ex-inmates. One such guide is Keith Bush, who worked in the gaol from 1976 until 1993, and, although sceptical about ghosts in general, admits that it is a very spooky place stating that: "A lot of bad things have happened in these walls—murders, rapes, suicides, hangings—and a believer would have to be a hypocrite to say ghosts weren't here." He has admitted that: "I've heard enough rumours of ghosts from others, and people on my tour have sworn they've experienced something."

Linda Snape, founder of the Hunter Paranormal Group, has visited Maitland Gaol numerous times and conducts overnight vigils in the old women's quarters. She recalls: "We've had phantom voices caught on digital recorders, there have been a lot of hits on our instruments that pick up electromagnetic fields, and we've also captured some photos of mysterious mist," and, on one night "a woman was scratched on her back even though there was nothing around her. We caught it on film."

Snape also admits that the gaol is a frightening place at night even without the prospect of ghosts as "the history goes back so long and there's a lot of people who died there. A lot of deaths in the gaol actually haven't been recorded, but you can see them in church records."

Others have reported slamming doors, disembodied voices, misty images of children, strange noises, as well as cold spots, even on searing summer days, and one witness even claimed to have seen the ghost of a stabbing victim. Others have also reported the ghost of a small girl who wanders the upstairs corridors apparently searching for something unseen, while some visitors complain of being tapped on the shoulder, or worse, pushed in the back. Whatever the case, Maitland Gaol, with its long and tragic history, is a place where even sceptics can feel uneasy about their beliefs.

And so it is for our next location, north across the border into Queensland, a place known for its beaches, steamy temperatures, and tropical climate. And with a history going back almost as far as Sydney and Newcastle, it too has a wealth of supernatural and paranormal tales, from ghosts in haunted jails to hotels and even a shopping mall.

CHAPTER THREE

QUEENSLAND

A DEVIL'S POOL, A HAUNTED GAOL AND THE CURIOUS CASE OF MIN MINS

By and large I've made a conscious effort to stay away from Indigenous reports of ghostly activities, mainly as a sign of respect and because it is not my culture; therefore, I cannot claim to have anything but a rudimentary understanding of the societal norms and beliefs. However, in this case, I will briefly explore the legend of the Devil's Pool in Far North Queensland.

Babinda Creek, south of Cairns, flows from Mount Bartle Frere through steamy rainforests and undergrowth, past rocky outcrops and pebble strewn banks toward the waters of the Coral Sea. Its waters are crystal clear, purified by the forests it has run through. On its way it merges with two other streams where the cool water tumbles over boulders and crevices to form an idyllic natural pool called Babinda Boulders.

However, as idyllic and attractive as the name sounds, it also has another, much darker name, the Devil's Pool, as this stretch of water is considered to be cursed. To the local Yidinji people, Babinda (meaning "water flowing over rocks") is sacred ground, the site of a dreaming legend—a legend that appears to have taken many lives.

The legend concerns a young woman called Oolana, who married a respected tribal elder called Waroonoo. However, over time another tribe wandered into the valley, and Oolana fell in love with a handsome young man called Dyga. The two lovers were soon found out and, as a result, ran away together. Later, when they were captured, Oolana broke free and threw herself in the water calling for Dyga to follow her. These days it is said that her spirit still guards the cold waters of the pool and that her voice can sometimes be heard, eternally calling for her lost lover and luring young men to their death.

Tragically, since 1959, at least seventeen young people have lost their lives in the waters of Devil's Pool. Of these, all but one have been young men, and while irresponsible behaviour and treacherous currents may account for a number of drownings, the high number of deaths of young males seems quite disproportionate. This is even more so when one realises that not all the victims were actually swimming at the time of their death.

In one case a young couple, twenty-year-old Nicholas Wills and his girlfriend, were standing on a rock platform admiring the view when they were suddenly

73

swept into the water by rapidly rising waters, and while the girl survived, the man did not. In 1979, according to Dulcie Schnitzerling, twenty-four-year-old Peter McGann "jumped across the short space between the rocks, slipped, and went missing." Other recent victims include an Adelaide tourist and, in 2006, a businessman from Sydney; while the last recorded death was that of James Bennett in 2009, it appears that visitors, rather than locals, fall victim to the curse.

In 1991, twenty-year-old John Peachey from Melbourne slipped off the rocks and fell into the waters. He was believed to be the fourteenth death at the pool. Previous to this, a forty-five-year-old German woman also slipped into the water and died. However, reports of deaths at Devil's Pool go back long before 1959.

In June 1933, a Mr. T. Winterbottom was swept over Barron Falls and, although the body was never located, it was believed that he ended up in the Devil's Pool. Searches of the pool, however, were unsuccessful. Then, in November 1940, eight-year-old John Dominic English also drowned in the pool.

So strange are the deaths at this place that it is said that the local Indigenous people refuse to go there. Indeed, it is said that if you disrespect the sacred site, the site will disrespect you, and legend has it that in one case, a young man who kicked a plaque commemorating those who had died at the pool slipped and fell into the pool and drowned.

Even television host Warwick Moss, while filming for the Australian television series *The Extraordinary,* suggested that there was no way he would swim in the cold waters, no matter how hot the outside temperature. To further complicate the legend, several photos purporting to show ghostly images staring from the waters have appeared over the years.

So, what are we to make of this apparently evil spot? Does the ghost of an Aboriginal woman haunt the waters drawing young men to their deaths? Or is it simply a treacherous place to swim, given the currents, depth, and freezing waters? Whatever the case, locals these days shun the pools; after all, one can never be too careful.

Interestingly, in 2014, Kim Davison was swimming with her friend Jessie Lu and three children at Murphy's Hole in Queensland's Lockyer River when they had a very strange experience. While swimming, Davison's daughter claimed that something grabbed her leg on two occasions, and Davison herself claimed that there had been strange occurrences that day as they swam in the water, which led her to believe that a spirit was present. She also stated that: "When I went back in for one last dip to cool off, I did feel something behind me as I was walking out of water but tried to ignore it."

Disturbingly, a photo taken of the group distinctly shows the two women and what appears to be four other children in the water. However, Davison and Lu, the other adult in the photo, were adamant that there were only three children when the photo was taken. The fourth figure is an eerie white head with what appears to be horns, or possibly hair buns on its head. Davison later stated that: "At the time of taking this photo there was nothing between us," and that she was "holding the little girl and that white head next to me with horns is not human, I can promise you that."

The story became even stranger when researchers discovered the story of Doreen O'Sullivan, a thirteen-year-old girl who drowned in the same creek in 1913 with the death notice in the *Brisbane Courier* saying that:

"Doreen O Sullivan, aged 13 years, eldest daughter of
Mr. James O'Sullivan was accidentally drowned whilst bathing in the
Lockyer Creek on Friday afternoon."

Did the ghost of Doreen O'Sullivan join in with the family as they splashed around in the water on that hot day in the Lockyer Creek? And if so, what circumstances brought her back to life, so to speak? Did she yearn to play with children her age once again? Whatever the case, the photograph is very compelling. (Visit www.thechronicle.com.au to find the article "Haunting 'child ghost' photo stumps experts.")

But if one eerie and isolated pool in the steamy mountains of Far North Queensland hold unknown secrets, then what of some more urbane, in fact, so urbane as to be a shopping mall in the heart of Brisbane itself?

In March 2009, Brisbane's Courier Mail reported that a shop manager was busy polishing a nineteenth century antique teapot in the old Brisbane Arcade when she saw something out of the corner of her eye. Looking up she was confronted by a woman with her hair up in a bun and wearing a black dress with a bustle as if she had stepped straight out of a television period drama. Since then she has also reported glass cabinet doors swinging open for no apparent reason.

The newspaper also reported that the founder of the "Room with Roses" tea shop, although never actually seeing a ghost, had reported doors opening and closing when no one was there, and, over the years, security guards in the complex have also reported sightings of a female figure walking along the gallery level as well as unseen footsteps that follow them at night.

Although no one is certain, it is believed that the woman in black is a former shopkeeper, although others believe that she is more likely to be Mary McIntosh, the wife of Patrick Mayne, an Irish immigrant who arrived in the colony in the early 1840s and who rapidly built up his wealth through cruelty and brutality. His reputation was such that people were in genuine fear of him, and for good reason as, on his deathbed in 1865, he made a shocking confession in that he had robbed, murdered, and then disembowelled a man by the name of Robert Cox, an itinerant worker who, while drunk, had boasted of his earnings from a big cedar find. Police reported at the time that it was one of the most savage slayings they had ever witnessed with the man's legs and torso being found in the Brisbane River, his entrails dumped in a well and his severed head deliberately propped up in a shed where it was later found.

Although shocking in itself, the confession was made worse as Patrick Mayne had escaped detection for the murder and allowed another innocent man to be charged, found guilty, and hanged for the crime. Apart from this, he was also suspected of two or three other deaths, and a suicide. Innuendo of scandal and rumours of depravity, murder, and insanity still poisoned the next generation, although none had any children of their own.

And so, is the Brisbane Arcade, a marvellous building whose design reflects the archetype of the traditional shopping arcade of the late eighteenth century Europe haunted in any way? Given the murder and scandal associated with the place I would not be surprised if it were haunted, although one would now be hard pressed to see any evidence of this today, given its elegant fittings and design, award winning fashion shops, designer jewellery stores, quaint cafes, and classy up-market shops. When I wandered through the lovely restored building I was more taken aback at the architecture and use of space and light than any wayward ladies in black or spooky shadows of disembowelled log cutters. But then again, it was a normal weekday lunchtime and not late at night and deserted.

Brisbane is the capital of Queensland; it sits on the Brisbane River, which was named after Scotsman Sir Thomas Brisbane, the governor of New South Wales from 1821 to 1825 and keen astronomer who built Australia's first observatory.

The first European settlement in Queensland was a penal colony at Redcliffe, just north of the central business district and was founded in 1824. This settlement, however, was soon abandoned and moved to North Quay in 1825. Free settlers were permitted from 1842 and Brisbane was chosen as the capital when Queensland was proclaimed a separate colony from New South Wales in 1859, although it was not incorporated as a city until 1902.

During the Second World War, the city became the central hub to the Allied campaign in the Pacific and used as the South West Pacific headquarters for General Douglas MacArthur, chief of the Allied Pacific forces. Approximately one million US troops passed through Australia during the war, and Brisbane, with its proximity to the South West Pacific, was flooded with servicemen, mainly from the United States of America.

In 1942, this flood of servicemen led to a violent clash between visiting US military personnel and Australian servicemen and civilians, which resulted in one death and several injuries. This incident, although covered up at the time, later became known as the Battle of Brisbane.

Incredibly, according to authorities, up to twenty brawls a night occurred between Australian and American servicemen and, in the weeks leading up to the Battle of Brisbane, there were several major incidents, including a gun battle between an American soldier and Australian troops near Inkerman, north of Brisbane, which left one Australian and the American dead. In addition, an Australian soldier was shot by an American MP in Townsville, and an American serviceman and three Australian soldiers were involved in a knife fight in Brisbane's Centenary Park, which left one Australian dead. In another incident, an American soldier was arrested for stabbing three servicemen and a Brisbane woman near the Central Railway Station.

But as interesting as this historical event is, it simply adds to the already dark history of the city, a history that has seen murder, depravity, and crime. Indeed, Victoria Park, originally called York's Hollow Swamp, has a rich history of tragedy from executions to murders and suicide. And, not surprisingly, it is said to be haunted.

Victoria Park itself is a heritage-listed area that covers twenty-seven hectares of undulating land bordered by the suburbs of Spring Hill and Herston. Named for the reigning British monarch at the time, Queen Victoria, it was gazetted in 1875. Initially spanning 130 hectares, the land was slowly encroached upon over the years with suburban development, schools, hospitals, golf courses, and show grounds all permitted to be built on the parkland. It is a place shrouded in mythology and mystery and recently has become a popular spot for paranormal investigation groups, especially the secluded pedestrian tunnel that lies at its heart. However, before we look at the ghostly tunnel dweller, we should at least explore some of the park's history.

In 1855, an Indigenous man named Dunalli was accused of murdering a number of white settlers in the North Pine area. He was duly caught and charged and was sentenced to be hanged outside the post office at Spring Hill. According to eyewitness accounts, when Dunalli was about to be hanged, the hills around Wickham Terrace became crowded with a large number of Indigenous people from the Bribie Island area. At this stage, Spring Hill was largely undeveloped, and settlers feared that violence might erupt at Dunalli's execution.

The execution went ahead as planned, but, as feared, a short time later Dunalli's brother, Ommuli, began to cause trouble for authorities, and, as a result, he too was arrested. At this arrest a number of Indigenous people began fighting with authorities. When the confrontation ended, a number of the people were killed, including Ommuli, although records are sketchy. And so began the long and tragic history of the park.

In the late-1800s, Victoria Park was the location of illegal gambling and other criminal activities and was also the scene of numerous suicides. In November 1871, students of St. Joseph's College Gregory Terrace discovered the severely decomposed body of John Davis, although medical examinations could not find a cause of death. Strangely, his body was found at a very popular spot for visitors, so it is unknown how his body had laid there without discovery for such a long time.

Then, in the evening of 2 June 1885, a steam train was rounding a bend on a line that runs adjacent to the park when the driver noticed a female figure lying on the tracks. The train could not stop in time and Ann Smith, who it was believed had fallen on the track, was decapitated. Gruesomely, the caretaker of Victoria Park was said to have ran towards the train and, seeing what he thought was a bag or a parcel, picked it up without thinking, only to later discover that it was the unfortunate women's head. As Smith did not move with the approach of the train, it has been suggested that she may have been killed by her husband and her body later lain across the tracks to cover his heinous deed. However, this is all speculation.

Then, only five years later in November of 1890, a young cabinet maker by the name of Mark Davis poisoned his three young children and himself after his wife was committed to Woogaroo Lunatic Asylum. Although the children survived, Davis died in hospital leaving the children essentially orphaned.

But Davis' attempted suicide is not the only one to have occurred in the park. In November 1892, Martin Rassmusson, after a trivial dispute with a post office, shot himself in the head with a revolver, while in March 1895, Hannah Downey, a barmaid at the nearby Criterion Hotel, committed suicide by slitting her own throat. In January 1896, Elizabeth Kenyon was found drowned, and in April 1913, Clara Jane Sumpton was found hanged in a tree, also in the park, and, although foul play was suspected, the case remained unsolved.

Apart from this, Polish immigrant Albin Cichon was found hanging twelve feet up a tree in March of 1954, and in late November of 1960, a migrant Swedish seaman by the name of Karl Dinass came to Victoria Park and slit his wrists before lying on the train track where he was then run over. Dinass, it must be noted, was a suspect in the murder of Kate Ryan, an elderly woman who was killed a few days earlier, but police had not arrested him due to a lack of evidence.

And, as Kate Ryan had been murdered, so too was James McGrath, a homeless man who was found dead of serious head injuries in October 1934, and in February 1937, Harry Brown, a relief worker, was found murdered near the tunnel. No murderer was found, although, during the inquest into his death, a man was said to have gone insane and was sent to Goodna Mental Hospital. Whether or not he was the killer is unknown to this day.

In September 1952, another homeless man, Walter Hall, was murdered in the Victoria Park tunnel and then dumped in a nearby lake, and, only a few days later, Noel Peterson was found in the park with severe head injuries. Although he died later in hospital, it is rumoured that he regained consciousness before his death but refused to say, or could not remember, details about his attacker.

And so, with such a history, it is little wonder that paranormal groups have flocked to the park trying to find evidence of ghosts and supernatural events. Indeed, in November 1965, a group of school children, after hearing rumours of a ghost in the tunnel, crept into the darkness hoping to see it. One of the boys, lagging to the rear of the group, was apparently accosted by a "misty green, armless, legless, headless apparition that seemed to materialise from the wall of the tunnel."

Terrified out of his wits and stupefied by his encounter, the boy was dragged by his friends to the nearby Royal Brisbane Hospital as his friends feared he had been possessed by the ghost. This in time made for sensational headlines in the local papers and before long thousands of people were making the trip to the tunnel to try and catch a glimpse of the ghost. The ghostly sighting became a major talking point for the residents of Brisbane over the coming weeks.

Speculation as to the ghost's origin was rife and included that of a man who had jumped off a pedestrian overpass into the path of a speeding steam train and was killed. However, upon greater examination of the report, including that the ghost appeared to have severed limbs, it was suspected that it could be the ghost of Dinass, as his horrible injuries matched the description of the ghost.

Others have suggested that the ghost could be none other than Ann Smith and that she was indeed murdered.

Whatever the case, dozens of people have died under tragic circumstances in the vicinity of the Victoria Park tunnel and, if the tunnel is haunted, then it could be a number of people, or a number of different entities. The area has been known for supernatural activity for a long time, including in 1903 when the ghost of a woman, described as looking like "a tall nun floating through the tunnel towards the lake on the Inner City Bypass side" was sighted. Then in 1932, there was another sighting of the ghost but this time less like a nun and heading for the lake.

Given the history of the place, I am surprised that there haven't been more reports of supernatural events, however, as time rolls on I'm sure more and more reports will surface. Having said that, there are plenty of other places in Brisbane that appear to be haunted.

Brisbane City Hall, the seat of the Brisbane City Council is adjacent to King George Square, where the rectangular Italian Renaissance style city hall has its main entrance. Considered one of Brisbane's finest historic buildings and on the Register of the National Estate since 1978, it was once the tallest building in Brisbane. Over the years, it has been used for royal receptions, orchestral concerts, pageants, civic greetings, flower shows, school graduations, and political meetings, and was officially opened on 8 April 1930 by Lord Mayor of Brisbane William Jolly.

From the 1950s, workers and visitors to the building have reported hearing strange footsteps in the hall and have reported sinister feelings in a series of small rooms on the third floor known collectively as Room 302. The rooms are close to the spot where a caretaker is believed to have committed suicide in the 1940s, and it is said that, for a time, the area, which was used as a photographic darkroom, was abandoned due to the ghostly activity.

Overall the building is reputed to be haunted by four ghosts: One is a female figure that haunts the foyer and the mezzanine overlooking the foyer, a second is rumoured to haunt an entire wing of city hall, a third is believed to be a World War II American sailor who was stabbed to death in the Red Cross Tea Rooms beneath the city hall, and a fourth, a ghostly lift attendant, who apparently haunts the tower of the grandiose building.

Although retold over the years with varying degrees of detail, it appears that a lift attendant or workman at the hall died in dereliction of duties in the 1930s. Over the years, he has been reported as "continually riding the lift since the 1930s" and, as published in *City News* in 2008: "When the clock tower was renovated a construction worker claimed to have seen a ghost, which presented as a silhouette of a man standing in an area off-limits to the public."

Somewhat different from the rumour is the fact that, on 31 October 1935, a building contractor by the name of George Edward Betts left his home in the morning to go to work. Although apparently in good spirits, he mentioned to his wife that he was visiting a doctor that morning about some unknown affliction, and that later he would drop into city hall to pay the council for a water connection on a project he was working on.

As he had suggested, Betts visited the city hall in the afternoon and, for reasons unknown, took the lift to the observation landing in the tower. Soon after, a large crashing sound was heard and a large hole was noticed in the roof of the hall facing King George Square. A search was immediately conducted, and Betts' body was found, having fallen over forty metres from the observation landing and through the galvanised iron roof of city hall, before landing on a concrete floor.

At a subsequent inquest, it was found that "the only way one could fall from the rail would be to climb up to look out at something," and that "it would be impossible for anyone to fall over the grill support near the telescope under ordinary conditions unless he climbed upon it." As a result, there were no suspicious circumstances and the inquest was closed.

What led to the events leading up to the death of George Betts? Did he climb out across the safety rail to get a better view of something? And why did he travel up to the observation deck in the first place? Is it possible that he had received some bad news at his earlier doctor's appointment, news that led him to throw himself off the tower?

Incidentally, in December 1937, Hilda Boardman fell and crashed through the galvanised iron roofing, dying of her injuries soon after. Whether her ghost has been seen is unknown but some believe a ghostly spectre of a woman seen in the foyer could be her. Indeed, in February 2012, the photo of a ghostly woman on the stairs of the hall was posted to a supernatural forum, and, if not faked, then the photo is extremely interesting to say the least.

Of course, no investigation of ghosts in Queensland would be complete without mentioning Boggo Road Gaol, and, although sceptics are quick to denigrate any reports of ghostly activity in the notorious prison, it still raises questions. And even though the official Boggo Gaol website run by the Boggo Road Gaol Historical Society seems to actively discourage a belief in ghosts, I am not so sure.

To be fair to them, they are committed to the history of the gaol, and, as a result, are keen to remove any references to ghosts who may or may not haunt the lonely corridors, rooms, and cells of the place. And to me, this is a pity as it all builds up a rich tapestry pertaining to the place—after all, who would deny the Tower of London its ghostly legends?

Having said that, I would encourage readers to keep an open mind and visit the site themselves—who knows what you may encounter?

Boggo Road Gaol is an infamous heritage-listed prison on Annerley Road in Dutton Park, an inner southern suburb of Brisbane. It is the only surviving gaol in Queensland that reflects the penal attitudes of nineteenth-century Australia and for years was Queensland's main prison. Officially known as Brisbane Prison, it opened in 1883 and was used mainly as a holding prison for criminals serving short sentences or on remand, although it did have a gruesome past of hangings.

In 1903, a new purpose women's gaol was created, while in the 1920s, the men of the St. Helena Island Prison in Moreton Bay were moved into the former women's gaol. This section, renamed Number Two Division, soon became home to murderers and violent offenders. As a result, the prison's notoriety grew. And with its stark red brick walls and imposing guard towers one can see why people now consider it to be haunted.

Many executions were carried out at the gaol, in all forty-two, including the hanging of Ernest Austin in 1913, the last execution in Queensland. Austin was born in Victoria and was convicted of raping and murdering twelve-year-old (or eleven in some reports) Ivy Mitchell at Cedar Creek Road near Samford in South East Queensland. He was duly found guilty and hanged and is now buried in South Brisbane Cemetery, another place reputed to experience supernatural events. Of course, Austin's ghost is reputed to haunt the gaol where he met his demise.

The legend of Austin includes that he laughed while on the gallows and claimed that he was proud of his crime, mocking the watching audience that he would return from the grave and cause more suffering. Years later this prophecy of sorts was reputed to have come true with prisoners reporting seeing a face that looked like Austin outside their cell doors. And legend also has it that he had made a deal with Satan to deliver their souls in exchange for his own and, once locking eyes, his spirit would enter the cell and try to strangle them, driving them insane.

Sadly for the legend, it is believed that Austin actually said something like the following: "I ask you all to forgive me. I ask the people of Samford to forgive me. I ask my mother to forgive me. May you all live long and die happy.

God save the King! God save the King! God be with you all! Send a wire to my mother and tell her I died happy, won't you. Yes tell her I died happy with no fear. Goodbye all! Goodbye all!"

Having said this, and realising that the legend of Ernest Austin is simply that, a legend, one still cannot discount that his spirit stalks the corridors of the gaol. True, it is fanciful to suggest that he made a pact with the devil and that his ghost strangled inmates who had the misfortune to lock eyes on him, however, reports of his ghost materialising or passing through walls is not a huge stretch, especially if we consider ghostly reports from other places, including the United Kingdom, where apparitions have done exactly the same.

For instance, let us have a look at a classic style haunting or ghostly apparition. Many people in the British Isles have reported seeing the ghosts of what they describe as Roman soldiers marching by, although only from the waist up, which suggests that these ghosts are marching along, not an existing path, but one that existed many years in the past. This makes perfect sense, and a great example of this sort of ghost is seen in the celebrated tale of Harry Martindale, an apprentice plumber who, in 1953, was installing a heating system in the cellars of the Treasurer's House in York when he witnessed the ghosts of Roman centurions. Apparently he first heard a horn in the distance and then a dishevelled Roman soldier on a horse emerged from the brick wall. This soldier was followed by others, all looking dejected and tired, carrying swords and spears. They appeared from the knees up which suggests that they were walking on a road that was buried below them. It was later confirmed that an old Roman road was located fifteen inches below the cellar.

After this bizarre procession had passed, Martindale made a hasty escape from the cellar and sat at the top of the stairs quite bewildered where an old curator saw him and asked if he'd seen the roman soldiers.

Austin's ghost, or what people believe to be his ghost, has been seen and reported by both visitors and staff alike, and they have reported seeing the shadow of a man in E Wing cell block, the same place prisoners saw Austin's spirit in the 1980s. Are these people simply lying or misinterpreting what they see?

Of course, it is possible as things like suggestion, infrasound, atmospheric condition, and simple states-of-mind can contribute to seeing things that may not exist; however, even if one of these were the real reason for seeing ghosts, and it is difficult to prove it so, is it possible that Austin's ghost does haunt the gaol but not as the devil worshipping strangler in legend, but more so as a lonely lost memory, a harmless Stone Tape theory apparition that appears at times due to atmospheric or emotional circumstances that we are yet to understand?

Admittedly, at the time, the *Brisbane Courier* described Austin's act as "one of the most horrible and abhorrent in the annuals of Australian crime," and noted his "callous indifference" and "silly grin" while in court. Having said that, do any of us know how we would react if sentenced to be hanged?

But if Austin's ghost is non-existent or, at the very least, nothing more than a replay of a historical event from many years previous, then what of the rest of the ghosts of Boggo Road? What about the so named "Warder," apparently a "black spectre with red eyes that peers down on intruders from a top floor cell."

The Warder is another of the famous ghosts that are reputed to haunt the gaol. It is reported that the spirit of Bernard Ralph, who was fatally bludgeoned to death with an iron bar by a prisoner in 1966, has been seen on numerous occasions. Indeed, witnesses tell of a ghostly figure that appears to be a warder and, therefore, by association, must be Ralph.

One report from the 1970s suggests that a prison officer, one Don Walters, was on duty and spotted a senior officer in front of him. He allegedly saluted the man who in turn saluted back and walked past him not uttering a sound. The next morning when Walters asked the gate officer if the regular night senior had been on duty, he was told that he had been away on holiday and that no senior officer had been on duty that night.

Whether or not this is a true account is now almost impossible to ascertain, and yet it does have all the hallmarks of a certain type of haunting that has been reported countless times all over the world. True, as the Boggo Road Gaol Historical Society like to point out, the story may have changed over the years, although they themselves state with some uncertainty: "What may have started out as a 1900s uniform became a 1960s uniform in later versions."

Of course, the important word here is "may." In simple terms they are telling us that they really don't know if the story started in the 1900s or whether it started at a much later period. And of course, who is to say the gaol isn't haunted by a number of prison warders? And the society also admits that "tales of a supernatural warder have circulated the prison for decades," which suggests to me that lots of people have been reporting the same phenomena over a long period of time, which leads one to suspect that possibly something very strange is happening within the walls.

Other visitors to the gaol, including ex-warders and officers, often claim to have felt Ralph's presence, and while I agree a feeling is nothing one can base a fact upon, it, at the same time, does not discount it.

Another story associated with Ralph's ghost is that officers on night duty on the "Track" near to where the workshops used to be, claimed that they would sometimes hear the jangling of a set of keys behind them, and when they turned around to see who it could be, found there was no one there. Yet, as the society rightly points out, it could simply be a trick, and, in many cases I have no doubt it was, yet this raises the question, what about the times when no one was there to perpetuate a fraud? What of those times when the officer who heard the jangling keys was genuinely alone?

There is also a legend of a ghostly cat called Tripod who, when alive, used to live in the grounds in the 1970s, something that was not uncommon given that cats are extremely adaptable and also very handy at controlling rodents. Tripod was apparently a very distinctive black-and-white-coloured cat whose name was derived from the fact that he only has three legs. Apparently, he became very well known to officer and prisoners alike.

Many years later, according to the legend, a visitor during a night tour felt something brush against her leg, and when she looked down she saw a cat walking away. At the end of the tour she told a tour guard about the animal, and he replied that he was unaware of any animals in the gaol. She then went on to describe it as black-and-white with three legs, and the guide recognised this as a description of Tripod, the long dead cat. And so the legend of Tripod the ghost cat was born.

The historical society writes off this sighting by implying that there are no other tales of ghost animals, indeed they state "no phantom rats, fish, elephants, lizards or budgies," and suggest that this is "a massive inconsistency in the whole 'ghost animal' concept," which would be correct if they were not so wrong.

In my previous book, *A Case for Ghosts,* I looked at a number of animal ghosts ranging from dogs to cats and even phantom horses, and in my research came across numerous references to ghostly animals, including chickens.

Indeed, at Pond Square, Highgate, a ghostly chicken is occasionally said to make itself known to passersby. And this chicken is said be attached to the ghost of none other than Sir Francis Bacon, who died in 1626 after conducting an experiment with, you guessed it, a frozen chicken. Since his death there have been numerous reports of a ghostly white bird, similar to a plucked chicken, which appears from nowhere to race round the square flapping its wings or to sit ominously perched on the lower branches of nearby trees.

In 1943, a Mr. Terence Long was crossing Pond Square late at night when he suddenly heard the sound of horse hooves and the low rumble of carriage wheels. Perplexed, he looked around only to be shocked by the appearance of the ghostly chicken, which shrieked and proceeded to race frantically around before vanishing as quickly as it appeared.

As well, during the Second World War, Air Raid Wardens patrolling the Highgate area often reported seeing the ghostly chicken, and one man actually attempted to catch it for dinner. However, the chicken simply disappeared by running into, and through, a brick wall.

Then in the 1960s, a motorist who was left stranded when his car broke down, found that he was subject to the whims of the ghostly chicken who once again ran around hysterically before disappearing. In the 1970s, an amorous couple were enjoying each other's company when it interrupted their embrace by dropping suddenly from above and landing next to them.

These reports, odd as they seem, are not the only ghost animals that have been reported. All over England, Scotland, Wales, and Ireland people tell of spectral black dogs that haunt lonely roads and thoroughfares and are harbingers of doom and death. In Yorkshire a ghostly goose has often frightened horses and drivers alike while in St. George's Church in York, it is said that a phantom rabbit scurries up and down the aisles. All attempts to catch it have failed and locals believe that it is the ghost of Dick Turpin. Athelhampton Hall in Dorset is another old building considered haunted, not just by the spirits of people, but also of a cat and a pet ape, which was accidentally imprisoned in the secret passage leading from the Great Chamber. Beyond this there are countless reports of ghostly horses, and not only in the United Kingdom.

The Boggo Road Gaol Historical Society also argues that: "This sighting could simply have been another cat with similar features, although no such animal was seen around the museum again," and that, "a more reasonable explanation is that the description of the cat in the dark was mistaken."

While this is undoubtedly true, how could a woman with no knowledge of Tripod the cat, who had died decades previously, describe a black-and-white cat with three legs? One has to ask, how many three-legged black-and-white cats have you seen? Coincidence? Perhaps. And yet one is left with the distinct possibility that, one night in the gaol a woman on a tour actually saw the ghost of Tripod, the three-legged cat.

Of course, when speaking of ghostly animals we must also recall the phantom bear of the Tower of London which, in 1815, emerged from a doorway where a terrified sentry lunged at it with a bayonet, finding to his dismay that it simply met with thin air. This encounter, and others, suggests that ghostly animals are no different to those of people.

These stories have been elaborated upon, however, this doesn't mean that they are untrue. How can so many people who have never previously met come up with the same stories over and over again? And for what gain? Whereas the society suggests that "Feeling a 'presence' or hearing the jangling of keys is hardly evidence of the supernatural," I would suggest otherwise as, what they omit to say is that, many people hear these things when there is no possible way any joker or fraudster could have done it. Put simply, a large number of the apparent supernatural occurrences cannot be explained.

At this stage I should explain that, although I am a fan of ghost tours, I find that they are simply entertainment and not serious investigations into the paranormal.

But if Boggo Road Gaol has raised some doubt in the minds of the reader, then where else can we turn to examine the supernatural in the Sunshine State? Indeed, what could be more appropriate than a cemetery, and not just any cemetery, but the largest in Queensland?

Established in 1866, and formally opened in 1875, Toowong Cemetery in Brisbane was established to cope with the growing population. Queensland's cemetery is on forty-four hectares approximately four and a half kilometres west of Brisbane. Now a popular tourist destination, it houses the remains of some of the city's most influential and well-known residents, famous and infamous.

As well as being heritage listed, it is rumoured to be haunted by a number of ghosts, and, although it has been reported as being the burial place of Jack the Ripper, this has never been substantiated. Still, while it probably does not hold the remains of the infamous Whitechapel murderer, it does contain the last resting place of Patrick Mayne, wealthy landowner and suspected perpetrator of one of the city's most gruesome murders, as we have previously read.

The Gothic headstones that dot the landscape cast eerie shadows, and even on the hottest days, there have been reports of people walking into odd cold spots and encountering strange misty shapes that look vaguely human. Others have reported being tapped on the shoulder or felt as if someone has blown in their ear, and there even exists a legend concerning a vampire.

In *A Case for Ghosts* I examined in detail all aspects of the Highgate Vampire, and it is believed that only two cemeteries in the world are known to have a vampire dwelling amongst the graves. One of these is Toowong and the other is Highgate Cemetery in London, and while I am not a great believer in this side of the supernatural, I feel it is my duty to report it anyway, if not in any great detail.

The vampire in question is said to be a black shadow with razor-sharp teeth that floats through the trees on Twelfth Avenue within the cemetery. Homeless people who frequent the location are said to be reticent to enter the area and are known to take a longer route if they have to pass the avenue rather than face the shark-like razor teeth of the Toowong vampire.

Local legend suggests that two gravediggers were asked to exhume a body and while they were doing so were puzzled by the softness of the ground, which appeared to have been recently disturbed. After they had removed all the soil they were equally puzzled to find that the nails of the coffin had been pushed from the inside out. Then, with rising trepidation, they removed the lid only to find the woman inside had not decomposed at all, even after many years. One of the men reached in and touched her face, then leapt back in horror as her head rolled to one side and she smiled revealing two rows of sharp teeth. Not surprisingly, the men shoved the lid back on the coffin and hurried to fill the grave back in with dirt.

Of course, this is a fanciful story and echoes numerous other vampire legends, including the previously mentioned Highgate Vampire as well as another, extremely well known case, the Croglin Grove Vampire, as documented by Augustus Hare.

The Croglin Grove Vampire is as famous in vampire lore as Dracula, although the story, which appeared in a book called *In My Solitary Life* by Augustus Hare, was probably fabricated at the time to impress guests or friends.

Having said that, in my 2014 publication, *WYRD*, I studied the Croglin Grove Vampire in detail and it does raise some interesting questions.

Apart from supposed vampires, the cemetery is host to many other spirits and entities, one of them being dubbed the "Angel of Death" who has been seen stalking the grounds of the necropolis since the Great Depression era. Who he is no one knows, but local ghost tour guide and author Jack Sim has claimed to have seen him at least eleven times. It is also rumoured that one tour group managed to summon the apparition.

Apart from the frightening "Angel of Death," it is thought that a much more benign spirit know as Mr. Macgregor can be seen in the form of a statue that wanders the lonely grounds, his coat fluttering in the breeze as dusk sets upon the gravestones. Edward Macgregor was a patron of the arts and the proprietor of the Lyceum Theatre, and after his death in 1939, a statue was erected in his honour. It is this statue that people report seeing.

There is an old English, or perhaps Anglo Saxon, legend that the spirit or ghost of the first person to be buried in a graveyard is doomed to haunt that graveyard for eternity. Is it possible that the "Angel of Death" is this ghost? Or maybe it is one of the myriad of other spectres that are rumoured to haunt these old, most encrusted tombstones?

In addition there is the legend of "The Black Prince," a boxer by the name of Peter Jackson who in 1886 became the Australian heavyweight champion. Many boxing aficionados maintain that Jackson would have become a world champion except that others refused to fight him because of the colour of his skin. Whatever the case, it is said that if you visit Jackson's tomb at midnight, by yourself, you will hear the sound of a ring bell sounding.

But Toowong has another odd legend that is very similar to one that is prevalent at the Air Disaster Memorial in Canberra in that cars are rumoured to roll uphill of their own accord. And yet, unlike the Canberra legend, there is supposedly a reason for this unnatural behaviour. According to the story, the graves of two young sisters killed in a car accident can be found at the top of "Spook Hill," which is a sloping road within the cemetery. The legend suggests that if you sit in the car and put it into neutral, the car will defy gravity and roll up the hill. People who have witnessed this believe that the two dead girls are dragging the car up the hill with the aim to kill everybody inside, although why the two want to kill everyone is completely unknown. Still, as an urban legend, it makes for interesting reading and, as much as such a legend can be dismissed outright, it doesn't negate all the other stories about this old cemetery.

But it's not just ancient civic buildings or grand cemeteries that seem to attract ghosts, and while Brisbane's youthful history betrays some sinister moments, there are many other places in the state that have been subject to supernatural manifestations, and one of those is the beautiful Lady Elliot Island.

Lady Elliot Island is the southern-most coral cay of the Great Barrier Reef and lies approximately 80 kilometres northeast of Bundaberg. Covering an area of approximately forty-five hectares, it is part of the Capricorn and Bunker Group of islands and is owned by the Commonwealth of Australia. The island is particularly renowned for its scuba diving and snorkeling due to excellent water clarity and hosts a small ecotourist resort and an airstrip.

It is also the site of some interesting stories, including the ghost of Susannah McKee, who has been seen peering out of a cottage window as well as walking across the island's airstrip.

There are two graves on the island and both tell a tragic story of isolation and loneliness, even in such an island paradise. One is the last resting place of Phoebe Jane Phillips, daughter of lighthouse keeper James Phillips, and who tragically died of pneumonia in 1896 at the young age of 30 due to a lack of medical attention. The other grave belongs to Susannah McKee, the wife of a later lighthouse keeper.

Susannah McKee originated from Ireland and with her husband, Tom, had four sons before accompanying him to Lady Elliot Island. Once on the island she found life much harsher than expected, supplies brought by ship were often late, perishables would not keep, the heat was often intense, and the living quarters cramped. Loneliness, boredom, and the sense of isolation became her constant companions, and, after her youngest son left for boarding school in Rockhampton, she decided that she could no longer stand the conditions she was living in. As a result, on 23 April 1907, she donned her best clothes, walked out onto the jetty below the lighthouse, and threw herself into the sea.

Of course, given the circumstances and the isolation of the place, rumours arose that Tom McKee had pushed his wife off the jetty. However, this could not be proven, and, after her body was recovered, she was buried next to Phoebe Phillips. However, for whatever reason, her spirit remained restless, and, in the late 1930s, the lighthouse keeper at the time, one Arthur Brumpton, reported seeing a women fitting Susannah's description walking between the lighthouse and the three cottages behind it. At the time Brumpton was looking down from the lighthouse balcony and was completely perplexed, given that there was no one else on the island who it could have been. His daughter, Margaret, also recalled that she felt that there was a presence of some sort in the lighthouse itself and that she was often afraid that whatever it was, it was going to push her off the balcony.

Later, in 1940, when the family returned to the mainland, the captain of the ship they travelled on showed them some photos of people who had lived on the island. One of these showed Susannah McKee, and Brumpton recognised her immediately.

Many decades later, in 1985, the lighthouse on the island was modernised and automated, and staff at a newly established resort were given the task of performing maintenance. Tali Birkmanis, the last lighthouse keeper duly handed over the three old cottages to the resort and reported that he had experienced numerous strange and unexplainable happenings while on the island. Indeed, after he left, the happenings became more prevalent, including staff hearing strange disembodied footsteps in the vacant cottages.

Soon after, two staff members, Jeff Raynor, a groundsman, and Chris Lister, a chef, moved into the same cottage. After moving their furniture in they decided to take a break and sat outside on a tractor parked in front of the cottage. Although it was a still afternoon, they were surprised when an empty plastic ice-cream container flew out of the front door and landed at their feet. Later that night the pair told some workmates about the strange event and the footsteps with Raynor proclaiming that, whatever it was, he didn't believe in ghosts.

That night, while sleeping soundly, Raynor was awoken and suddenly hurled out of bed by an invisible assailant. Landing on the floor puzzled and in pain, he decided to sleep on the veranda instead. A few nights later while asleep on the veranda he awoke and, to his horror, could plainly see the transparent figure of a woman standing in the cottage doorway.

The resort is powered by generators, which are kept in a locked room. However, it is reported that they often stop, plunging the resort into darkness, only to restart again before staff can unlock the doors to find out the problem. In addition, staff have heard old fuel cans crashing around in the locked generator room, and in one particularly frightening event, painters contracted to paint the old lighthouse found that every time they scaled the scaffolding, it began to shake violently only to stop once they got down.

Susannah McKee's ghost has also been seen peering out of the cottage windows as well as walking across the airstrip, sometimes on her own and at other times with a young women who is believed to be Phoebe Phillips. In some cases she is seen in the company of an old man in blue overalls, but no one has any idea of his identity except that he was possibly a maintenance man from previous years. Oddly enough, staff and guests also report seeing a boy in a cowboy hat between two of the cottages, and somewhat alarmingly, bloodstains sometimes appear on the steps inside the lighthouse. In addition, people have reported hearing the plaintive voice of a little girl calling for her mother, yet again, no one has any idea who she could be.

And speaking of the plaintive voice of girls, we shall leave the Lady Elliot Island and move farther north on the mainland to Rockhampton, which lays some 600 kilometres north of Brisbane.

Rockhampton itself was officially proclaimed in 1858, and, in 1859, gold was discovered at nearby Canoona. Miners rushed to the area using Rockhampton on the Fitzroy River as the nearest navigable port. Sadly, the Canoona field proved to be less than profitable and many people were left stranded in the town, unable to afford to return to Brisbane or wherever they had come from.

However, disappointments aside, the town began to boom, and, by 1861, it had a regular newspaper, banks, court house, and a school of arts, and soon it was the main port for developing the Central Queensland hinterland with the main export at that time being wool. Before long sea ports were well established and rail links were constructed, as were schools and other public buildings.

And of these schools, one was the Rockhampton Girls Grammar School, which was officially opened in 1892. Designed by E. M. Hockings, the school was constructed to accommodate fifty day and twenty boarding students. However, to meet growing demands as student numbers increased, the school was enlarged in 1897, 1899, and again in 1901.

The school's motto is "Non scholae, sed vitae," which translates to "not only for school but for life we are learning." This motto was adopted in 1894 and reflects the philosophy of Miss Helen E. Downs, the first headmistress of the school, apparently a no-nonsense figure who believed in female education, women's emancipation, and the rejection of female frivolities, such as beauty, among other things. Apparently, during a speech in 1898 she reminded parents that "the senior classes in her school were for training cultured women who would exert an uplifting influence in social matters—and not waste their time on prettiness."

Whereas no one today would be shocked by her progressive attitude, it was almost unheard of in the late 1800s. Having said that, the school's scholastic achievements were exceptional, and as such she was tolerated by her critics. Without doubt Downs was a woman ahead of her time and a strong-willed individual. As a result it should come as no surprise that the school is believed to be haunted by her intimidating spirit, and it is said that once a year, at 11:00 p.m. on 11 November, she comes down from the bell tower, selects the girl with the longest blonde hair, and, with a pair of spectral scissors, snips off the locks.

Of course, this is simply folklore, and no girl has ever had to encounter a ghostly headmistress intent on snipping off their hair. Having said that, girls at the school have reported strange happenings, cold spots, and misty, indistinct woman-like figures, especially near the bell tower, and, in one encounter, on the night of the eleventh, a group of schoolgirls heard noises on the roof that sounded like footsteps, and all screamed until a mistress came in and told them to be quiet, suggesting that it was an animal. The girls themselves, however, were adamant that it was indeed Ms. Downs.

And yet the rumours continue, and to the girls of the school the ghost is very real, even if it doesn't engage in midnight haircuts. Not surprisingly, given the age of the school, it is also believed that it has three student ghosts, one a girl who died of scarlet fever many years ago. Whatever the case, Rockhampton Girls Grammar School has managed to find itself a part of Queensland folklore whether haunted or not.

But if the previous girl's school has a haunting that is dubious in the least, then what of our next building, Townsville's historic West End Hotel on Ingham Road, now the Bruce Highway?

Built in 1885, the West End Hotel was constructed by Townsville builder Peter Dean, who was also the first licensee. The building is significant in that it is a rare surviving example of an intact balconied hotel in North Queensland as very few hotels now exist with their balconies intact, and of these, even fewer survive with an intact 1880s balustrade. It is a two-storied building constructed of brick with a concrete floor throughout the ground level. The timber balustrade balcony overlooks the showgrounds and the mountains to the south and west and, by the time it was constructed, Townsville had grown to a thriving supply town for the pastoralists and miners in North Queensland.

The hotel is reputed to be haunted by the ghost of a Chinese cook named Jimmy Ah Sin who was stabbed to death in 1891. Records show that, on the afternoon of 2 May 1891, PD Bourke, the publican and J McLaughlin were arrested on suspicion of murder.

Interestingly, on 21 July 1924, Terence Rooney, aged fifty-six, fell from the balcony and died soon after from his injuries, and, in 1921, Peter O'Neill, licensee of the pub, passed away on site. In 1891, a Miss Cathleen Hodgson, aged only twenty-one, died upstairs in the building.

Does the ghost of Jimmy Ah Sin wander the creaky old corridors and rooms of this old pub? According to locals he does, and they have recounted their experiences to the local press for North Queensland. One commented that: "I've seen the ghost many times. It's like a mist and follows me around when I go upstairs at night." The same man also claimed that the ghost's presence was strongest in the kitchen at the spot where he was murdered. One of the hotel waitresses also told of how she had seen the ghost several times and could feel its presence whenever she entered the upper floor of the building. "He's quite harmless. He just follows me around like a shadow."

The West End Hotel is not the only haunted pub in Queensland. Indeed, there are many, one of those being the Royal Hotel in Harrisville, which was established in the mid-1870s. And according to some paranormal groups, it is one of Australia's top ten haunted sites.

Darren Davies, president of Paranormal Paratek Queensland, has gone on record saying that the Royal Hotel's links with paranormal activity were the result of an alleged seven deaths when the pub burnt to the ground in 1916. However, as he pointed out, no lives were actually lost in the fire. Having said this, he still concedes that the pub could be haunted, and a number of patrons and workers agree.

Hotel manager Monika Patrick, although having no paranormal experiences herself, is open minded on the subject given that patrons have recounted strange tales to her, such as one woman who "saw a short, slightly tubby-looking man. He was older and had broad shoulders. She couldn't say what he was wearing."

Davies and his paranormal investigation team also witnessed a misty figure pass before their eyes and heard footsteps along the hardwood floor whilst conducting a night-time vigil at the pub. Apparently the 1.5-metre high full-figure appeared to be female and was seen in the entry to the kitchen, the same location a ghost was spotted by previous patrons.

Davies noted that the amount of activity was more than even he'd expected and that: "We had some very strange things happen visually. It was creepy. It was so dark and quiet we could hear those movements."

Whether or not claims of the pub being in the top ten haunted sites are justifiable is up for conjecture, although it would appear that, in comparison to many other haunted places, the hotel is remarkably untouched by the paranormal. And yet, this doesn't mean that it is not haunted, and as we have seen, patrons and investigators have had supernatural experiences within its old walls.

And so it is for our next destination, another hotel, this time south of Townsville in a small town called Ravenswood, a small mining town with a large number of historically important buildings. However, of all these buildings there is one that really concerns us, and that is the Imperial Hotel, a fantastic example of a building seemingly preserved in time and existing almost exactly as it did a century ago.

The first Imperial Hotel was built on the site in 1901 by James Delaney during the gold rush heyday, but tragically it burnt down only six months later. Not deterred, Delaney built another structure, and it has lasted until the present day with the Delaney family only moving out in the 1990s. Current owner Martin Josselyn explained why the building has kept its unique heritage untouched: "During the '70s there was a big push to renovate all these buildings and modernise them, and of course now that's all out of date, and a lot of these building don't look quite right. But this building was left alone and essentially because the same family owned it from when it was built in 1902 right through to the mid-'90s."

From the exterior to the tables and chairs and stained glass windows, almost everything you encounter at the hotel is original, which certainly helps when it comes to stories of ghosts and things that go bump in the night, as it is a place where you really could imagine that ghosts exist.

Josselyn and his wife, Tracey, came to Ravenswood and took over running the Imperial in 2007, and despite being newcomers, locals and visitors have been only too willing to pass on the stories of the hotel over the years. Especially stories of ghosts which, although Josselyn hasn't seen anything himself, he noted that: "Some of the stories in relation to people that have since passed in the hotel and some of the incidents that have occurred here in the hotel over the last 100 years have meant that those stories could ring true," and that: "there are too many people that have seen, heard, or had another experience for there not to be something."

Apart from that, Josselyn has had to deal with patrons who have had ghostly encounters while staying in the hotel. "I saw a miner that was probably twice my size come rolling down those stairs one day, white as a ghost, and he would not go back up the stairs. One of the chefs we had here came out of the kitchen and looked through where the old ladies parlour used to be, which is now a cool room, and swore black and blue he saw a young lady in period dress. Now that lady had been seen a number of times throughout the hotel as has the older gentleman."

Stories over the years also include a ghost who haunts room 12A, which is technically supposed to be room 13. Why the room number was changed is not known, but one could suspect that at some stage in its life the owner decided that a haunted room with the number 13 was not a good deal for patrons wishing for a good night's sleep, especially those with a superstitious nature.

But ghosts do not simply wander the corridors and rooms of old hotels, gaols, and public buildings for, near Lake Bindegolly National Park just east of Thargomindah, is a stream called Crying Woman Creek. The road from Cunnamulla crosses the creek and travellers are warned to be wary of a banshee as they pass as the place is reputedly haunted by the ghost of a woman who died after her hair was caught in the wheel of a buggy some 100 years ago. These days her anguished screams can still be heard along the creek.

In 1941, on the remote Parrabinna Waterhole on Bulloo Downs, southwest of Thargomindah, a group of drovers decided to camp in an old decrepit hut. During the day and night they were surprised when stones bombarded the hut and the men. Later, a wheezing sound was heard on the roof, and one of the men claimed he felt a cold, clammy hand on his arm. Despite this strange phenomenon, the men stayed and later reported their experiences to the Thargomindah Police. The police investigated but, apart from a burnt out fire and a number of stones, found nothing. This event was later dubbed the Parrabinna Poltergeist.

Another poltergeist-like incident happened on the Palmer River and involved a Chinese tin miner named Ah Quay who was working a claim on Granite Creek. Living with him was another much older Chinese man who suffered from leprosy. Ah Quay cooked meals and generally cared for the old man until he died and, on advice from authorities, due to his leprosy, burned the old man's hut and all his possessions as a safeguard against contracting the disease.

Soon after Ah Quay and his offsider, Willy Hip Wah, found themselves subject to what could only be described as a poltergeist-like attack. Sticks, stones, horseshoes, and empty tins were hurled at their hut by unseen hands and plates, cups, and bottles flew around inside, often striking the two men. Twice Willy Hip Wah woke to find something invisible trying to strangle him with his own blankets and, completely bewildered and at a loss of what to do, the men sought the help of some nearby European miners.

The European miners laughed at the two but said they would see what they could do, believing it to be simply a Chinese superstition. When they arrived at the campsite they were amazed to see lamps getting thrown around by invisible hands and spontaneous fires bursting out all over the place, spooking their horses. One of these fires leapt up inside Ah Quay's hut and it quickly burnt to the ground, after which the activity stopped. It is reputed that Ah Quay philosophically remarked, "Ah well, no matter I burn him, he burn me."

But stories of poltergeist-like behaviour and ghosts that haunt lonely roads and billabongs are nothing unusual in this country, after all, the quintessential Australian pioneering song *Waltzing Matilda* concerns a ghost haunting a billabong. And yet, still we are drawn back to the towns and cities that dot this harsh landscape, towns like Ipswich.

Ipswich is Queensland's oldest provincial city and boasts a rich history, including superb 1800s architecture. Centrally located in the southeast, it is forty minutes drive from Brisbane, although the delineation between the two is now blurred by urban sprawl. Beginning as a mining settlement, it was proclaimed as a municipality on 2 March 1860, and became a city in 1904. And according to historian, author, and ghost tour operator Jack Sim, it is extremely haunted, especially the Warwick Road cemetery, which he calls "a morbid museum of Ipswich's past" in which graveyard hauntings "take many interesting forms. Silhouettes of people moving have been observed darting across the tracks, and footsteps can be heard walking on the gravel that covers the tracks."

The first recorded burial in this cemetery, officially called the Ipswich Cemetery, was a four-year-old boy named John Carr and took place in July 1868. And, if one is to wander around the lonely headstones, one will quickly realise that infant mortality rates in those days were extremely high. Indeed, statistics show that in 1862 there were 117 deaths in the Ipswich area and 47 of these were children under the age of five, while in 1863, there were 146 deaths, 80 of them children.

People who have visited the cemetery have reported strange phenomena, such as gravestones suddenly lighting up, and on cold still nights, a strange mist that can be seen hanging low to the ground in the oldest section, almost as if crawling through between the graves. Others have reported seeing soldiers marching on their graves and a lady in historic dress with a young child are often seen on the side of the road to Warwick.

Apparently before each ghost tour, guides walk the track the group will go on to check whether it is safe as, in 2012, it was reported that a guide and his son were walking the grounds before a tour when, as was stated: "My son was at the back of the cemetery, checking the path before the tour. As he made his way along the path toward the front gates, he was pelted with pebbles. Shining his torch around he could not see anyone, yet still the pebbles were flying out of the darkness toward him. For the next five months, the pebbles were seen flying through the air and heard bouncing off headstones and the tour guide's car."

Warwick Road cemetery isn't the only haunted place in Ipswich. The Old Flour Mill that houses the Inkuku Arts and Crafts Centre is supposedly haunted by the ghost of a young man by the name of Hubert who worked at the mill. He apparently died after a bout of scarlet fever when he came back to work before he had recovered sufficiently and, after being ordered to work harder, collapsed and died.

Staff and visitors have reported seeing a shadowy figure in a coat lurking around the interior of the building, while others have reported footsteps that follow them around. In addition, staff have reported that radios and lights turn themselves on and off, and once, an unplugged sewing machine started up and ran without any power source for a couple of minutes.

It is said that when the Flour Mill was being used as a restaurant, cutlery on tables in the hallway leading to the kitchen would often be moved around, and Hubert's ghost was often seen at functions, especially when a particular waitress was working, which led staff to believe that the ghost was particularly interested in her. Having said that, it is generally felt that Hubert is a benign spirit who simply haunts the building where he died and causes no more than a minor disturbance every now and then.

Other reputedly haunted places in Ipswich include Limestone Hill, St. Mary's Church, the North Ipswich Railway Workshops, Goolloowan and the Goodna Mental Asylum and, according to local ghost hunter Jack Sim, the city "seems to attract ghost stories. Unlike Brisbane, the pace is slower in Ipswich. Unlike busier towns, people remember their local ghost stories."

Elsewhere, the old Ipswich ambulance station is said to harbour the ghost of one W. C. Tomkins, a superintendent who died in 1934 in the upstairs residence of the building. Tompkins founded the Ipswich City Ambulance Transport Brigade in 1901, and he lived on site. These days his ghost is said to rattle blinds and move from room to room and floor to floor scaring visitors and staff alike.

Sim said of the ghost: "A few of them spoke of seeing the ghost and others of feeling like they were being watched and followed. These are ambos who attend some horrible accident scenes, and some of them said they wouldn't go upstairs at night. But this ghost has never hurt anyone, and I don't think he would. He founded the ambulance in Ipswich, and he is a nice bloke."

However, with the ambulance station being moved to new premises it is unclear whether Tomkin's ghost has followed and, if we recall the Stone Tape theory whereby a ghost is the energy of a person somehow captured by the fabric of a building, then one would suspect not. However, having said this, it is not unknown for a spirit to follow certain objects as if attached to them across the divide of life and death, and a good example of this is at the National Museum of Australia where it is thought that a collection of Indigenous material has a number of ghosts attached to the objects rather than the building.

Leanne Dempsey, who I consulted while writing *A Case for Ghosts*, used to work at the National Museum, and she was gracious enough to take me on a tour of the building explaining the strange experiences she and others had witnessed.

The room in question is in the lower Gallery of First Australians, which holds the Open Collections and is long and thin with a large glass-fronted display cabinet on either side and a floor to ceiling cabinet that run down the centre of the room. Entering the room the visitor feels a certain presence, and some have simply refused to enter. Conversely, others have said that they feel peaceful and at ease in the room.

Walking along the corridors the artifacts take on a slightly menacing air, and reflections and shadows look like human shapes moving amongst the displays. During one visit I suddenly felt a chill, and the hairs on the back of my neck stood up. I mentioned this to Leanne, who said that the spot was one of the spots that lots of people seem to mention. Strangely, it felt colder in this area than anywhere else in the gallery.

But this is not proof of a ghost. Museums are big airy buildings with air conditioning units, and for all I know I could have been walking past an outlet duct. Indeed the clicking of some sort of electronic device in the ceiling sounded very odd and out of place to me, yet as Leanne pointed out, it was simply a normal noise associated with the gallery. She also put forward the theory that glass cabinets, artifacts, and shelves tend to throw up some unusual shadows when viewed by someone walking along in the dark, and this could account for many sightings of ghosts in museums or like places. However, conversely, she also agreed that it could be possible that the ghosts of this room were attached to the artifacts themselves and not the building.

Whatever the case, it is unknown whether superintendent W. C. Tomkins' ghost has made an appearance at the new ambulance station. Maybe he is happy with what he now sees, and, as a result, has simply ceased to exist? However, this is not the case for another Ipswich ghost known by locals as Bluestone Betty.

Bluestone Betty has been haunting the overgrown pioneers' cemetery and nearby Bluestone Corner on Pine Mountain Road for more than a hundred years. Her real name was Elizabeth Cox, and she died aged seventy-six in 1883, the first person to be buried in the cemetery. Apparently, according to local legend, she was seen not long after wandering the grounds of the cemetery, and many people recognised her.

Interestingly, as we have previously seen, there is an old English, or perhaps Anglo Saxon, legend that the spirit or ghost of the first person to be buried in a graveyard is doomed to haunt that graveyard for eternity. And maybe this is the case for Bluestone Betty?

Elaine Peet, a member of the Pine Mountain and Districts Historical Society, remembers the story from her childhood days. "We know it was her because the sightings started soon after she was buried, and people recognised her." She is also on record as saying: "Over the years, many people reported seeing a woman standing on the corner in a long dress."

While attending the local primary school Ms. Peet used to ride a horse to school and recalls that the horses "always used to shy away and walk sideways, so we had to go the back way. They just wouldn't walk past the corner; there was something about it that made them uneasy."

Apart from this, Ms. Peet has been frightened by the ghostly figure on numerous occasions, recalling how she "used to work as a night duty nurse in Ipswich, and I'd be on my way home when I'd run into mist on Bluestone Corner and get the fright of my life. I've run my car off the road five times on the corner, because the mist rising in tendrils looks exactly like Betty standing there."

However, despite all this, it is believed that Betty is completely harmless; indeed, locals believe she is a protector of the cemetery. Other reports suggest that she rides a ghostly black horse and that to see her is bad luck; however, given the affection locals seem to have for her, I am more inclined to believe the former.

But if Bluestone Betty is harmless, what of strange, unexplained lights that regularly appear all over the country or phenomena such as the Min Min lights of the Channel Country of Queensland? Are they a ghost? Or ghosts? And if they are, then what can we make of them? And if they are not, then what in the world are they?

Many years ago, when I was in my early teens, I recall watching in amazement, if not some apprehension, as a flickering greenish light hovered over a morass in Victoria some fifty metres from where I stood. It was night, and a few of us were walking alongside the edge of the swamp when it caught our attention. At first we thought it must be a fisherman with a lantern, but then realised that it seemed to be hovering. Of course, it could have been a boat, but at that distance we should have been able to make it out.

At this stage of my life I had never heard of a will-o'-the-wisp or swamp lights, let alone read about them. However, after a period of about ten minutes, the light seemed to start moving, at first across our path and then receding further into the morass until it abruptly disappeared.

But was this strange light a famed will-o'-the-wisp? In hindsight I would have to say yes. However, I am still no closer to actually understanding what it was given that it hovered, moved left and right, and then disappeared.

Min Min Lights

Min Min Lights are the names given to strange light formations that are often reported in eastern Australia. They have been reported as far south as Brewarrina in western New South Wales to as far north as Boulia in northern Queensland although the majority of sightings are reported to have occurred in Channel Country of Queensland.

These sightings have occurred from well before European settlement in Australia, and stories about them can be found in Aboriginal myth predating western settlement. However, overall they seem to be a fairly recent phenomenon and over time have become part of wider Australian folklore. Interestingly, Indigenous Australians seem to think that the number of sightings has increased with the increase of Europeans into the region, which makes sense given that more people would be likely to see the event if it were to happen at any given time.

Generally seen in the Boulia District of Queensland, the lights may have got their name from the old Min Min Hotel and mail exchange. The site, approximately 100 kilometres east of Boulia, is now no more than a deserted pile of dirt and dust and the remnants of a cemetery, but its name lives on in the evocative and mysterious lights.

The old Min Min hotel burnt down in 1917, and it was around this time the lights first started appearing in the area, although lights had been reported in other places from earlier times. Legend has it that in 1917 or 1918, a stockman late at night, was surprised to see a light hovering over a grave near the settlement of Min Min. The glowing object floated towards him, and panicking, he galloped off to the next station followed by the ball of light.

Since that day the light has been reported many hundreds of times throughout northwest Queensland. Descriptions of the light appearances vary, though they are most commonly described as being fuzzy, disc-shaped lights that seem to hover just above the horizon. They are usually described as being white, although some reports suggest that they can change colour from white to red to green to orange and blue and back again.

Generally, they are seen about a metre off the ground or roughly the height of a fence. Sometimes they even seem to run along the top of a fence line. In some accounts they are dim, while others describe them as brilliantly bright and strong enough to throw shadows on the ground around them.

On occasions they have been seen high in the sky, sometimes oscillating up and down like a yo-yo. It is also frequently mentioned that, unlike a car headlight, its light emanates from all around it. Strangely, it appears to have some sort of intelligence and appears to be curious, although in no way threatening. Of course, this is not to say that its appearance doesn't cause some consternation in witnesses given that it has been reported that the lights are able to keep pace with cars whilst driving along the lonely outback roads.

The lights have been seen by tourists, farmers, stockmen, miners, bush walkers, truck drivers, and car drivers alike. They have been seen by large groups, small groups, couples, and individuals at all times of day and any time of year. Oddly enough, cattle seem unperturbed by the lights although dogs and cats generally take fright.

In her book *The Mystery of the Min Min Light*, Maureen Kozicka mentions a report from a shearer who stated that: "I was shearing on Clio station north-west of Winton for a month, and night after night the Min Min light would come from behind the shearers' quarters, around, and into the bore drain. Always the same pattern." As well, a near neighbour of Clio station remembers seeing the light on the station as a child and, apparently braver than most, chased it across a paddock.

In the case of the Min Min lights there does appear to be a very rational, if not completely foolproof scientific explanation that has been put forward by Professor Jack Pettigrew, from the University of Queensland, and this involves a phenomenon called Fata Morgana where, due to atmospheric conditions, light, either man made or natural, can actually bend over distances of hundreds of kilometres. Put simply, it is an inverted mirage.

This inverted mirage is named after the fairy Morgana, who was reputed to be able to conjure up cities on the surface of the sea ice. Indeed, in one widely observed and documented case, the Irish sea cliffs were seen floating in vivid greens and browns above the calm Atlantic by observers on a ship more than a thousand kilometres away.

However, as rational as this explanation is, it still doesn't explain why the light sometimes seems to show intelligence and moves towards people, and then away when they advance towards it. Perhaps Pettigrew is correct in his theory, but as with most things supernatural, maybe his is not the only explanation.

And so, from ghosts in pioneer cemeteries and old hotels to strange intelligent lights that apparently interact with people, where now do we go to continue our paranormal journey? Indeed, what has the Northern Territory got to offer us in the way of ghosts and other unnerving tales?

Weetangera Cemetery (Australian Capital Territory). An old pioneering cemetery just alongside suburban Canberra, the start of our quest and where people have witnessed the ghostly figure of a tall, thin man in old-style clothes walking along a nearby road. (Photo: JG Montgomery)

Old Parliament House (Australian Capital Territory). Sitting serenely at the base of Capital Hill on manicured lawns in the middle of the parliamentary triangle, security guards have reported having their walkie-talkies ripped off their belts and thrown across rooms while others have reported a ghostly pair of legs wandering through the courtyards. (Photo: Kirsten Willcox)

Blundell's Cottage (Australian Capital Territory). A quaint, almost English cottage sitting quietly on the shores of Lake Burley Griffin in the ACT. Could it really be haunted by the ghost of Flora Blundell? (Photo: JG Montgomery)

The National Film and Sound Archives (Australia Capital Territory). A splendid neo classical building and once the home of the Australian Institute of Anatomy. It is reputed to be haunted by a number of ghostly presences including one that pins people to the walls of the basement. (Photo: Kirsten Willcox)

The Royal Hotel, Bungendore (New South Wales). Built in 1882, the colonial-style two-story building is the site of one of the more remarkable ghost photos ever taken. (Photo: Steve Salliard)

The Bushranger Hotel (New South Wales). Built in the 1860s, this quint colonial pub was the scene of a horrific murder in 1865, when Constable Samuel Nelson was brutally gunned down by bushranger John Dunn. Some believe that the tragic figure of Nelson's ghost still haunts the pub. (Photo: JG Montgomery)

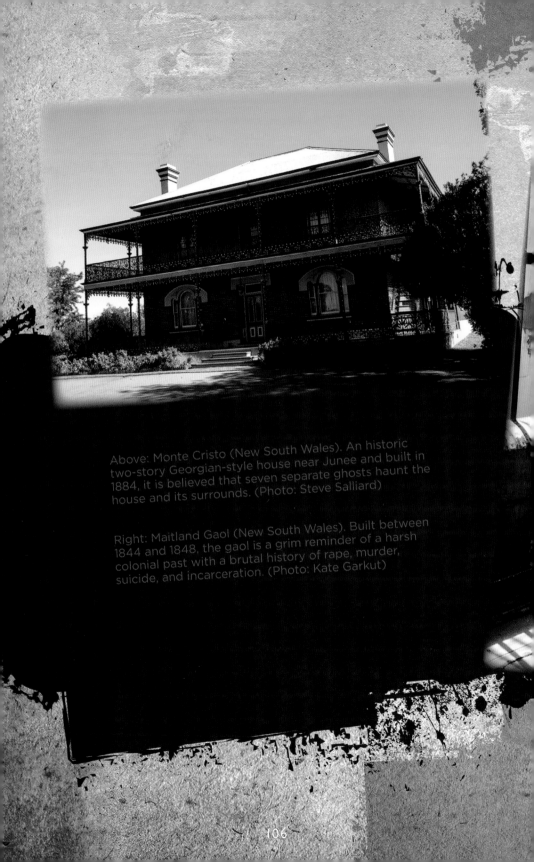

Above: Monte Cristo (New South Wales). An historic two-story Georgian-style house near Junee and built in 1884, it is believed that seven separate ghosts haunt the house and its surrounds. (Photo: Steve Salliard)

Right: Maitland Gaol (New South Wales). Built between 1844 and 1848, the gaol is a grim reminder of a harsh colonial past with a brutal history of rape, murder, suicide, and incarceration. (Photo: Kate Garkut)

Opposite: The Russell Hotel (New South Wales). One of the oldest buildings in The Rocks, it has seen murder, crime, plague, and death and is believed to be haunted by several ghosts, including an old seaman and a number of women, assumed to be prostitutes. (Photo: Nic Montgomery)

Below: St. Johns Orphanage, Goulburn (New South Wales). Now abandoned, it remains a lonely reminder of a past probably best forgotten. Many believe it to be haunted by the spirits of the children who once lived there, and there have been reports of the sounds of children playing from within the building. (Photo: Dan Backhouse)

Berrima Gaol (New South Wales). Built between 1836 and 1839 to imprison the bushrangers who preyed on the travellers between Goulburn to Sydney, the gaol has seen many tragic and grisly events. It is little wonder that people report strange noises and voices as well as visions of dark shadows in the corners of cells. (Photo: JG Montgomery)

Berrima Courthouse (New South Wales). Built in a Roman-style between 1836 and 1838 from sandstone and featuring four Doric columns supporting a classical pediment, it is said to be haunted by the spirit of Lucretia Dunkley, who was hanged at the nearby gaol in 1843 for the murder of her husband. (Photo: JG Montgomery)

Burnima. (New South Wales). Built in 1896 for grazier Mr. Henry Tollemache Edwards, this remote and isolated Victorian Gothic mansion is rumoured to be haunted by a number of spirits, including Miss Edith whose ghost has been seen wandering the grounds. (Photo: Tim the Yowie Man)

Green Cape Lighthouse (New South Wales). The scene of a terrible shipwreck in 1886, when the *Ly-ee-Moon* steamed onto the rocks near the lighthouse leaving seventy-one people dead. It is rumoured to be haunted by a phantom sailor who lurks in the cottage's hallways. (Photo: Tim the Yowie Man)

Brisbane City Hall (Queensland). Adjacent to King George Square, this Italian Renaissance-style construction was once the tallest building in Brisbane. It is reputed to be haunted by four ghosts, including that of Hilda Boardman, whose ghostly spectre has been seen in the foyer. (Photo: Stuart McCallum)

Above: Brisbane Arcade (Queensland). A marvellous building whose design reflects the archetype of the traditional European eighteenth-century shopping arcade, it is believed that a woman in black, thought to be Mary McIntosh, the wife of an Irish immigrant, haunts these elegant corridors and shopfronts. (Photo: Stuart McCallum)

Opposite: Brisbane Arcade (Queensland). Now a stylish, up-market shopping mall full of award-winning fashion shops, designer jewellery stores, and quaint cafes, it hides a murky past that includes murder and scandal and, not surprisingly, ghostly tales from yesteryear. (Photo: Stuart McCallum)

Boggo Road Gaol (Queensland). Officially known as Brisbane Prison, it opened in 1883 and was used mainly as a holding prison for criminals serving short sentences or on remand, although it did have a gruesome past of hangings. It is said to be haunted by a number of spirits, including that of Bernard Ralph, who was bludgeoned to death with an iron bar in 1966. (Photo: Stuart McCallum)

IN LOVING MEMORY OF
MARGARET
BELOVED WIFE OF
THOMAS KEATING
DIED 29TH DEC. 1902,
AGED 42 YEARS.
ALSO THEIR DEAR CHILDREN
MABEL,
DIED 4TH OCT. 1893,
AGED 3 YEARS.
JOSEPHINE,
DIED 23RD MARCH 1895,
AGED 9 YEARS.
MAY,
DIED 16TH OCT. 1896,
AGED 13 YEARS.

Toowong Cemetery (Queensland). Formally opened in 1875, Toowong Cemetery is Queensland's largest cemetery. Now a popular tourist destination, it is rumoured to be haunted by a number of ghosts. Bizarrely, it has also been reported as being the burial place of Jack the Ripper, although this has never been fully established. (Photo: Stuart McCallum)

CHAPTER FOUR

†HE
∏ORTHER∏ †ERRITORY

A Disruptive Poltergeist, a Mad Miner, and an Eerie Outback Photograph

So far we have looked in the main at simple ghost sightings, although, in the Queensland chapter we examined the phenomena of the Min Min lights. However, through our journey we have rarely mentioned poltergeist behaviour, a common if not frightening aspect of some hauntings. And whereas poltergeist activity is regularly reported in countries such as England and the United States of America, here in Australia we seem to see little of this phenomenon. This is not to say that it doesn't exist, indeed, if one is to delve deep enough, one will find numerous accounts of this behaviour and, as we have seen, the National Museum of Australia is sometimes subject to poltergeist-like activity.

What is a Poltergeist?

Poltergeists have been described as being noisy, mischievous, and occasionally malevolent spirits who manifest their presence by making noises, moving objects, turning electrical equipment on and off, and even assaulting people. The term poltergeist comes from the German words *poltern,* which means "to knock," and *geist* meaning "spirit."

Poltergeist activity ranges from the non-threatening to the inexplicable with anything from moving and hiding keys to throwing stones and smashing glass or pottery. As well, reports of large furniture being moved around rooms and even levitation of people have also been reported in some circumstances. In the most severe cases people have allegedly been attacked and have shown bites and scratch marks on their bodies.

In general, poltergeist activity starts and stops abruptly, although the duration of the occurrences may last up to several hours spread randomly over a period of up to a few years. The activity almost always occurs at night when someone is present. Strangely, poltergeist activity is usually associated with a person who seems to serve as a focus for the activity—more often than not, a prepubescent female.

It has been suggested by some researchers that most poltergeist occurrences are not caused by spirits or ghosts, but by a person suffering from intense repressed anger, hostility, and sexual tension, which makes perfect sense in the case of the presence of a teenage girl. It is also suggested that the activity is a way for the child to express hostility without the fear of punishment.

Whether a poltergeist is a ghost or not is an interesting question and one we shall look at further. However we can say, without doubt, that poltergeist activity falls well within the scope of ghostly or supernatural occurrences. And as such, the reader starts to get the idea that ghosts come in many different shapes and forms.

Interestingly, the Northern Territory, although not unhaunted, appears to lack the ghost folklore of such older places, such as Melbourne, Sydney, and Perth. This is not to say that it is a place where strange things do not happen as it seems to have a greater percentage of UFO reports than other places. Why this is I have no idea, but as this book is solely about ghosts we will not be delving into the subject of UFOs.

Having said that, the Northern Territory does have one well-known story about a poltergeist, indeed, a story that rivals even the greatest poltergeist tales, including the famous Enfield poltergeist of the 1970s in London. And this is the so-called Humpty Doo poltergeist that made itself well and truly known to the residents of a small house over a five-month period in 1998 in the outback Australian town of Humpty Doo.

As with most poltergeist reports, the Humpty Doo story involves what one could describe as typical poltergeist behaviour in that objects of all kinds—spanners, knives, glass, gravel, live ammunition, and even baby bottles—seemed to have been thrown randomly, and sometimes not so randomly, by unseen hands within the house. In all, it was reported that more than seventeen people witnessed this strange phenomenon, including a security guard and a television newsman.

The house in question was nothing special: a quiet timber bungalow sitting in a two-hectare property planted with mango trees and without any history of strange events. However, beneath the peaceful facade, the five people living there complained that something unnatural was going on.

Before long, journalists from the *Northern Territory Times* and another local newspaper, the *Litchfield Times*, attended the house to report on what they were sure was a hoax. However, all soon came away believing that they had witnessed something supernatural and beyond the realms of modern science. What they had encountered was the Humpty Doo poltergeist.

As mentioned previously, the phenomena was quite violent with the thrown objects seemingly having no pattern and occurring twenty-four hours a day at random intervals, so much so that sleep was almost impossible. The tenants, Dave Clarke, his partner Jill Summerville, Andrew and Kirstie Agius, their baby, Jasmine, and a friend only known as Murph, were understandably at their wits' end.

Strangely, apart from the random throwing of objects, it seems the poltergeist was trying to get some sort of message across as on the floors and ground outside the house Scrabble® tiles appeared spelling out words such as "Help," "Skin," "Car," "Fire," and eerily, "Troy," the name of a young man and friend of the tenants who had recently died in a car crash when he was burnt to death. So odd was the story that when ABC television news reporter Tracey Farrer sat down to interview Kirstie Agius, she received a shock from her microphone. But if this could be explained as being simple equipment failure, then what happened next is completely and utterly inexplicable as a small object simply fell out of the air and landed in front of her. Puzzled, she picked the object up and realised that it was a small brown shell, something she had collected the previous day at the beach.

Another reporter, Nikki Voss, this time from the *Northern Territory News*, was extremely sceptical when she first came across the story. However, this scepticism disappeared rapidly when she visited the house and found herself ducking a flying beer mug that then smashed a window. Later, while standing with their backs to a wall in another room, she and another reporter were inexplicably pelted with gravel, which hit them painfully on the neck. Where the gravel came from they could not tell.

By this time the story had gained international attention, and sceptics the world around derided the accounts of the tenants and local media, one sceptic even suggesting that the tenants "loaded up" the indoor fans with rocks and knives and debris so as to be able to surreptitiously launch missiles upon the unsuspecting media whenever they visited. Kirstie Agius, however, rightly pointed out that she was already worried about her child's safety without having to resort to such dangerous tricks.

Another news crew, this time from Channel Seven, spent five days in the house and were subjected to almost nonstop phenomena. However, photographic evidence was almost impossible to capture as the entity, or whatever it was, seemed to stop performing whenever the television cameras were turned on—either that or it started playing up behind the cameras and stopped when they were turned around. Like most reported poltergeist cases around the world, the Humpty Doo poltergeist seemed to possess intelligence.

Interesting and somewhat frightening, when the Channel Seven news crew arrived they found, on the bathroom floor, Scrabble tiles arranged in the words "Go" and "No TV." The tiles were later found to have changed to the words "No Camera." Sceptics of course would point out that the lack of compelling evidence proves that it was all a hoax and that, in fact, nothing untoward or supernatural was happening. However, the weight of witness reports of strange activity was unceasing and came from not only the tenants but respected news crews, journalists, priests, sceptical reporters, and others.

The Channel Seven crew and some priests reported almost nonstop activity that included scissors splashing into a pool, a bullet apparently thrown across a room, a knife being plunged into a cameraman's car, a spanner violently thrown into a kitchen cupboard, and bedding being hurled against a wall.

Another newspaperman, Max Anderson from *The Australian*, a conservative broadsheet, described in an article how he witnessed knives, glass, and a bullet fly through the house, seemingly thrown by unseen hands. Frustratingly, the phenomena always took place when the cameras were pointed another way, which led to one cameraman to shout out in exasperation for the ghost to cooperate for once, which, in one instance, it did as three separate cameras managed to catch a baby bottle as it toppled from a microwave oven.

Over time the phenomena became more aggressive, including some Scrabble tiles that appeared from nowhere and fell directly onto a cameraman's boom mike where they landed and spelled the words "Go." As this was the crew's last day on site, they were quietly relieved when they left.

The Channel Seven news crew used cameras from all sorts of different angles, including some cameras that used thermal imaging to detect heat signatures left on objects. This was to presumably catch out hoaxers as a human hand will tend to leave the blurred outline of a hand on an object when filmed with a thermal camera. Oddly enough, the objects did have a thermal image, but not a tell-tale hand print, more so a rapidly dissipating heat that was spread evenly all over the object, as if it had been encased in something warm. Thermal imaging experts were reportedly baffled by this and could not explain it.

Damning, however, one piece of film footage did appear to prove something. On, *Today Tonight*, a national current affairs program, footage taken after their investigation and later enhanced appeared to show a reflection in some glass of what could possibly have been a person throwing a plastic bottle top. Confronted with this evidence, Kirstie Agius, owned up, claiming that she had done it because she was desperate to convince people that something unnatural was happening in the house.

Having noted this, everyone else who witnessed the phenomena was adamant that no one was hoaxing the incidents and that, if she had thrown it, then it was only a minor thing in comparison to everything else that was happening.

Surprising, in light of the previous enhanced footage, another flying object was filmed by a freelance cameraman, and it clearly showed a small ball or some other round-shaped plastic object bouncing off the top of a cabinet with glass doors. In a freeze of one particular frame, an indistinct reflection appeared in the glass near to the cameraman: a face where no one was standing.

Also of note, a Catholic priest, Father Tom English, performed an unsuccessful exorcism and, whilst in the middle of the ceremony, was astounded when something slammed onto a steel table in front of him. Examining the object he realised it was a bullet. He also reported that, as he was about to sprinkle holy water, a medicine bottle appeared out of nowhere and smashed against a wall. As well, his Bible was later torn from his hands by some unknown force and when retrieved was found to be missing a number of pages.

Whatever the case, the Humpty Doo poltergeist remains unsolved. Even with the admission from Agius that she had thrown an object, it still in no way explains the countless eyewitness reports of objects flying around rooms or how gravel could fall from the ceiling or be pelted at unsuspecting people. Unfortunately, however, the Agius incident will always cast doubt upon the whole story

But if poltergeists in the rough and tumble Australian outback towns doesn't scare you, or at least pique your interest, then what of the next amazing and quite unbelievable story that reportedly happened to Jennifer Mills-Young of Durack, near Darwin.

Mrs. Mills-Young told her local newspaper, *The Northern Territory News* that: "I was asleep (and) I woke up when someone grabbed my wrist. I thought, 'Hmmm, hubby wants a bit of romance', when I suddenly remembered he wasn't even at home. The moment I opened my eyes, the grip was gone and the room was empty."

The ghostly visitor, named Kevin for some reason, had been rumoured to be haunting the house for a number of years and that Mrs. Mills-Young, her husband Geoff and two children, had always thought that something was not quite right about the house. Her daughter once reported that someone was in her room and that she had seen a "tall black shadow standing at the door."

Mr. Mills-Young also said that he had seen the ghostly figure, stating that he "saw someone walking past our back door inside our yard, which I had locked. I jumped up and ran to the door to see what this guy was doing in our yard and he just vanished."

Mrs. Mills-Young said she was the "worst sceptic" when it came to ghosts, although one would suspect that her views may have changed since.

Later, in 2010, Mrs. Mills-Young wrote to a local blog claiming that her son, Aaron, had recently encountered a "tall male figure standing in the doorway that leads into our lounge room" and that it was "white and misty and definitely of male physique." Apparently, Aaron drew the ghostly figure which, when viewed by Mrs. Mills-Young the next morning was exactly what she had been experiencing around the house.

A few days after this Aaron woke his mother at around 10:00 p.m. and claimed that he had seen "a white face with eyes and mouth in the back window, but a low window only one foot off the ground." A later search proved futile as, whatever it was, was gone.

Whether or not this was the alleged "Kevin" we will never know, although Mills-Young believes that it is and that he still haunts the modest family home for reasons unknown.

Meanwhile, also in 2010, another Darwin-based family, this time in Jingili, a northern suburb of Darwin that was built in the early 1970s, claimed that a ghost they named Harry was scaring their children and rattling cupboard doors.

Jahmaine Sheridan, who was ten at the time said she was relieved to hear there were "more ghosts out there" and that her house wasn't the only place that was haunted, stating that: "I was so glad to see it was happening to other people, too. It's not just us; we are not mad."

She also mentioned that her family has encountered "something very creepy and scary" in their home since moving in three years previously and that her first encounter was when she saw a "white shadow" just after moving into the house. Later she explained that she was "sitting on the toilet and I looked behind me and there was this white shadow." And that: "Only a couple of days ago I was sitting on the couch with my sister and someone was playing with the cupboard doors; we couldn't see anyone, but the doors were making a flicking noise."

Nathalie Sheridan, Jahmaine's mother, who works at the Royal Darwin Hospital, said the spooky encounters were "not something made up by children with too much fantasy" and that: "We all see things out of the corner of our eye and when you turn your head it's gone." She also added that when the family is downstairs, they often hear footsteps walking around in the upstairs rooms and vice versa when they are upstairs.

But whereas Harry seemed to be reasonably benevolent, it is said that the ghost of a beautiful Asian woman who haunts the Poinciana trees at East Point now stalks the night enticing young men to their deaths.

The Poinciana Woman was believed to have been raped by Japanese fishermen at East Point after which she became deranged, and, when she discovered she was pregnant, she hanged herself from a branch of a Poinciana tree. She has since become a wraith who stalks and kills men at night by initially appearing as a beautiful white-robed, long-haired young woman who then transforms into a hideous wild-haired eagle-clawed hag just before she disembowels her victims and feeds on their intestines.

She has a distinctive shrill scream and can be summoned on moonless nights by spinning three times and calling out her name, somewhat like the American legend of Bloody Mary, who appears after someone says her name three times into a mirror.

Of course, the legend of the Poinciana Woman is just that, a legend, no more a real ghost than Bloody Mary. Having said that, just as going to the Air Disaster Memorial in Canberra is a rite of passage for Canberra teenagers, so too is a trip to the tip of East Point at night for Darwin teenagers.

But if the Poinciana Woman is no more than an urban myth, then what of the ghost reputed to haunt Fannie Bay Gaol in Darwin?

Fannie Bay Gaol is now a museum and operated as Her Majesty's Gaol and Labour Prison, from September 1883 until September 1979. In this time eleven executions took place, even though some believe there were another sixty that were either not recorded or the records were lost.

Of these executions, Romanian immigrants Jerry Coci and Jonus Novotny, were hanged for the murder of a taxi driver on 8 August 1952. These were the last two executions to be carried out in Darwin, and it is now believed that the souls of these two men haunt the old gaol with prisoners and officials reporting hearing sad moans coming from empty cells and doors opened and slammed at times when there were no guards around. Although the gaol ceased operation in 1979 and is now a museum, visitors have reported feeling an invisible hand glide over the steel bars and have heard sounds of a body being dragged along one of the corridors.

Others have reported being touched by unseen hands in the cells while the sensation of being watched is not uncommon. As well, some have reported the frightening phenomena of having the sensation of male bodies pressed up against them to the point of near suffocation.

But if gaols are well known for their tragic and violent pasts, what then can we make of our next destination, far to the south of Darwin and just outside Alice Springs? A place called Corroboree Rock.

Corroboree Rock Conservation Reserve is about an hour's easy drive from Alice Springs. It is an outstanding dark grey column of dolomite and is of great importance to the Aboriginal people of the region. The rock outcrop itself is made of dolomite and was originally laid down in salty lakes 800 million years ago. Dolomite is a soft, sedimentary, fine grained rock and is very similar to limestone except magnesium carbonate is the dominant compound rather than calcium carbonate. This contributes to the strange colours of the rock.

Corroboree Rock was probably used as an important storage site for ceremonial objects by the Eastern Arrernte Aboriginal people, although it is doubtful that it was ever used as a corroboree site due to the lack of water in the area. Having said this, there is no doubt that the place holds great spiritual significance, even though this would have been a tightly held secret. What is known, however, is the area is considered spiritually dangerous for Aboriginal women, children, and uninitiated men. It is also considered taboo to climb the rock itself.

And it was here that one of the most intriguing and compelling ghost photos was taken in 1959 by Adelaide Presbyterian minister R. S. Blance, who was visiting the sacred site when he took a photo of the seemingly empty scene. When the photo was developed, he was shocked to find the image of a semi-transparent woman in a white dress standing amongst the scrub surrounding the open clearing.

Curiously, although the woman appears to be wearing an old-fashioned dress, she appears to be holding her hands in such a way that it could be construed that she is holding a pair of binoculars or a camera.

Of course, this has led to speculation that the photo is simply a double exposure or that Blance simply didn't notice the person in the shot. However, upon inspection, one gets the feeling that this is not the case and given that it was taken in 1959, it would be difficult to fake. For one, the ghostly woman appears to be semi-transparent and yet she fits into the landscape as if she really was there when the photo was taken. As such, one would have to suggest that a double exposure is out of the question, as if it was, the figure would appear to be out of synch with the landscape.

But if it is a double exposure, then surely Blance would have remembered taking a photo of the woman previously, which he denied. Therefore, if it is not a double exposure, we are left with the sobering thought that this photo could possibly show a real ghost. Having said this, what of her hand position and what is she looking at and why? One theory that has been suggested is what is known as a "time-slip" in which the camera has somehow recorded a scene from a different period of time.

Time-Slips

To understand what we mean by a time-slip I shall briefly discuss the subject. Imagine walking into a completely familiar place, say a shop that you know quite well, and finding that the complete interior has changed and that the people behind the counter and the actual products themselves seem to be from a different era, indeed, from an era well before your lifetime? Imagine also that you are walking along the street when you pass a friend or an acquaintance who is going the opposite way. You acknowledge each other and continue on your separate ways only to turn a corner and come face to face with that person once again, even though you know it is completely impossible for that person to be where they are. Perhaps, you think, he has an identical twin or this person is just very similar in appearance, right down to the exact same clothes and shoes. But no, you acknowledge him again and have no doubts. This is the same person and you have seen him twice in completely unexplainable circumstances.

Even though these situations seem completely and utterly implausible, there have been many occasions when perfectly rational and sane people have reported instances as such. And such instances are what are commonly referred to as a time-slip.

Imagine time being a piece of string stretched out tightly and tautly in a perfectly straight line. Then imagine people moving along this piece of string as time passes. All are going the same direction at the same pace and will apparently, never meet. However, what if this piece of string suddenly developed a loop of some kind? If this were to happen, then the occurrences previously described could actually happen. Either you or your friend has somehow managed to step off the straight and narrow part of time and found yourself on the loop.

Previously, while discussing ghosts in the Australian Capital Territory, we looked at the National Film and Sound Archive where a Professor Jeff Brownrigg encountered something that he has never been able to fully explain when he was astounded to find over a hundred people standing around in the foyer as if there for some official function. In addition, he reported that they appeared to be sepia-like in colour and from a different era, almost like a costume or fancy dress party. This strange event could be seen as one of two things, that being, a large gathering of ghostly figures, or a time-slip whereby, for a brief moment, Brownrigg had somehow—by what means we do not know—glanced into the past as if it were an old movie playing in front of him.

And this isn't a one-off as, on the morning of 18 June 1968, in Tunbridge Wells, England, Charlotte Warburton was shopping with her husband when they decided to separate for a while with the view of meeting later. Unable to find a particular brand of coffee that she liked, Mrs. Warburton went into a supermarket on Calverley Road. Once in the shop she noticed a small old-fashioned café that for some reason she had never seen before. The place had wood panelled walls and no windows but was lit by electric lighting. Two women in long dresses were sitting at one table and a number of men in dark suits were milling around chatting and drinking coffee.

Mrs. Warburton did not stay and indeed didn't really think about it much at all until the following day while passing the supermarket with her husband when she decided to call in to the little cafe. When she entered the supermarket there was no sign of the place and, although the two searched up and down the street, they could find no evidence that the place had ever existed. They later learned that the Kosmos Kinema used to stand on the site of the supermarket and that the cinema had a small bar with tables for refreshments, exactly as Mrs. Warburton had described.

The cinema, bar, and assembly room had all disappeared many years previous, and yet it appears that on that day in 1968, Mrs. Warburton had somehow stepped into the past.

In another celebrated case, in 1935, Wing Commander Victor Goddard, while flying from Andover to Edinburgh in a Royal Air Force Hawker Hart biplane, had an equally perplexing incident when he reportedly flew over an RAF base that, at the time, did not exist in the form he saw it in.

So, time-slip or ghost? I am inclined to suggest the latter and dismiss the hands of the woman as simple coincidence. And even though some have speculated that the ghostly woman might actually be a time traveller or inter-dimensional being who was photographed in the act of watching the minister, I think this is simply too farfetched to consider. Which leaves us with the possibility that yes, just maybe Blance photographed a ghost.

Tennant Creek is approximately 1,000 kilometres south of Darwin and some 500 kilometres north of Alice Springs. It is named after a nearby watercourse of the same name and has a population just larger than 3,000 people. It is well known for tourist attractions such as the Devil's Marbles and is situated in the centre of the Barkly Tableland, an elevated plain of black soil and grasslands that covers more than 240,000 square kilometres.

It is also known for its gold mining past, which is where we become interested in the place, as, if you are ever in the area fossicking amongst the now abandoned gold claims around the Warrego mines area, you may bump into the ghost of an old miner known locally as Mad Mick.

Although the majority of the gold mines closed down in 1942, there was still enough present for prospectors to survive, although the extraction of the gold was tough, hard work. One of these was a company called Peko Wallsend Mining Company, which was capable of doing all its own crushing on site. Besides this there were a number of men mining their own small claims. One of these men was Mad Mick.

Mad Mick appeared in the 1970s and worked for a while with Peko Wallsend. He was described as of eastern European heritage and spoke in rapid, broken English. Not long after he had arrived, he found a large nugget of gold and decided to leave the company and strike out on his own, taking out a miner's lease. Although people were aware of his claim and the area he was working, no one dared go near him as he had a habit of firing his shotgun at people as a warning to stay away.

In the 1980s, a man went missing in the vicinity of Mad Mick's claim and, although people searched for him, it was not until a few years later that his body was discovered. In the meantime, locals realised that no one had seen or heard from Mad Mick for quite a while.

Fearing the worse, police extensively searched the area for a week, but Mick was never found. His four-wheel drive vehicle was still at his shack and it didn't appear as if he'd decided to move on. His disappearance was a complete mystery, and some wondered if a murder-suicide had occurred.

These days local legend suggests that strange wailing sounds and moans can be heard coming from the old shack as well as the clattering of tools. Others report seeing the shady outline of a figure near the diggings, which locals say is Mad Mick himself. Indeed, prospective miners surveying the area often refuse to camp near the old shack, citing the ghost as a reason.

Others believe that the figure is the dead man's ghost and that Mick himself had killed him in some sort of disagreement before leaving town and creating a new life for himself elsewhere. Whatever the case, if you are ever in the area, be sure to watch out for a shadowy figure, whoever it may be.

The Northern Territory is a vast an inhospitable place where haunting presences seem to lurk constantly just out of reach and eyeshot. It is a place of primeval landscapes, deep-rooted culture, of rock art and mythological figures that walk the land or hide in the crevices and cracks of ancient rock formations. And although we could have explored the spiritual side of Indigenous people of the area, I believe that it is not for me to do so.

Although there are not that many ghost reports from the Northern Territory, this is not surprising given the small population spread out over such a huge area. But if this is so for the NT, then what of WA, that huge expanse of sand and desert that encompasses nearly half of Australia's total land mass?

CHAPTER FIVE

Western Australia

Another Haunted Gaol, a Tragic Island Prison, and a Cursed Ship

The city of Perth is a far flung outpost of the Australian nation, almost closer to Asia than any other mainland city. The nearest city with a population of more than 100,000 is Adelaide in South Australia, some 2,100 kilometres to the east. And due to this, it seems a world away from the hustle and bustle of better-known cities such as Melbourne and Sydney. And yet, to think of it as unmodern and backwards is completely wrong.

These days Perth is a thriving, bustling and busy city known for its cultural history, climate, easy living, and tourism. Set beside the beautiful Swan River with superb waterside restaurants and miles of clean beaches, it is a jewel in the desert that surrounds it and the home for nearly 2,000,000 people. But don't be fooled into thinking that this is a town full of glitz and glamour and, as such, lacking in history, as its roots go all the way back to 1829, and like most Australian cities, it has a dark convict past.

And with this dark convict past, one is not surprised that it has a long history of ghosts and hauntings from old gaols to asylums and hospitals. And of these, the logical place to start would be the Old Fremantle Prison, or Fremantle Gaol.

Built between 1851 and 1859 using convict labour, the gaol sits on a six-hectare site and includes cellblocks, an ornate gatehouse, huge and imposing stone perimeter walls, cottages, tunnels, and these days, an art gallery and museum. Initially known as the "Convict Establishment" or simply "The Establishment," it was constructed as a prison for convicts.

In 1886, the gaol was transferred to the colonial government and opened to locally sentenced prisoners, and it continued in this way for much of the 1900s, resisting change and modernisation until it closed in 1991. In 1992, it reopened as a cultural centre. Remarkably, the place never had flushing toilets at any stage of its operational history.

Walking from the car park to the entrance of the prison, one is filled with a sense of awe. The gatehouse itself is a two-story limestone building with two turrets flanking a large arch, which leads into a harsh stone-surfaced interior courtyard. Entering the arched doorway, one is suddenly transported back to another time, another age when this place was the site of brutality and violence.

And yet it is quiet, very quiet, as if the place has the power to suck all energy from those who enter.

Given that the gaol held some of the most notorious and violent criminals in the country and that forty-four people were executed there, it is not surprising that it is rated as one of Perth's most haunted locations.

The building is very eerie and cold, and the long, lonely corridors echo as if the pain encountered by the former cellmates still exists in the very walls and floors. The cells, basic and dark, are small and dank, and during a tour one gets to see these cells, plus the gallows, the morgue, the solitary cells, the whipping post, and the exercise yard. Wandering around, one gets a feeling of despair and loneliness, once again, as if the building itself is forcing its emotions onto the visitor. It is a creepy and unnerving place.

Over the years, people have reported numerous supernatural occurrences within the walls of the gaol, including strange noises and lights, doors opening and closing of their own accord, ghostly shadows, whispered voices, unexplained screams, cold spots, feelings of dread and depression and, in some cases, full-body apparitions—one of these a woman in grey, believed to be Martha Rendell.

Martha Rendell, who was hanged in October 1909, was the only woman to be hanged in the gaol and the last woman to be hanged in Western Australia. She was convicted of murdering her de facto husband's son, Arthur Morris, in 1908 and also suspected of killing his two daughters, Annie and Olive by swabbing hydrochloric acid on the back of their throats. Although she protested her innocence, maintaining that she was treating the children for diphtheria, there was considerable public outrage at the time, and her fate was sealed. She now rests in Fremantle Cemetery.

A day after Rendell was hanged an unusual image seemed to appear on the outside of one of the church windows. It was said to be the portrait of Martha who watches over the prison. Interesting, and somewhat confusing, the image can only be seen from outside the window, as from the inside of the church, no image is evident.

Death row is especially disturbing and legend has it that mass murderer David Burnie's ghost has been seen in this part of the prison, even though he later suicided in the newer Casuarina Prison, in October 2005, after the closure of Fremantle Gaol. Burnie and his wife, Catherine, were sentenced to life imprisonment for the murders of four women in Perth in the 1980s in what the press later dubbed "The Moorhouse Murders."

The fact that Burnie's ghost is seen in a place where he did not die is not unheard of, and it seems to suggest that ghosts are not simply the lost souls of a dead person. Rather, it suggests that there is some sort of emotional attachment or trauma involved in at least some of the hauntings people have experience all around the world.

An example of this is to be found in the wonderfully serene setting of Hever Castle in Kent, England, where the ghost of Anne Boleyn has been seen on regular occasion, even though she was later executed in the Tower of London. Hever Castle, it should be noted, was the childhood home of Anne Boleyn so it would seem natural that a part of her spirit has remained in this wonderful medieval building. And yet she is also reported to have been seen at the Tower of London, at Blickling Hall in Norfolk and Rochford Hall in Essex. Indeed, at Blickling Hall it is said that she appears once a year on the anniversary of her execution travelling in a coach pulled by a headless horse driven by a headless horseman with her severed head in her lap. Once the coach reaches the hall it is said it disappears leaving the sad and pathetic figure of Anne alone on the steps until she disappears before being seen again in the halls and corridors of the great house. Local folklore also suggests that these ghostly visions are said to be followed by eerie blue lights through the back roads of Norfolk. What they are is unknown.

Similarly, at Rochford Hall in Essex, once belonging to Thomas Boleyn and the marital home of Anne's sister Mary, it is said that a headless woman dressed in silk and said to be a witch haunts the grounds for the twelve days after Christmas. This spirit is also said to be Anne.

But if Anne's ghost is seen all over the place from the Tower of London to Blickling Hall and Hever Castle, is there any other evidence that ghosts can haunt more than one place? Is it possible that ghosts are not simply the spirit of a dead person and are something much more complex, for instance, a memory or event in history that has somehow become attached to a place, somewhat like a holographic recording? The spirits of Sir Francis Drake and Sir Walter Raleigh are just two more examples of this multiple ghosts theory.

But not all of these out-of-place ghosts appear in medieval English castles or dwellings as, in Canberra at the Australian War Memorial in the Hall of Memory, the ghost of a soldier is often reported to staff even though no one is buried there, and the place only opened relatively recently in 1941. Is it possible, as in the case of Anne Boleyn and Walter Raleigh, that this ghost has somehow returned without his remains to this most poignant of places? Why does his spirit haunt these hallowed halls and not the green, overgrown battlefields of First World War France? Or is it something else? Is the significance of the place something that can generate intense emotions, enough to somehow produce what one could call a ghost? And if this is the case, then is this really a ghost or do we need to readjust our beliefs as to what ghosts really are?

It would seem, given what we have read, that ghosts are more than just the souls of the tormented dead. Indeed, it would seem that they are something much more substantial and even less understandable, and this is something that we shall look at further as we delve into this strange and misunderstood world.

But whereas Anne Boleyn and Raleigh's ghost are well known at the Tower of London, this book concerns itself with Australian reports of ghosts and, as such, we shall move on from the Old Fremantle Gaol to another well-known haunting in the city of Perth: the Fremantle Arts Centre.

The Fremantle Arts Centre is another site that is widely known as being haunted and these days is a community multi-arts organisation offering exhibitions, residencies, art courses, and music. The building itself was constructed using convict labour between 1861 and 1868 and was used as a psychiatric hospital, initially called the Fremantle Lunatic Asylum and later known as the Asylum for the Criminally Insane.

After the 1890s gold rushes, the asylum became seriously overcrowded, which forced a reorganisation of the facilities, and although it operated up until the early 1900s, two suspicious deaths saw the government set up an enquiry that concluded that the building "be demolished as unfit for purpose for which it is now used."

As a result, patients were moved to alternative locations. After this, the building was used for housing homeless women and later operated as a midwifery school. During World War II it became the headquarters for the American armed services based in Western Australia.

With such a rich history, one would suspect that stories of ghosts and hauntings have some grounding in reality and Cal Greatbatch, the founder of the paranormal research and investigation organisation Perth Ghost Hunters, believes that the building is haunted by at least ten separate entities, including one whose voice was picked up on a digital recorder saying, "Those are chains." This voice was recorded next to a display showing leg chains from the convict era.

Along with the voices, people have reported cold spots, voices, banging noises, movement of objects, footsteps, smells, physical contact, black shadows, and, terrifyingly, part or full apparitions.

Alex Marshall, who runs Fremantle Ghost Tours, also estimates that the old Gothic-style building is haunted by at least ten restless spirits, including an elderly lady believed to have been a mental patient in the asylum. Legend has it that after her daughter was abducted, she jumped from a first-floor window of what is now the Investigator Gallery, and as a result, her spirit still roams the building searching for her daughter. Indeed, in the room where she jumped, people often say they've seen or felt her around them, and on one tour, a woman was startled when she heard a child singing. Not long after, the whole group agreed that they could hear the singing, although there was no one around.

Marshall himself had a frightening experience when a shadowy figure of a man dressed in black walked across a courtyard in front of him before disappearing into thin air, leaving him somewhat shocked and thinking, "Oh, my gosh, it's true! I've seen one."

Another to see a full apparition at the Arts Centre is medium Anthony Grzelka when he joined a television team staying overnight in the building to film a ghost documentary. The crew was locked in the asylum for the night when he saw the figure of what he described as a "very tough and hardened spirit of a man standing halfway down a corridor." He later described that the temperature in this area dropped from 22 degrees to less than 16 degrees in that exact area, and that he was filled with a nauseating feeling of unease.

Grzelka also recalled that his "impressions were that he was not an inmate of the asylum when it was operating but a very nasty nurse or warden type," and that he couldn't "begin to fathom the types of things he did to those poor souls who were patients in that place many years ago. This very unpleasant man had been here a long time—perhaps 100 years or so from the look of his demeanor and dress."

Grzelka later discovered that a number of security guards simply refused to enter that part of the asylum after a couple had been pushed down a stairwell. He has since concluded that this spirit is that of a particularly evil man, who probably worked in the institution a century or so ago.

Alex Marshall also speaks of frightening encounters, including one when he was taking a group through the painting studio, when one of the men on the tour started shaking violently. Marshall initially thought he was putting it on, but when he turned on the lights realised that the person was not joking, and that he was sweating profusely and staring blankly into space.

Then, as soon as it started, the man stopped shaking and came to his senses. When he did, he shook his head and said, "She's gone now. That was pretty scary!"

In another frightening encounter a woman standing at the top of a set of stairs witnessed something and became frozen in fear, so petrified that she could not speak or move and, as a result, fainted. When she came to, she fled the building leaving no one the wiser as to what she had seen.

Of course, mental asylums at the turn of the century were harsh, heartless places where people were sent to remove them from society. There was little compassion shown for the patients, and cruelty and mistreatment were commonplace. Research suggests that the inmates were often subjected to unwanted sexual advances and other forms of exploitation and abuse. This includes three sisters from a well-to-do and well-known local family who were confined to the building to keep them out of sight of the public. The spirits of these poor girls are said to now haunt a bath area, the place where they were supposedly molested by staff.

In addition, research has shown that a number of American soldiers stationed in the building during World War II reported hearing odd whisperings, bangings, and noises at night, and some even reported being touched by ghostly hands. Add to this heavy footsteps in empty rooms and the ghost of a woman or child who kisses people and you have a recipe for supernatural mayhem. Whatever the case, the Fremantle Arts Centre appears to live up to its reputation.

But, as with other states and territories, it is not just old gaols and asylums that seem to attract supernatural entities.

The Kalumunda Hotel, some 20 kilometres east of the CBD, is another old building reputed to be occupied by a number of ghostly entities, including an angry old man, a woman in her thirties, an unknown man that seems to stay in the shadows, and a young mischievous girl.

Built in 1902, the original Kalamunda Hotel was the centre piece of social and commercial life of Kalamunda well into the 1950s, although a fire in 1985 seriously damaged the building and the whole ground floor was converted into a bottle shop. The current Kalamunda Hotel, designed by Perth architect George Herbert Parry, was built in 1928 and featured a beer garden, bars, and restaurant with function rooms and guest rooms.

The new Kalamunda Hotel played an important part in the life of the town and was conveniently situated near the railway station until 1949 when the railway closed. With such a location it was well patronised by businessmen, workers, and general travellers. In fact, the building is a significant part of the social and cultural history of the area and was classified by the National Trust.

Apart from the aforementioned ghosts, it is also believed to be haunted by a young woman who, after finding she was pregnant by the hotel's original owner, Paddy Connelly, committed suicide by jumping off the hotel balcony. People on this story have complained of disembodied voices and, on one occasion, reported an angry voice saying: "Get out!"

Whatever the case, if one is looking to have an encounter with the other side, the Kalamunda Hotel may be worth a visit, or even an overnight stay; after all, who knows what one may encounter? It seems Kalamunda has its own version of the hitchhiker ghost, much like Lake George just north of Canberra.

Apparently, as the legend goes, a bus driver was travelling down Kalamunda Road towards Great Eastern Highway when he stopped to pick up an elderly lady who was waiting at the bus stop outside the cemetery. She got on and sat in the front row of seats and for a couple of minutes held a pleasant conversation with the driver. The conversation then stopped, and the bus driver thought nothing of it, continuing to drive. However, the next time he looked behind him, the woman had disappeared, and, although he later searched the bus throughout, he could find no trace of her. Because of this it is said that bus drivers no longer stop outside the cemetery at night

Roughly 100 kilometres east of Perth, in the town of York, is an old hospital reputed to be haunted by some quite malevolent spirits, although no one is quite sure who, or what, they are.

York itself is a pretty town and is the oldest inland town in Western Australia, being settled in 1831, only two years after Perth. Although the township didn't start to appear until 1836 when an army barracks and store were built, it soon began to attract new settlers from Perth, all eager to make their fortune from the land, including, in the 1880s, miners and fossickers all seeking gold. From 1885 to 1900, the town was booming, and a large number of impressive civic buildings were constructed, including the tailway station buildings, the Imperial Hotel, the York Roller Flour Mill, the court house and police station, and the York Hospital.

The hospital itself is a two-story building constructed in 1896. The site also included a morgue, a laundry, nurse's quarters, and a maternity block. Designed by George Temple Poole, chief architect in the Public Works Department, the building continued as a hospital until the early 1960s when tenders were called for the construction of a new hospital. In 1963, it was used by the Methodist Church, which renamed it "Mirambeena" after which the place continued to be used as a youth centre until it was sold to the National Trust of Australia (WA) in 1976. Since then, it has mainly operated as a youth hostel, a hostel that not everyone was happy to stay in.

A former matron who worked at the hospital in the 1920s said: "There was always something terrifying about the upstairs rooms. The hospital staff refused to go up there alone, and even when the ward was full of patients, the nurses always made their rounds in pairs."

In 1980, a children's athletic club booked into the hostel for a week-long stay. Although only a two-hour bus trip from Perth, it took six and a half hours in the hired bus due to breakdowns and holdups, which, in over 100 degree heat, ensured that the journey was exhausting. However, if they thought this was the end of their troubles, then they were very much mistaken as, in spite of ordering their food requirements some three weeks earlier, there was absolutely nothing there for them, not even a drink of cold water. Still, this was obviously a minor oversight and was quickly rectified, and soon the children and parents were comfortable.

However, late on the first night sounds of moaning and whimpering started to come from inside the walls of the dormitory they were staying in and, even with a search, the source was never found. This was to repeat over a number of nights. The next morning, after a fitful night's sleep, two of the women woke early and went down to the kitchen to prepare breakfast for the children when, to their amazement, a large jug slowly lifted into the air, a foot or so above the bench, travelled through the air toward the window, and then suddenly dropped to the floor smashing into many pieces.

Amazed, and somewhat concerned, the two women searched for an answer or a reason as to how the jug could have acted as it did, but no matter what they thought of, none of it made any sense, and they were none the wiser as to what had happened.

Breakfast, however, was uneventful, and the two women were soon at ease. However, not long after, two girls, who were in a passage outside the dining room, were apparently attacked by an unseen entity with one of the girls screaming; "Hold me! Hold me! I can't sit down! Stop them! Stop them!"

The other little girl grabbed her by her clothing, but there seemed to be some sort of tussle going on between the two girls and some unseen force, which, according to the girls afterwards, seemed to be trying to lift one of them off the ground. After a few moments one of the girls was thrown against a glass-paneled door at the end of the hall with the impact being so hard that it shattered the thick glass, gashing her arm to the bone. She was rushed to the hospital and received seven stitches to the wound.

Justifiably angry about the events of the morning and the previous night, one of the mothers sought out the caretaker of the building who simply laughed it off, although he chillingly mentioned that they "had heard the matron," the rumour being that a previous matron had been raped in the building, and that one could sometimes hear her running around trying to find her assailant.

The woman, however, was perturbed and asked if the caretaker could bring one of his dogs with him later that night while they checked out the upstairs room to see what had been making the moaning noises. Upon coming to the room, the group of adults were assailed by a terrible stench, and the dog refused to go any closer, raising his hackles and looking frightened. The group then opened the door and looked in the room only to find it completely empty. One of the group said that the atmosphere of the room made him feel violently ill. They locked the door and left. Later the group found out that the room had been used as a "dying room" for terminal patients and may have also served as a morgue in earlier years.

Not surprising, everyone was now on edge, and a series of small incidents made sure they stayed that way. One boy managed to get his leg wedged in a bannister (something that could have happened anyway), a woman was kneed or pushed in the back by an unseen force, another woman complained that a needle was stuck in her head, and one of the coaches ended up with a large bruise on his head when a door flew open, violently striking him.

In addition, a putrid smell seemed to invade the building as if something was dead in one of the rooms, even though it was not evident from the outside. Spookily, the doorknob on the dining room door keep spinning around even though this was a locked, unused door.

Tuesday night was similar to Monday night, and the children showered and went to bed. The moaning noises could still be heard, so the adults stayed close by, and a check of the children later found an eleven-year-old boy sitting in his bed absolutely terrified and unable to speak. After he had been consoled and had calmed down, he described seeing a person beside the door; however, it was not a complete person, more so the side of a face, a shoulder, and the hand on the door handle. The rest of the figure was simply missing.

Although the place was relatively quiet in the mornings, it appeared as if the intensity of the haunting increased in the afternoons and nighttime. By the end of the third day, both adults and children decided to sleep in one room in hope of protecting themselves against whatever it was that was attacking them. Another night of fitful sleep passed by.

The next day was unremarkable, although the group was made aware of a nurse who had died upstairs in the hospital, which made her wonder whether this was her spirit that they were experiencing, and if so, why?

Later that night, a couple of the men did a thorough search of the grounds, and the women checked the dormitory. Nothing unusual was heard or seen, and the children were sleeping peacefully. The group then decided to check the upstairs part of the building and found that their torch lights mysteriously flashed on and off in relation to where they were standing. As well, to their amazement, they heard running water, and, flashing their torches at the wash basin, they observed steaming hot water disappearing down the plug hole, although both taps were firmly turned off and there was absolutely no way anyone could have snuck past them to turn the tap on and then sneak back out without being seen.

Now thoroughly spooked, the group checked everything for signs of an intruder but, finding nothing, decided to go back downstairs to the dormitory where the children were sleeping. Happy that nothing untoward was going to happen, they made cups of tea, left their torches on a kitchen bench, and moved to a small adjoining sitting room. Just as they did, they heard the kitchen door slam shut leaving them without supplementary lighting.

Then an explosion-like noise shook the building, and they thought that the hot water system had exploded. The group immediately ran out of the room and checked the children, but they were still sleeping soundly as if they hadn't heard the noise. At this time, one of the women, according to a witness, became possessed by "something" and swore that she had seen a cloudy, ghostly figure. As a result, she promptly lay down on a bed and pulled the covers over her head.

Completely terrified, the group armed themselves with cricket bats and stumps and anything else they could find and waited in the dark. In the meantime, the woman who had seemingly been possessed returned to normal just as the woman who had hidden under the bedsheet began to convulse as if fighting with herself. She began screaming and shouting: "Why didn't you help me?"

The group looked at her puzzled having no idea what she was talking about, and she explained that something had leapt on her and was strangling her. She opened her shirt and showed them her neck, which was bruised as if someone had tried to strangle her. "Didn't you see her? She had me by the throat. She tried to kill me."

At this stage the group, already frightened enough, heard a record player they'd brought along for the trip begin to play. However, no one was prepared to leave the room to switch it off. They all agreed to wait until daylight.

Not long after, one of the women, sitting next to a window, drew back the curtain to look out. To her horror she came face to face with an apparition of a person. Surprisingly calm, she simply dropped the curtain back down figuring that it would go away. When she opened it again, it was still there, floating grotesquely outside the window. Again she waited for a moment before lifting the curtain; this time the figure had disappeared.

In the morning the caretaker arrived, and the group explained the loud bang they had heard. As a result they all went upstairs to see what it could have been, and, to their surprise, found the old morgue room door wide open. This was enough for the group, and they hurriedly gathered the children and left on the bus, leaving the old hospital to whatever spirits haunted its rooms and corridors.

The building was sold as recently as 2004 and is currently rumored to being renovated into a bed and breakfast. As for the ghosts, well, they seem to have quietened down for the moment. Either that or the new owners are simply remaining quiet about this spooky old building.

But not all ghostly encounters concern malevolent ghosts. For instance, the Old Bakery in Nannup, approximately 280 kilometres south of Perth, was built in the early 1900s and later abandoned in the 1930s. It appears to be haunted by the ghost of a baker with visitors sometimes reporting the smell of freshly baked bread and the noise of an old-fashioned cash register, which, while it may seem a little disconcerting, is hardly frightening.

Likewise, the Mahogany Inn in Mahogany Creek, roughly a forty-minute drive east of Perth, was built in the early 1800s and is said to be haunted by famous bush ranger Moondyne Joe. Originally named "The Prince of Wales Inn," it was built on a three-and-one-half-acre block from local stone, and it is rumoured that Moondyne Joe used the attic at the inn as a hideout when evading the police. Staff and visitors have mentioned ghostly noises and experiences.

Moondyne Joe, whose real name was Joseph Bolitho Johns, was born in Cornwall in 1826, and, although nothing more than a petty criminal and robber, he became known as Western Australia's best known bushranger. He died in 1900 of senile dementia in the Fremantle Lunatic Asylum, now the Fremantle Arts Centre, and was buried in Fremantle Cemetery. Whether it is his ghost that haunts the inn is unknown, but as previously seen, it is not impossible that it could.

Toodyay is another Western Australian town that is reputed to be haunted. It is known that Moondyne Joe lived in the pioneering town during the 1860s. Situated 85 kilometres northeast of Perth, the first European settlement occurred in the area in 1836. Today it is a town rich in heritage and history with a huge number of impressive turn-of-the-century buildings dotting the urban landscape. It is also a town rich in folklore and tales of ghosts, mysterious lights, and other occurrences generally associated with the supernatural.

Toodyay Jail, completed in 1864 and used as a state prison until 1909, was where Moondyne Joe spent some of his time. Now, although restored as a museum, is believed to be the haunt of a number of malevolent spirits, one of which could be Moondyne Joe.

As we have seen, gaols seem predisposed to ghosts evidentially due to the torment and pain felt by prisoners over the years. However, Toodyay has many supposedly haunted buildings, and one of those, conveniently located on the main street, is directly connected to what used to be a shoemakers shop.

No longer a shoemakers shop, it is believed to be haunted by the ghost of one Miss Constance Ellory who worked there in the 1900s. Legend has it that she would arrive at work in her horse and buggy, make a cup of tea, and with cup and saucer in hand, would visit every shop on the main street wishing them all good morning. Always dressed very conservatively in a long black skirt and white blouse with a lace collar, she never married and later died in the 1950s. Since then, however, it seems that she regularly makes her rounds of the main street, dressed in her regular fashion complete with a cup and saucer in hand.

Also on the main street is another place of interest, this time an antiques shop, originally built in 1897 and with a long and colourful past. Currently there are at least two resident ghosts in the building, one called Paddy and the other the ghost of a sixteen-year-old boy who died in an accident many years ago. Paddy is believed to have been of Irish Catholic descent and fought in the Crimean War before arriving in Australia and eventually ending up in Toodyay. His presence is usually marked by the overwhelming smell of burning tobacco as apparently he was a heavy smoker. Paddy also lost one of his legs sometime before he died and had it replaced with a wooden stump. The noise of a wooden leg scraping the floor is regularly heard in the shop. Interestingly, and maybe due to his Catholic upbringing, he seems to have a dislike for the colour orange and it is reputed that orange items on display in the shop are often found on the floor as if he has thrown them there in disgust.

But whereas Paddy can sometimes be a nuisance, the other resident ghost, the sixteen-year-old-boy, doesn't make his presence felt often but has been seen at the back of the shop near the rear door, and a number of photographs of this area have shown orbs, which some suggest are an indication of a ghostly entity.

Farther along the main street is the old Connors Mill. It is a three-story building constructed in the 1870s, and many people and visitors have reported hearing noises and voices in its empty rooms.

The Toodyay Tavern, built in 1862 and licensed in 1863, sits on Stirling Terrace and is another place in the town that boasts ghostly activity. Originally named the Newcastle Hotel, for a short period of time Toodyay was called Newcastle; it has an old well under its dining room. According to local legend, a businessman was having an affair with a local nun and promised that he would take her away. Unfortunately for the nun, he was already married and had no intention of fulfilling any of his promises. When she confronted him, he panicked and killed her, throwing her body in the well. Now her ghost is said to haunt the building, especially rooms 8 and 10 where her forlorn spirit has been seen.

The historical Toodyay Cemetery on the outskirts of the town is also reputed to be haunted by a number of ghosts, and yet, for all this, perhaps the most supernaturally active building in Toodyay is the Freemasons Hotel, the oldest public house in the town and built in 1861.

The building itself is a two-story red brick structure with a corrugated iron roof and a decorative cream-covered federation-style parapet with a verandah on the first-floor level, complete with timber posts and balustrades. The ground level also has an additional set back verandah and a single-story brick extension.

In 1977, it was given a permanent listing on the Register of the National Estate.

As the visitor enters the front door, they will see the original staircase where Toodyay residents have seen up to seventeen ghosts congregating on the stair's landing, all dressed in what has been described as evening wear as if they were going to a ball or something similar. Of these, one of the ghosts appears to be a lady holding a bunch of lavender and rosemary, the aroma of which can be smelt on and around the staircase. Upstairs, outside one of the hotel rooms, visitors often report a strong smell of burning feathers. Apparently, in the past, a man burnt to death when he caused a fire while smoking in bed.

This sighting makes one recall the sighting by Professor Brownrigg at the National Film and Sound Archive in Canberra and leads to one questioning whether or not this is a ghost sighting or a time-slip. Whatever the case, there is no doubt that something strange is going on in the little town of Toodyay.

Oddly enough, the town also has reports of animal ghosts, such as the ghost of a cat that is seen outside the Fruit and Vegetable shop on the main street. But as surprising as this may seem, it is not that unusual, as in Kalgoorlie a ghost cat has been reported. During the renovation of an historic house, the curator felt that he was being bitten on the ankles by something like a cat or a small dog, but bizarrely he could see nothing there. Later, as the work progressed, the body of a cat was found under the building, and it was suggested that it may have been there since the 1890s. Once the body of the long-deceased cat was removed, the strange phenomenon stopped.

But ghostly cats aside, where else in this enormous tract of land can we find reports of ghosts and hauntings?

Oakabella Homestead, some 450 kilometres north of Perth, exudes a certain colonial historical charm. Built in 1860, the site includes the homestead itself plus numerous outbuildings, including a cookhouse, barn, shearing shed, stables, and blacksmith's workshop. The museum on the property has an impressive display of relics found on site, including a mid-1800s bottle collection, Indigenous artifacts and historic farm utensils. It has also been called the most haunted house in Western Australia.

Oakabella sits on 50,000 acres of grazing land and changed hands three times until being purchased by the Jackson family in 1910. The present owners, Alan Jackson and his partner Loretta Wright, have restored the heritage listed place with such dedication that, instead of renewing material, they kept the original furniture accessories of the early twentieth century, including kitchen utensils, cutlery, and crockery. For all purposes, it appears to have been frozen in time.

And while the current owners do not live in the old homestead, preferring a newer house on a hill that overlooks the old building, there was a time when they did. And this coincided with a number of supernatural events, which considering the history of the place, is not entirely unexpected.

In 1879, one of the property's owners perished while fighting a fire, and, in 1918, a seven-year-boy by the name of William died from influenza. In addition, another child died in 1885 by falling out of a window and breaking his neck, and George Jackson, a family member, died in 1973 by accidentally shooting himself while cleaning his gun.

The room where the child fell from a window has a spooky and slightly disturbing ambience, and it is said that dogs refuse to enter the room. Visitors have also reported hearing children's voices, sometimes singing, but upon entering the room have found it completely empty.

In another bedroom, called George's Room, there exists a stain on the wall, said to be the blood of George Jackson after he shot himself. One of the current owners, Ms. Wright, once moved the furniture in this room only to find that there was a constant banging sound coming from the room until she moved it back. As she put it, George "did not like it."

As well, electrical equipment is known to fail when in the house, indeed, Wright has stated that: "Every vacuum cleaner that entered Oakabella left days later, broken. And the kettle and radio would turn on and off constantly." As well, during the refurbishment, she discovered cat bones concealed in the door frames and later learnt that the first settlers in the area did this to ward off evil spirits. It would seem that Oakbella has been haunted for longer than people had expected.

Other strange things have happened in the building, including doors that open and close by themselves, the feeling of a presence, strange lights, smells, and temperature drops. Indeed, on one occasion, a mother brought along her three-year-old daughter who, when she entered the room, started talking to apparently thin air saying: "Do you like my dress?"

Other visitors have also been touched by the spirits as well, including a man who called Wright to tell her that, after visiting the homestead, he'd been having nightmares about his legs being on fire before completely coming off. Interestingly, a man by the name of Elliot suffered a serious fishing accident in 1901, where his legs caught fire and were so badly burnt that they later had to be amputated.

Rumours of murder and suicide also plague the place, and, if historical documents are to be believed, it was also a sacred site to the local Aboriginals, and some consider the place to be a spiritual portal, a place that is built on native sacred ground and magnet of spiritual energy. Visitors are warned not to take any souvenirs away from the homestead or the surrounding land—not even rocks or pebbles as those that do are said to be at the mercy of a curse.

Whether the homestead deserves the title "Most Haunted in Western Australia" is debatable. However, what is not debatable is that it does have an interesting past and one that would suggest that ghostly comings and goings are not out of the question. This is much the same for our next location: the lonely and isolated Camp Quaranyup, a former commonwealth quarantine station in Albany, a port city in the Great Southern region of Western Australia,

418 kilometres south-east of Perth and the oldest permanently settled town in Western Australia, predating Perth and Fremantle by over two years.

During the 1890s, it was the main gateway to the Eastern Goldfields and for many years was the colony's only deep water port, playing an important part of the shipping services between Britain and its Australian colonies. The opening of the Fremantle Inner Harbour in 1897 saw its importance as a port decline, and local industries turned to agriculture, timber, and whaling. As well, Albany played an important role in the ANZAC legend, as it was the last port of call for troopships departing Australia in the First World War. Today the town is a major tourist destination and is well known for its natural beauty and heritage.

The Commonwealth Quarantine Station in Albany was established in 1875 and, as immigration increased, more buildings were added, in particular between 1898 and 1904. With wars in Europe and South Africa and a subsequent huge displacement of people, plus the lure of vast agricultural lands and gold, the temptation of the west was all encompassing, and before long people from all over the world started pouring into Albany.

Of course, given the time, many immigrants brought deadly diseases with them thus starting epidemics. As ships were quarantined, the passengers were sent to the Quarantine Station.

By the late 1900s, immigration was beginning to decline and, with increased medical advances, the Quarantine Station became used less and less until the 1950s when it was closed. Although a number of community groups used it over the next thirty or so years, it soon fell into serious disrepair until leased by the Wheeler Family in 1956, who changed its name to Camp Quaranup. Eventually, the state government took over the lease and ran it primarily as a recreation camp. It is now back in private hands but still runs as a venue for conferences, weddings, and as a school camp and is now one of the few intact, working ex-quarantine stations in the world.

And it is reputed to be haunted by a number of ghosts. Indeed, apart from ghostly handprints that are said to appear on the ceilings of some of the buildings and footsteps, sightings of a young girl in an old-fashioned nightgown have been reported, and the ghost of a young man whose body was buried under the floorboards of a house in the camp can be seen walking around on certain nights. As well, paranormal groups have reportedly caught disembodied voices on tape, and the apparition of another child has been witnessed by several people.

Not surprisingly for an historic seaport, Albany has a number of ghosts with nautical connections. One of these is a former Albany lighthouse keeper by the name of John Reddin who died in 1940. There are many tales of the ghostly lighthouse keeper appearing to help sailors in difficulty, and he has been described as smoking a pipe and wearing a duffle coat.

Also not surprising is that the old Albany Gaol is also considered haunted.

Built in 1852, the gaol is a complex of men's cell blocks and some warders quarters and was last used as a police lockup in the Great Depression of the 1930s. Extensive restoration from 1989 to 1996 returned the gaol's condition to its original state, and today the cells, warders quarters, and the Great Hall contain historic displays of the times.

There is said to be a ghost in Albany's Old Gaol, although it is not clear who this ghost may be. However, some suggest that it is the ghost of a young woman falsely imprisoned for theft, as the gaol at one stage housed a separate women's prison. Another legend suggests that one particular cell once held a woman who had been sexually abused and died in childbirth, and it is she that now haunts the cell and corridors of the gaol. People who have heard noises in the cell say that they are the cries of a woman in great torment. According to tour guide Joy Bradley: "Some of the rooms do often have activity in them," and that "visitors and staff alike have seen or felt presences within the building from people to animals and tugs on arms and legs."

Patrick Taylor Cottage, also in Albany, is an eleven-room wattle and daub house and is the oldest surviving dwelling in Western Australia. Built circa 1832, the cottage consists of an entry, boxroom, parlour, nursery, bedroom, dining room, family room, sewing room, kitchen, laundry, and side veranda and is surrounded by a neat English cottage garden. It is believed to be haunted by Boer War army doctor Major Frederick Ingoldby, who rented the cottage and then died there in September 1942. As a result, his ghost is said to appear each September, materialising firstly in military uniform, complete with a wounded right arm cradled in a sling, then vanishing, to later reappear lying on the bed in which he died.

At the harbour side around Seamen's Walk is the ghost of an Irish woman by the name of Catherine Spense. Ten years previous, her husband, Cathal, was transported to Western Australia for ten years, and being illiterate, he was unable to write to her to let her know of his whereabouts. During these long ten years of separation, Catherine found work with a wealthy lawyer who, when he died, left her a small fortune in his will. Now wealthy and still yearning for her husband, Catherine arrived in Albany in 1877 and was told by a local priest that there was a man who might be her husband and who was living at Oyster Harbour.

As it transpired, the man was her husband, and he told the clergyman that he would cross the harbour at twilight in a small boat in two days time and that Catherine should meet him on the shore. At the appointed time, Catherine went down to the shore and, to her overwhelming joy, soon saw a small boat sailing towards her. As it got closer she recognised that her husband was piloting the boat. However, upon seeing his wife, Cathal became excited and stood up and waved to her, overbalancing the boat. It capsized and he fell into the waters, never to be seen again. Heartbroken, Catherine collapsed on the spot and died, presumably of a broken heart. As a result, it is said that her ghost still haunts the shoreline. However, there have been no reports of Cathal's ghost appearing at any stage.

But whereas Albany is a thriving coastal town full of historical attractions and tourist opportunities, what of less populated regional centres? Towns for instance, like Cue?

Situated about roughly 620 kilometres northeast of Perth is the near ghost town of Cue. Before the First World War, Cue was home to over 10,000 residents as gold was found in the region. Tragically, the town was also hit by typhoid, and, without proper medical help and sanitation, the town was a place of death and suffering. It was said at the time that at nights one could not tell the difference between dingoes howling in the surrounding bush and the feverish cries of sick and dying diggers. The disease killed the majority of prospectors, leaving the town virtually abandoned and seemingly frozen in time.

These days most of the abandoned buildings are open to the public, and people can explore the old crematorium, the abandoned mine, the Masonic hall, the old shops, and deserted houses. The ruins of the old hospital still stand, and people have reported seeing strange lights, shadowy figures, and odd, ethereal sounds, especially at night.

A local paranormal group investigating the site once noted that they: ". . . became aware of shadows moving around the ruins. By the light of the UV torch we could definitely identify the shape of human figures, but as soon as we used the LED torch, there was nothing there. These shadows kept lurking around while we were there."

But whereas one could expect a place as such to be haunted, other places are not so obvious.

The Mundaring Weir Hotel in Mundaring, roughly 34 kilometres east of Perth, was built in 1898, partly to service the workers on the Mundaring Weir and Kalgoorlie pipeline project. Nestled in the hills, the hotel gardens and federation design provide an attractive setting for weddings and corporate functions or just a cold beer on a hot, dusty day. It is also haunted by a couple of ghosts, one being the spirit of a worker who has seemingly decided to remain on at the hotel for the rest of his eternal life.

The resident ghost is known as Paddy and was supposedly killed while working on the pipeline project. A number of staff members and visitors have reported seeing his spirit lurking around the hotel, and it is reported that he has been known to smash beer glasses, hide tools, turn on electric appliances, and even lock and unlock doors and windows. He usually only appears when the pub is quiet, and witnesses report that he takes the form of an outline, usually seen through the glass doors to the bar.

Another less well-known ghost is also said to haunt this beautiful turn-of-the-century building, that of a lady that appears in the recently constructed units behind the main hotel building. Guests have reported having glasses spun around the table and seeing the figure of a woman simply staring out of the window. Although there seems to be no historical explanation for her presence, it is likely that she may have been a longtime resident at the hotel or in the building that preceded the new accommodation.

As with Sydney and Brisbane, many of Perth's hotels have ghost traditions. These include the 152-year-old Guildford Rose and Crown Hotel, the historic Fitzgerald Hotel in Northbridge, and the Leederville Hotel.

The Leederville Hotel, which has recently experienced a multimillion-dollar redevelopment, was built in the late 1800s and, up until recently, had been known as the "Seedy Leedy" due to its patronage and a less-than-good reputation. However, it was not just the clientele that was frightening as it is reputed to be haunted by a ghost by the name of Kanga.

Apparently, Kanga was the nickname of the man who managed the local betting shop for many decades, and he lived in the tower bedroom of the hotel. Local legend suggests that he died alone in the tower of natural causes. However, even though there is no story of violence and terror or untimely death, it seems Kanga does not want to give up his place of abode so easily.

Residents, visitors, and staff are said to regularly come in contact with the ghost of Kanga, generally in the kitchen area and sometimes along the hotel corridors. Usually his presence is reported as a feeling, although many claim to have seen a shadow or outline of some kind. Others report cool breezes as if someone has rushed past them, footsteps, and odd noises in the night, and on one occasion he is said to have caused the massive jarrah bar in the hotel to shake and rattle. His spirit is said to be particularly strong on the stairs leading up to the tower and in the tower room itself as this was his residence and the place of his death.

Not unusual for a hotel ghost, the alarm system in the hotel seems to be affected by his presence. Over a period of about eight months in 1986 the alarm would go off frequently throughout the night causing the manager to get up and search the hotel for intruders. In each instance no one could be found. As a result, electricians were called in, but none could find any fault in the alarm or the electrical system.

The manager, suspecting something strange, then decided to write a note to the ghostly visitor saying: "We know you like to walk around the hotel. We know you like to look and make sure everything is safe and secure, but please try not to set off the alarms."

The note was then left in the tower room along with a pen, and local legend suggests that the next morning the pen was found in exactly the same place but the note pad had disappeared. Even more remarkably, ever since then, the alarms have remained silent.

But not all ghosts hang around turn-of-the-century pubs as, in Broome, a coastal pearling and tourist town in the Kimberley region some 2,240 kilometres north of Perth, is the ghost of a pearler by the name of Abraham Davis.

Davis was a prominent Jewish entrepreneur in the Broome pearling industry around the turn of the century but was tragically drowned, along with all other passengers and crew in the wreck of the *Koombana* off Port Hedland in 1912. His grand house later became the residence of the first Anglican Bishop of the North West, a man by the name of Bishop Gerard Trower, who remained in the job until 1927. Trower, obviously a God-fearing man and not taken to flights of fancy, later related that one night he awoke to see a ghostly figure dressed in the garments of a rabbi standing in a pool of light. When he called to the figure, it promptly vanished. Noticeably, this same figure has been seen by others on numerous later occasions, usually late in the afternoon or early in the evening.

Writer Ion Idriess, in his book *Forty Fathoms Deep,* put forward the idea that Davis, at the time of his death, was carrying the allegedly priceless "Roseate Pearl," which was believed to be cursed and to bring bad luck to whoever possessed it.

Equally, on the foreshore at Broome is a beacon that is said to unaccountably dim from time to time. No cause of this mysterious dimming has ever been found despite the light being regularly checked and having been overhauled on many occasions. As well, no natural phenomenon appears to be the cause and locals suggest that the dimming is a result of the ghosts of drowned pearlers slinking around the beacon on certain nights of the year.

But not all lighthouses it seems are haunted. Indeed, the Wadjemup Lighthouse, also known as Rottnest Island Light Station, which sits on Rottnest Island some 18 kilometres west of Fremantle, appears to be ghost free. However, this cannot be said for the island itself as local folklore suggests that at least two ghosts exist upon this tranquil, low-lying sandy island.

The island has its own dark history that ranges from executions to murder and death from disease. Indeed, for much of its colonial life it served as the site for a penal settlement with all the hardships one would expect from such a place.

In August 1838, ten Aboriginal prisoners were brought to the island, and not long after that the colonial secretary announced that it would become a penal establishment for Aboriginal people. As a result, the crown resumed all land on the island and compensated the disgruntled settlers with land on the mainland. At its height the penal colony held a remarkable 3,700 Aboriginal men and boys from many parts of the state.

From the late 1830s until the relatively recent 1930s, it is believed that 369 Aboriginal prisoners died, and while most deaths were caused by disease, five prisoners were reported to be hanged. Poignantly, an Aboriginal cemetery is located within the Thomson Bay Settlement. While on the island the prisoners were put to work building a large number of buildings and other structures, including lighthouses, the seawall, and others, now all heritage listed.

Most of the infrastructure development took place in Thomson Bay and of particular significance is the Quod that was the prison accommodation for the Aboriginal men. The Quod is now part of the modern-day Rottnest Lodge.

Rottnest Lodge is the premier accommodation on Rottnest Island and, if you believe the advertising, offers visitors quality hotel-style apartments and suites with private facilities. It also boasts at least two ghosts, one being a woman by the name of Ethel and the other an unknown woman who committed suicide after being spurned by a lover.

Ethel appears to be a benevolent ghost and simply appears now and then to guests and staff in some of the guest rooms, while the other unknown figure makes itself known by the crying of a baby and a frightening presence in the part of the building where her body was found.

It is believed that the second ghost is that of a women who was a housemaid and worked there almost half a century ago. One day she discovered she was pregnant and returned to the mainland to tell her boyfriend, who refused to acknowledge responsibility, and, in despair, the woman returned to the Rottnest Lodge where she committed suicide. Indeed, even Lonely Planet gives this helpful tip when visiting the place: "There are ghosts in this comfortable complex, which is based around the former Quod and boys' reformatory school. If that worries you, ask for a room in the new section, looking onto a salt lake."

Whether or not the place is haunted by the ghosts of the incarcerated Aboriginal men and boys is unknown, but given the appalling and horrendous treatment they endured, one would not be surprised if it was. Indeed, as Wadjuk elder Noel Nannup has stated: "Aboriginal people don't come here because it's a sad place for us." And one could add, tragic.

Farther afield, some 130 kilometres north of Perth, is the small town of New Norcia. Located on the banks of the Moore River, it is the only monastic town in Australia, and, according to many, has a number of ghosts. As with most country towns, these ghosts, including a pesky poltergeist, seem to congregate around the local pub, although it is said that the figure of a nun dressed in blue can sometimes be seen fluttering around the clock tower of the monastery just as the bell tolls midnight.

Of course, Western Australia is now a state full of ghost towns, a result of long gone gold rushes and failed agricultural ventures. It is a place where fortunes have been made and lost in remote, inhospitable locations. It is natural that there are numerous ghost towns, places where fortune seekers rapidly arrived when gold was discovered and just as quickly departed once the gold ran out, leaving behind haunting remains of their lives on the harsh landscape in the form of mullock heaps, rusting machinery, broken shards of pottery, and at others, magnificent crumbling stone buildings, ramshackle hotels, and long forgotten graveyards. And who is to say that these places are not haunted?

But far from the crumbling remains of colonial buildings in the outback is our next story, and this one, although strange, is not concentrated on an abandoned gaol or a suburban pub or even an asylum built by convict hands.

Instead, it is a ship, and if the legend is to be believed, a haunted ship that holds a curse against all who go near her or sailed on her.

The *Alkimos* was a Greek-owned merchant ship that was wrecked on the coast north of Perth in 1963. Like all wrecks, it is now a popular diving place. Over time it has earned the reputation as a haunted, cursed ship, both during its working life and since it was wrecked, due to numerous, unusual events such as inexplicable accidents, recurring bad luck, and the appearance of ghostly apparitions.

Originally named the *George M. Shriver* in Baltimore in 1934, the *Alkimos* was constructed in ten days during World War II as one of the 2,751 Congress-approved American Liberty ships. Later, she was sold to Norwegian hands and became the *Viggo Hansteen* before finally being sold to a Greek shipping line when she was named the *Alkimos*.

During 1944, and then-named the *Viggo Hansteen*, the *Alkimos* was steaming toward a Russian port when two ships ahead of her were bombarded by German U-boats. Although the *Viggo Hansteen* escaped any damage from the attack, she inexplicably became stranded on an unmarked reef until she was able to break away six hours later, again lucky not to be attacked and sunk.

After nearly twenty years on the high seas, the *Alkimos*, on a journey from Jakarta to Bunbury, ran aground at Beagle Rocks, south of Geraldton in Western Australia. With her propeller badly damaged, authorities decided to tow her back to Fremantle for immediate repairs and then be towed to Hong Kong for permanent work. Remarkably, the ship managed to refloat itself and, with a seriously damaged propeller, steamed under its own power to reach Fremantle.

In 1963, while awaiting repairs at Fremantle, the *Alkimos* mysteriously caught fire resulting in many thousands of dollars of repairs. In 1964, after being repaired, the ship was then prepared for the long trip to Hong Kong although, while being towed by a seafaring tug, the tow line broke and the *Alkimos* drifted away and once again became stuck on a reef. An attempt to pull the ship from the reef was short lived when the boat responsible, the *Pacific Star,* was placed under arrest for monies owed to a company in Manila and was ordered to return to Fremantle. Although the *Alkimos* was anchored, it soon broke away from the reef and became beached, where it was abandoned.

The *Pacific Star* was then set ablaze whilst in port awaiting legal proceedings. Over the years, the *Alkimos* had several salvage crews and caretakers living on board as any ship abandoned can be legally towed away by anyone. And yet, no matter how many tried, all ventures to salvage her failed, and today she exists as a rusted landmark sitting 50 kilometres north of Perth, being pounded by the relentless Indian Ocean.

Why it is considered haunted is anyone's guess; however, a number of strange things that have happened on the ship over its lifetime could certainly be considered. Indeed, in 1944, the ship witnessed a murder-suicide.

Maude Steane was a Canadian radio operator on what was then the *Viggo Hansteen,* and, although women were not allowed to serve in combat zones in the army or navy, they could do so on Norwegian merchant ships. As a result, she signed up as the radio operator on the *Viggo Hansteen.*

Steane served on the ship for roughly six months as it was used to transport gliders to Naples. One day, while the ship was in dock unloading the gliders, Steane was shot dead by another member of the crew who then committed suicide. Because the incident was so horrific, the military stated that Steane had been killed by enemy fire and she was later buried in Italy.

Since then the ship has been said to be cursed by the spirit of the dead Canadian radio operator and many blame her ghost for its running around, snapping of tow ropes, and inexplicable fires. However, the ship has had a long and strange history, including reports that, during its construction, a number of ship welders were inadvertently sealed within its hull. If this is so, then could it account for some of the weird occurrences?

Apart from the murder-suicide of Steane, an apparition known as Harry has been sighted on the ship by various people. He is said to be dressed in rubber boots and an oilskin, a dark grey seaman's coat specially designed to keep out the spray of the ocean.

As well, during salvage operations, numerous tools were reported to be moved by unseen hands. Workers would report the tools missing only to find that they reappeared the next time they were on the ship, and, although it cannot be completely confirmed, it is believed that the *Alkimos* was bought and sold at least eight times whilst it was stranded, and each person who purchased the ship suffered unexplainable bad luck from bankruptcy to life-threatening illnesses. Remarkably, this seemed to disappear when the person later sold the vessel. In all, it is believed that up to twelve unsuccessful attempts were made to salvage the ship between 1963 and 1970, but all failed due to a series of bizarre and completely unexpected circumstances.

At night salvage crews on the ship would not leave their cabins alone as ghostly footsteps would follow them. Footsteps were also heard on ladders when all salvage crews were accounted for, and cooking smells and noises would emanate from the galley even though, upon investigation, it was empty.

Another to feel the wrath of the supposed cursed ship was Wayne Morgan, an American exchange student employed as a caretaker to deter looters. In the end, he locked himself in a cabin and refused to come out after seeing a misty figure that walked around the ship both day and night.

At one stage, a married couple took over as the ship's caretaker and they too struck misfortune when the woman, pregnant at the time, fell and seriously injured herself. Later, after being rushed to hospital, the baby was delivered stillborn. Then in 1969, Herbert Voight, a champion long-distance swimmer, disappeared while trying to swim from Cottesloe to Rottnest Island. Bizarrely his skull reportedly turned up washed into the wreck of the *Alkimos*.

Cray fishermen who regularly worked the area often reported seeing a man in an oilskin coat aboard the ship, and although some believed he was a local hermit taking refuge for free aboard the ship, subsequent searches have never been able to find anyone living aboard the ship. Whether or not this is Harry the ghost is unknown.

Ted Snider, a US Navy submariner who was called in to make preliminary assessments of the wreck, was later killed in an aircraft crash after visiting the ship. He was a passenger in an Auster aircraft, which was northbound for Onslow when it crashed, killing all occupants. Jack Sue, author of the book *Ghost of the* Alkimos, suffered from a strange respiratory disease and was not expected to live.

Indeed, Tim the Yowie Man, while examining the wreck, suffered from a badly gashed hand, inexplicable blackouts and car troubles, caught pneumonia, and was knocked out after being head-butted by a camel, all while investigating the wreck.

Worried about his run of bad luck, including the death of his grandmother, Tim explained that he flew all the way back to Perth from Canberra and made his way to the wreck where he yelled: "I believe in your curse. I'm sorry for trying to question your existence. I promise not to mess with you again; please free me of it."

Coincidence or not, Tim rapidly regained health and his luck took a change for the better. Add to this numerous curious coincidences of near drownings, boat engines failing, and visitors slipping and hurting themselves in and around the *Alkimos* wreck and one must wonder if the rusting hulk is indeed cursed.

Having said that, the Internet is full of strange half-believable stories as such and whether the former are products of some vague curse or haunting is debatable. What is not debatable, however, is that a rusting wreck in a high surf area is a dangerous place, and to venture near the wreck is undoubtedly inviting some sort of disaster. And, as in the case of many curses, for instance Tutankhamun, there appears to be a lot of dubious links to what appear to be unrelated events that are then attributed to the curse of the ship.

As of the present, the *Alkimos* is almost fully disintegrated above the water line to the point where it is rarely visible from the beach. It seems that the ship and the seas it once sailed will take their secrets to the grave, and as Jack Sue pointed out in an interview to the *Sun Herald* in 1998: "It's probably just coincidence, but you can never tell with the *Alkimos*. I can't help thinking of the number of people who've driven down that beach in four-wheel drives to photograph the wreck and had their cars break down, or their cameras fail, or their watches stop. That ship is bad luck."

But if there are some doubts as to the authenticity of the *Alkimos* and its ghost stories, then what can we make of our next port of call, South Australia, and in particular, Adelaide's very first gaol.

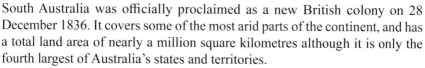

CHAPTER SIX

South Australia

A Ghostly Clairvoyant, Haunted Pubs, and a Haunted Winery

South Australia was officially proclaimed as a new British colony on 28 December 1836. It covers some of the most arid parts of the continent, and has a total land area of nearly a million square kilometres although it is only the fourth largest of Australia's states and territories.

Adelaide, the capital of South Australia, was established in 1836 as a planned colony of free immigrants, promising civil liberties and freedom from religious persecution and, as a result, it was believed that in a colony of free settlers there would be little crime. As a result there was no provision made for a gaol in Adelaide's original plan. However, by mid-1837, escaped convicts from New South Wales were said to be headed for the new state, and tenders for a temporary gaol were sought.

In March 1838, following a burglary, a murder, and two attempted murders in Adelaide, the governor at the time, Rear Admiral Sir John Hindmarsh, a career naval officer, created the South Australian Police Force. Soon after, the first sheriff, a Mr. Samuel Smart, was wounded during a robbery, and on 2 May 1838 one of the offenders, Michael Magee, became the first person to be hanged in South Australia. By 1840, George Strickland Kingston was commissioned to design Adelaide's new gaol, and construction commenced in 1841.

Located in Thebarton, the Adelaide Gaol operated from 1841 until 1988, and although it is now a museum and tourist attraction, it housed approximately 300,000 prisoners during its 147 years of operation. At the time of its closure it was the longest continuously operating prison in Australia, and a total of forty-five people, including one woman, were hanged inside its walls.

Not surprisingly, many people, including staff and visitors, have reported paranormal activity in many places of the gaol including full body apparitions, disembodied voices, cold spots, and EVPs. Witnesses have reported being touched, pushed, scratched, seeing ghostly apparitions of guards, and numerous other paranormal events.

Alison Osborn, who runs Haunted Horizons Ghost Tours, believes without doubt that the old gaol is haunted. Located in the northwest corner of the Adelaide Parklands, it has plain, small cells and exudes an air of menace, possibly a hangover from the desperate men who once inhabited these dank cells. Some of the cells still have graffiti on the walls, a reminder that the men incarcerated in this place dreamt of a life outside the confines of the huge stone walls. Add barbed wire and a hanging tower plus burial sites for the condemned and you have all the ingredients for a haunted site.

Osburn herself claims to have seen evidence of unexplainable happenings, such as video footage of a heavy steel door opening and closing on its own, lights flashing inside electricity free cells, and noises of pool balls being played in the dead of night. "We've just had so much happen that we couldn't rationalise or explain, which is why, eight years after first starting investigations, we're still there."

And yet, for all this, Osburn is still puzzled at two specific incidents that happened in the gaol while she was conducting her ghost tours. She recalls that she "was taking a tour for two documentary film-makers. We were in the new building, but it was still built in the 1870s, and there is an old metal staircase there where I stand and tell the stories. I'd only just started the story about the apparition of a guard that is seen in here, and as I was talking about that, footsteps started on the top of the gantry and we could literally hear the click of the heel and squeak of the leather boots, and it came right to the top of the stairs."

Osburn recalls being both thrilled and apprehensive at the time. "Then it came down the stairs. The two filmmakers just stepped aside to let it through, because it felt like an authoritative figure was coming through, and they needed to step aside. If you've ever rubbed a balloon against your arm and it's made all your hairs stand up on end, and it tingles, that was what it felt like when it went by; it was just like a static breeze going by."

In another bizarre encounter, Osborn suggests that a ghost possibly walked straight through her. "It was a hot night and we'd finished up doing an investigation and it was about 4 a.m. I was standing against one of the walls. We weren't even talking about ghosts; we weren't even thinking paranormal. Then, you know that little shudder you get when someone's walked over your grave? It's something we all get; it's a normal human body thing—but if you multiply that by about fifteen times, that's what happened to me. It was so violent my head just went whack backwards against the wall. And then every bone literally just turned to ice. I just froze and it was like: Yuck. I felt unclean and cold. I had to sit on the steps and it took me twenty minutes to thaw out. I don't know what it was; was it something to do with my brain? I hadn't had it before and I haven't had it since, so I'm not prone to that. But I haven't stood next to that door since either."

Others have reported other strange events. Indeed, a former guard recalled that: "In the New Building some of us were looking up the stairs for one reason or another, especially with the stories of the old guard, so we spent most of our time looking up there. I remember seeing this head up there because that was a canteen for the years I was here. The head looked out very quickly and went back in. I saw it quickly out of the corner of my eye, but I wasn't the only one, as there were three or four others that saw it exactly the same time, which I found interesting. I would have said male."

In 2002, a paranormal investigations group reported that they had witnessed "a person who was very solid and described as wearing dark clothing with a beanie hat." One of the group stated that she had watched him, hands in pockets shuffling along a wall and then turn into the long tunnel that leads through to the New Building. Not surprisingly, her first thoughts were that it was a real flesh-and-blood person and not a ghost, and knowing that a far end gate had not been unlocked and that the person was trapped, the group ran over to the entrance to the New Building fully expecting to find an intruder. However, upon entering the area, they found it empty. The person had vanished into thin air.

Equally as strange, the group managed to photograph what appeared to be a single wet footprint on the cement, although there were no other footprints leading to it, nor from it. Indeed, they reported that the footprint was so fresh that there were drip marks after the toe as if freshly lifted out of a puddle.

It is quite common for people working on their own in the office in the Governors Quarters to hear footsteps upstairs, and the sound is thought to come from the very first governor, William Baker Ashton, who lived and died in the gaol. A former manager of the gaol, Deanne Hanchant-Nichols, recalled that she was working alone when she heard heavy footsteps walking around on the second floor above her. Having heard them before, she assumed that they were from an artist who had been renting a room above, until she realised that the artist was not in residence at the time.

Growing curious she was suddenly shocked as her two dogs, which were downstairs with her, suddenly started barking. Thinking that someone had broken in, she decided to take the dogs and confront the intruder. Letting the dogs go first, she pushed the door open and the dogs ran into the room where, curiously, they started wagging their tails and rolling over as if playing with someone. The room, however, was totally empty, and Hanchant-Nichols beat a hasty retreat.

Interestingly, in this case, is the behaviour of the dogs given the fact the animals in general, especially domestic animals, usually become aggressive or defensive when confronted with such things as ghosts. As to why these dogs acted completely different, and unexpectedly, is unknown.

Also of interest, and very unlike the Boggo Gaol group, the South Australian government website for the gaol actively promotes its haunted credentials noting that it is said to be "regularly visited by some of the inmates and prison officers who once wandered its halls. Innocent people who were hanged have been heard and seen seeking exoneration to this day. More frightening and ominous are the reported sightings of the Gaol's hangman."

It is generally believed that, apart from a number of unknown entities who haunt the building, the gaol is haunted by three prominent figures: Frederick

Carr, who was hanged at the Adelaide Gaol on 12 November 1927 for the murder of his wife; Ben Ellis; the Adelaide Gaol hangman from the mid-1860s to the mid 1870s; and Governor William Baker Ashton, who we have already discussed.

Frederick Carr, who protested his innocence up until his final moments, is said to be a happy spirit and appears regularly near the stairs leading to the upstairs cells of the New Building. Witnesses have described him as being neatly dressed in dark clothes. Strangely, previous to November 2000, it was said that he appeared without a face. These days, however, people have suggested that he is smiling. Why this is so is yet another mystery of the gaol.

Having said that, with these types of sightings it is often bizarrely reported that the ghosts in question have very little facial features. In fact, sometimes it is reported that the ghost actually has no face whatsoever. Why this is so I have no idea and I cannot even begin to put forward any explanation, except to suggest that there exists many different types of ghosts and that faceless ghosts could possibly be completely different from those with visible facial features.

An example of this is Anne Boleyn who, apart from being seen without a head, is often described as not having a face. In 1882, a Captain of the Guard saw a light burning in the locked Chapel Royal at the Tower of London and, wondering how this could be, given the place was locked and silent, went to investigate. When he opened the door he witnessed a figure who he thought was Anne leading a slow, stately procession of knights and ladies in plush medieval clothing. Strangely, in this case, although Anne had a head, the man reported that she appeared to not have a face or that it was averted in some way. The complete procession then disappeared leaving a slightly shaken and confused witness.

Of interest here is the report that, although the figure had a head, it appeared to not have a face, or if it did, its features were somewhat indistinguishable, which matches with numerous other ghost reports from all over the world where ghosts are reported as being, almost as if flesh and blood but without facial features. Of course, if a ghost is lacking facial features, then one must ask, how is it that a person can identify who the ghost is? Is it the case that, knowing that the ghost of Anne Boleyn is said to haunt these corridors, a witness seeing something simply assumes that it is her ghost? And if so, then who is to say that this ghost is not Anne but someone else? After all, it is not as if Anne was the only person ever horribly killed, tortured, imprisoned or executed in the tower.

Having said this, people are adamant that the ghost they see on the top of the stairs in Adelaide Gaol is Frederick Carr, but one must ask, how can they be sure of this?

Governor William Baker Ashton is another of the ghosts who regularly seem to appear in the gaol. The first governor of the Adelaide Gaol, he was said to be a reasonably fair man although, at one stage of his life, he was embroiled in a scandal that undoubtedly led to his demise.

Ashton was a huge man, believed to weigh in excess of 130 kilograms, and when he died in 1854, his body could not be carried down the steps from his apartment. Instead, he had to be lowered out of a window to the waiting undertakers. Three months after his death he was cleared of any wrongdoings, although it seems that this did little to pacify his angry spirit, who is said to tread heavily in the upstairs apartment, sometimes moving the furniture about.

Ben Ellis was the Adelaide Gaol hangman for a decade and lived at the gaol in a small apartment below what became the female dormitory. Apparently taking great pride in his work, each of his executions were expertly carried out, although one, that of Charles Streitman in 1877, did go awry when the victim got caught on a platform and took much longer to die than usual.

Ellis was said to be the hangman who, in December 1873, executed Elizabeth Woolcock, the first and last woman hanged in South Australia, and it is believed that his restless spirit now haunts the gaol seeking forgiveness for what he later considered a heinous deed.

But gaols, although seemingly hotbeds of paranormal behaviour, are not the only places where we can seek out ghosts and associated hauntings. Indeed, sometimes lonely highways can be equally as frightening and perplexing as any old building. And such is the case with the Anzac Highway where a phantom hitchhiker, much like that seen at Lake George in New South Wales and Kalamunda in Western Australia, can be seen.

And as in most phantom hitchhiker legends, the story is roughly the same but with slight regional differences leading us to believe that either phantom hitchhikers are very real and very common, or they are simply a retelling of an urban myth. Personally, I am of the latter opinion; however, this doesn't take away from the tales, and neither does it disprove that the ghost exists.

In the case of the Anzac Highway, travellers see a young distraught woman standing by the side of the road. When they stop to lend a hand they notice that she appears to have been in an accident and so put her into the back seat of the car and decide to drive her to the nearest hospital. As they drive along, one of them asks where she is from and is shocked to find that she is no longer in the car. She has completely vanished as if into thin air.

For the people who have reported this happening, the experience of seeing her has been nothing short of terrifying. However, the phantom hitchhiker story is known all over the world from Australia to England to South Africa. Indeed, a popular South African story reads like this; on Good Friday, 1978, Corporal Dawie van Jaarsveld was riding his motorcycle on the N9 heading toward Uniondale at 9:35 p.m. when he encountered a girl on the side of the road. Van Jaarsveld stopped and offered her a lift, and she climbed on the back of his bike, taking the offered spare helmet and earphone. Van Jaarsveld later stated that: "After a few, say a kilometre or two, the bike had a twitch. I thought she fell off. A lot of things went through my mind. I turned around; I wanted to see if I still had somebody with me. There was nobody. I turned around; I went back with the motorcycle, [and I] looked to see if there was anybody lying in the road." While searching the road for the missing girl he noticed that the spare helmet was back on the bike as was the earphone, which appeared to have not been used.

Ghost or urban legend we cannot say. However, the Anzac Highway hitchhiker is only one of the reported thousands of ghosts across South Australia who are said to wander the streets, churches, pubs, houses, old jails, and other historic sites, including the Adelaide Arcade.

Built in 1885, the Adelaide Arcade was Australia's first retail centre to have electric lighting. However, as fantastic as this was, in 1887, caretaker Francis Cluney, while investigating a flickering light, slipped and fell into the arcade's generator where he was crushed by the fly wheel. His mangled body was found shortly after, and his ghost is now said to haunt the upper levels of the arcade.

According to the centre's management, Cluney's ghost is most active when works are taking place, and despite his gory death, traders and shopkeepers who report his presence regard him as friendly and are not put off by his ghostly presence. However, on one occasion an electrical contractor working in the ceiling heard some footsteps behind him and then felt a bitter chill before leaving the place and telling management that they didn't have enough money to make him do the job.

And, according to the arcade's resident psychic, Joan Lesley, he's not alone as, in 2004, she stated that she saw Francis "every day" and even suggested that there was another ghost called Ken, who was his friend.

Others suggest that in all there are five ghosts in the arcade, including Bridget Byron and her three-year-old son, Sydney.

In 1902, Bridget Byron, known as Madame Kennedy, and her son, Sydney Kennedy Byron, lived in the arcade as the upper level was once apartments for the shopkeepers on the ground floor before being converted into shops in the late twentieth century. Madame Kennedy and her husband, Professor Kennedy, were advertised as "intuitive palmists, phrenologists, and clairvoyants," although, when Sydney was a year old, his parents split up and his father took Sydney with him to Tasmania. Madame Kennedy used a detective to trace her son and recovered him before Christmas 1901 and subsequently took him home to Adelaide. Apparently, during Sydney's absence, Madame Kennedy admitted that she used drugs and alcohol to help her sleep.

On 11 January 1902, Madame Kennedy's cleaner arrived at the arcade in the morning to do the cleaning and noticed a strong small of gas coming from her rooms. Entering she found Madame Kennedy and Sydney lying on the floor of the dining room. Although Madame Kennedy was able to be roused, both Sydney and a pet bird were dead. A doctor later confirmed that Sydney had died of coal gas poisoning.

Madame Kennedy was unable to be interviewed at the time, and the attending doctor suggested that he could smell alcohol on her breath, and that he believed she had also taken chlorodyne, a mix of laudanum, chloroform, and cannabis. He also noted that she had advised that Sydney often turned on the gas and was punished for doing so. At the time, the doctor believed her to be mentally unstable and not responsible for her actions. However, in time, it was revealed that her husband, Professor Kennedy, had, in the meantime had an affair with an abortionist. As a result, Madame Kennedy was sent to trial for the murder of her son.

The case proved to be immensely popular involving as it did an attempted murder-suicide and a cheating husband with an abortionist for a mistress. In the end the case was not heard by a jury and did not go to trial as it could not be proven that Mrs. Kennedy turned on the gas, so the case was dismissed.

Sadly, eight months later, in August 1902, the body of a woman was found in the West Park Lands near the railway line. The body was later identified as Bridget Lauretta Byron, aka Madame Kennedy, and the cause of death found to be poisoning by either caustic potash or prussic acid, as bottles of both substances were found in her belongings.

Today her forlorn ghost is still said to wander the quiet corridors of the arcade as if searching for something, possibly her long-dead son.

The arcade is also said to be haunted by Florence Horton, who was shot dead by her estranged husband, Thomas Horton, at the Rundle Mall end of the arcade in February 1904. On the night Florence Horton died, she was with two friends, Frances Isabel Smith and Nellie Linnett, and they had been walking up and down Rundle Street for about an hour. Tom Horton approached them and tried to coax Florence away from her friends, but she refused. He then attempted to get her to follow him up a side street, but again she refused. Suddenly enraged, Horton shot Florence in the back three times before running away. The mortally wounded girl was dragged into a tobacconist's shop in the arcade where she died.

Thomas Horton was found guilty of murder and was sentenced to execution at Adelaide Gaol, and on 12 May 1904, he was hanged. Florence had earlier been buried at the West Terrace Cemetery on 1 March 1904, and her ghost is said to frequent the alley where she was fatally shot.

Apart from this, people have also reported a dark, shadowy figure walking by, footsteps pacing on the second floor, a child's voice and laughter, doors being slammed after hours when the building has been locked up, cleaners mop and buckets moving on their own, people being pushed in the back by an unseen entity, alarms playing up, and most frightening, the ghost of a little boy who simply stands in front of witnesses and stares at them before vanishing. Whether or not this is young Sydney Byron is unknown, but whatever the case, it appears that the arcade has cemented its reputation as a haunted building for many years to come.

Elsewhere in Adelaide is the heritage listed Carclew Youth Arts Centre, which was built in 1901 and is said to be haunted by a ghostly grey lady or a lady in a purple gown who was believed to have fallen or been thrown to her death from the tower in the early 1900s. In one tale, Sir Bonython, a wealthy South Australian socialite, businessman, and philanthropist apparently had a mistress and a wife and, after his wife found out that he was having an affair, he lost his temper and threw her out of the spire. Gruesomely, it is said that when he went downstairs to check on her, he found that she was still alive and so carried her back up the spire and threw her out once again, this time ensuring that she was dead. Visitors also report smelling her perfume throughout the arts complex as well as hearing disembodied voices, footsteps, and reporting objects that seem to move of their own accord.

At Martindale Hall in the Clare Valley, built in 1879 and used for the interior shots of the classic Peter Weir movie *Picnic at Hanging Rock*, the ghost of a man has been seen sitting on the back stairs while a guest reportedly once woke up and found a ghostly child in bed with her. One owner also got the shock of his life when he awoke to find a child standing at the end of his bed before disappearing.

South Australian pubs are also extremely active when it comes to ghosts and supernatural happenings. The Old Spot Hotel at Gawler, built in the 1830s and rumoured to have once been used as a morgue, is just one of these and has seen its fair share of death. In 1868, Charles Donaldson a thirty-five-year-old local passed away in the hotel, while in 1889, a serious accident occurred directly in front of the hotel when an eight-year-old boy was crushed to death by the wheels of a cart. It is also the site of an incredible photo taken by Scott Pearson in 1993 that appears to show a ghost, a white, shadowy figure that police forensics and photographic experts have all described as unexplainable.

The Exeter, another typical Adelaide pub, is reputed to be haunted by the ghost of a former manager by the name of Gwendolene Joseph, who was stabbed in the pub's kitchen by an upset lover. Her ghost is said to be felt and sometimes seen at the scene of the murder and in her old room. On some occasions her steps can be heard pacing along the old corridor upstairs.

Meanwhile, the Port Dock Hotel, which opened in 1855 and has long been rumoured to have tunnels under the hotel out to the harbour where drunks would be shanghaied into becoming crew members, is said to be haunted by a "blue lady," who is often seen in the basement. She is believed to be the spirit of a prostitute who worked in the hotel in the late 1800s. Witnesses have reported her descending the stairs of the brewery into the dark and dank basement where it is believed she plied her trade. The cellar is also said to be haunted by the ghost of a lost sailor, and, according to owner John Cowled, "strange things have happened, lights going out, taps getting turned on, the old moaning and groaning sound" and, "We had one girl who had such an experience with the madame that she wouldn't come back."

Apart from that, the Union Hotel on Waymouth Street, which has been in service since 1855, the Ambassadors Hotel on King William Street, and the Colonist Tavern at Norwood, open since 1851, are only a handful of the pubs in the city that are rumoured to be haunted.

But it's not just city pubs that are haunted as the Overland Corner Hotel, commissioned in the 1850s and situated on the bend of the Murray River between Renmark and Barmera, is also believed to be haunted. Indeed, apart from the ghosts, the isolated old pub was the haunt of two of Australia's most infamous Bushrangers. The Ned Kelly Gang often drank in the pub as did Captain Moonlight and his gang. As for ghosts, some believe that the spirits of the Brand Brothers, the original owners and builders of the hotel, still wander around the building. Other spirits reputedly include a local aboriginal girl and, oddly enough, Queen Adelaide.

The pub's owner, Heather Wynand, who lives in the hotel, certainly believes the place is haunted and recalls how one night she was lying in bed when she heard the sound of music. As the bar was closed and the doors locked, she thought someone must have left the jukebox on. However, as she contemplated getting up, she came to the realisation that the sound wasn't that of modern music but that of old-time fiddle music and the sounds of men and merriment. Going into the pub she found, to her surprise, that it was dark, quiet, and empty.

But it is not just Wynand who has experienced something strange in the pub. Her partner, Andrew Mader, had a frightening experience one night when he decided to sleep in one of the bedrooms that had previously been used as a makeshift morgue as Wynand had a dose of the flu. As he slept he became aware that the bed he was in was shaking. As he lay there, the shaking became more and more violent, and Mader, terrified, leapt out of the bed only to find the room completely unoccupied except for himself.

A previous owner, Jim Kane, believes a ghostly experience saved the pub from burning down one night when he was woken by the sensation of his arm being pulled. Puzzled, he had a strong sense that he was being led somewhere and walked into the bar to find someone had emptied an ashtray into a bin where it had ignited some papers. Kane has no doubt that something otherworldly helped him save the hotel from burning down.

The hotel's gardener, Bill Medley, also believes in the ghosts of the place as, one night after closing time, he saw the figure of a bearded man in a white nightshirt leave one of the bedrooms and walk into the courtyard.

Ms. Wynand says that sometimes the ghosts are playful and move things around so that they aren't where she left them. "I could be doing my bookwork at a table, get up to do something, and then go back and find that my paperwork has been moved. It will turn up later in a place I know I didn't leave it."

Hanging above the bar is an old photo that locals believe shows one of the pub's ghosts. The photo itself shows the four Brand brothers who built the hotel and another disembodied face. Of course, being such an old photograph it could be a flaw in the original negative or even a trick of light. Having said this, it is reasonably compelling.

And from one haunted pub to another: this time the North Kapunda Hotel, in the town of Kapunda near the Barossa Valley and established as a town after a discovery of copper deposits in 1842. The hotel itself started life in 1849 as the North Kapunda Arms before becoming the Garland Ox in 1853 and then the North Kapunda Hotel in 1856. Later, it was known as the Sir Sidney Kidman Hotel until 2010 when it was renamed the North Kapunda Hotel once again.

Now a National Trust property, it is said to be haunted by a number of spirits, including ex-residents, publicans, prostitutes, and miners. Indeed, so haunted is it said to be that it appeared on the television program *Haunting: Australia* where one of the crew was allegedly possessed. In addition, Allen Tiller, a self-professed ghost-hunter experienced what he believes is the spirit of a young girl called Sarah. The hotel once served as a brothel, and it is thought that when a prostitute was murdered inside the hotel, her young daughter Sarah was taken in by the hotel's madam. Tiller recalls that he was "closing up the top of hotel after a tour and I saw a little girl standing in hallway. She ran down the hall to take her out of the hotel and she looked solid; she was laughing."

The North Kapunda Hotel **is not the only haunted place** in this small outback town. In 2002, a television documentary, *Kapunda, Most Haunted Town in Australia* hosted by Warwick Moss, was shown on national television leading to a rush of ghost hunters flooding the town, especially the ruins of St. John's Reformatory, which was used as an orphan girl's school from 1897 until 1909.

The television show retold the stories of ghostly apparitions and happenings at St. John's Reformatory, which from 1897 until 1909 was a boarding home for troubled girls. Originally opening in 1854, it started life as a Catholic school, and had something of a troubled beginning with three priests dying a few years apart from each other.

The program suggested that in 1909, eighteen-year-old Ruby Bland, who was pregnant at the time to a Father James Martin who ran the boarding school, died from a botched abortion with the implication being that Martin had forced her into the procedure that killed her. Following her death, it was said that she was hastily buried in an unmarked grave and, as a cover up, the place was shut down leaving Martin as the sole occupant of the building until he too died.

The documentary also suggests that these days her ghost haunts the cemetery, while Martin's spirit has been seen in the ruins of the school. To further add to the story, it was also said that fifteen students from Kapunda saw a marble slab move back from one of the graves at the cemetery before witnessing a semitransparent girl carrying a lantern moving through the grounds. As well, it was alleged that the students found a circular spot with strange markings in the soil where the ghostly girl allegedly disappeared. Others described feelings of being watched by unknown eyes.

Sadly, the place was demolished soon after, probably due to its derelict and dangerous state. However, demolished or not, the legend of Ruby Bland grew, which is a pity as most of the story has been proven to be false. For example, there were no girls from the school buried in the cemetery, and Ruby Bland never lived there. In fact, Ruby Bland was actually training to be a nurse at the local hospital and died after an operation to remove kidney stones went wrong. She was subsequently buried, coincidentally on the day that the boarding school, which had been scheduled for closure anyway, closed.

As for the priest alleged to have impregnated the girl, there is absolutely no evidence to suggest that he was an evil rapist, as the legend says. True, he did die at the site and was known to be harsh on the girls, but he was never suspected of the deeds suggested in the documentary. He later died of starvation due to senility.

Having said that, in 2002, a grave monument to Ruby Bland was found buried under a pile of rubble, and people still report strange things coming from the cemetery. Whether or not it is haunted is up for conjecture. But if Kapunda is not the most haunted town in South Australia, then what is?

Tailem Town Pioneer Village, next to the Princess Highway just north of Tailem Bend on the River Murray, was established in 1982 and is Australia's largest pioneer village. Portraying a period of time from the late 1800s, many of its buildings were transported in one piece from their original locations, while others were taken apart piece by piece and reconstructed in the town and, while most of the buildings are over 100 years old, the place is completely fake, including the cemetery which, although resplendent with ancient cracked tombstones, is free of any actual graves.

The buildings are all furnished with original artefacts as are the shops while the picture theatre has working projectors and is fully functional as a seventy-seat cinema. It is, at first glance, as if the visitor has stepped back in time, and according to some, it is the most haunted town in South Australia.

Visitors to this admittedly creepy-looking place have described seeing solid, shadowy figures darting between the buildings or in windows to having been touched or tapped on the shoulder by unseen entities. Many others report feelings of dread and doom in certain areas of the village while others feel as if they are being watched.

And of course, the town holds its own ghost tour that offers paying customers a thrilling walk around the old buildings. Still, one must ask, why would a tourist attraction be haunted? Indeed, it's not as if Tailem Town Pioneer Village is even a real village, even though it has been suggested that a number of people have died on the site.

The fact that many of these buildings are original and were once people's homes might hold a clue, remembering that most are over 100 years old with the earliest dating back to 1890. Is it possible that somehow the spirits are attached to the building in which they once existed and not so much to the place? A good example of this may be All Saints Church in Canberra.

All Saints Church is a quaint limestone building in the sleepy suburbs of the gentrified inner north of Canberra. Built in the 1860s, it was originally the Rookwood Cemetery funeral train station in Sydney up until the 1920s when it fell into a state of disrepair. In 1957, it was bought by the Parish of North Canberra and rebuilt in its current location.

It is reputed to be haunted, but one must wonder, if the church is haunted, then where do the ghosts come from? Or more to the point, where do they belong? Are they ghosts from the old Rookwood Cemetery who have been unwillingly transported from their previous abode to Canberra? Or are they recent ghosts who have just sprung up in the past fifty years?

I suspect the former. If a ghost is the built-up collective energy of people over a period of time, which seems possible, then it would seem prudent to suggest that the ghosts of this building have been transported to their current location within or as a part of the stones.

Often one will walk into an abandoned building and feel as if there is some sort of unexplained ambience to a certain room or area. Quite often these buildings have been associated with large gatherings of people in an emotional state, for instance, a funeral, a wake, a wedding, or even a party. If these certain areas have been used for that specific purpose for decades, then is it not possible that the energy expressed from the people there at the time is collected in the actual building itself and, over time, gathers more of the same until at some stage this energy becomes strong enough to be able to be felt by outsiders, and in some cases, manifest itself as some sort of conglomerate entity consisting of years and years of memories, emotions, and feelings?

As with the National Museum of Australia, which we looked at previously, is it possible that ghosts can somehow be attached to historical items? In the example of Tailem Town Pioneer Village is this maybe the case?

With this in mind, let us move from one heritage site with unanswered questions, to another, albeit one with true heritage as in it has existed on the same site for over a century: The Cape Northumberland Lighthouse is the most southerly lighthouse on the South Australian Coast and the first to be built on the mainland of South Australia, being established in 1859. The lighthouse was originally built as a consequence of one of the worst maritime disasters in Australian history when the SS *Admella* steamship was shipwrecked on a submerged reef in 1859 off the coast of Carpenters Rocks, claiming eighty-nine lives. Survivors of the initial grounding clung to the wreck for over a week, and many people took days to die as rescue attempts failed.

Sadly, although built to last and to protect shipping from the treacherous seas, the lighthouse was inexplicably built in the wrong place. Indeed, it was built too close to the cliff edge and was being undermined by the pounding ocean waves, so much so that it was thought that it would collapse into the water itself. Described as "exceedingly exposed, on a narrow point, with perpendicular cliffs falling to the sea on either side without any shelter from the most violent winds," the original lighthouse only stood for twenty-two years.

In 1882, a new lighthouse was built, this time farther back from the cliff face and some 400 metres to the east of the original site, and it still stands today. Like all lighthouses around Australia, it is now fully automated. Sadly, there are no public tours, which is a pity as the building is said to be haunted by the ghost of a woman described as wearing 1950s clothes and she has been witnessed on numerous occasions.

As reported in the *Advertiser* in February 1978, a Mr. Jordan, who lived at the lighthouse, reported that he was "lying in bed when this woman appeared at the end of the bed. She was looking at my wife and smiling. Oh, I smiled back at her and all that." The clothes she was wearing were "a bit out of date, but not really old-fashioned. She was playing with ends of a scarf she had on her head. I've no idea who she was either. All of a sudden she just vanished."

Interestingly, Jordan also noted that: "I didn't tell anyone about it, but the next morning the chap from next door came up and told me he had seen exactly the same thing, which was strange."

Haunted lighthouses do not seem uncommon in Australia, indeed, Tim the Yowie Man in his book *In the Spirit of Banjo* describes staying in a lighthouse at Green Cape on the New South Wales South coast that is rumoured to be haunted by a phantom sailor who lurks in the cottage's hallways.

And like the Cape Northumberland Lighthouse, Green Cape was also the scene of a terrible shipwreck when, on a cold winter's night in 1886, the *Ly-ee-Moon* steamed onto the rocks near the lighthouse leaving seventy-one people dead. Tragically, only twenty-four bodies were recovered and they are now buried in unidentified graves marked by white painted rocks.

Likewise, the lighthouse at Cape Otway, which sits on the most southern point of Victoria's coastline, is said to house a ghostly presence as does Cape Leeuwin Lighthouse in Western Australia.

A haunted lighthouse is somewhat understandable given their isolation and role. After all, a lighthouse is a lonely and remote place where one could all too easily lose their mind. However, another place where one could lose their mind, not from loneliness but from the products available, is Seppeltsfield Winery in the heart of the beautiful Barossa Valley. But just why a winery is haunted is unknown except to suggest that somehow the place has retained the spirits of previous workers, whether due to tragic circumstances or otherwise.

Seppeltsfield, one of Australia's oldest wineries, was founded in 1851 by Joseph Ernst Seppelt and is well known for its outstanding wines. Known locally as one of the most haunted places in the Barossa Valley, visitors regularly report disembodied footsteps on floors that no longer exist, phantom gunshots, unearthly screams from the surrounding vineyards, indistinct moaning and whispering in the dining hall, and a mysterious blood-like substance seeping from the mausoleum walls on the anniversaries of family deaths.

Joseph Seppelt, who emigrated with his family from Prussia to Australia in 1849 to escape political and economic unrest, never saw his winery come to its full fruition. He died in 1868 leaving the majority share of the property to his eldest son, Oscar Benno Pedro Seppelt, who later bought out his brothers to take full control of the winery. Oscar, it was said, slowly turned insane in his later years, apparently from spending so much time alone in a private retreat.

And, of course, if one wishes to do so, they can go on a ghost tour to learn all about the place and its resident ghosts where people feel as if they are being watched all of the time and where footsteps are often heard in empty rooms. As well, the apparition of a maid is said to haunt the homestead, while screaming is sometimes heard coming from the vineyards themselves.

The mausoleum of the Seppelt family, locked and inaccessible to the public, is said to leak blood on the interior walls on the anniversary of the deaths of the inhabitants, and it is said that, due to this, its doors remain sealed. In some areas of the homestead disembodied moans and voices have been heard, and many visitors have complained of feeling chilled to the bone in certain areas or being pushed by invisible hands. Others have described feeling waves of depression and loneliness flowing over them while visiting the gardens. Whatever the case, the winery at night seems a spooky and unnerving place.

Equally unnerving is the Adelaide Migration Museum, which was originally Adelaide's Destitute Asylum and previously housed thousands of people who were unable to meet society's monetary standards for the era. Operating from 1850 until 1918, it was a result of South Australian policies that dictated that Adelaide would have no poor or destitute. According to the theory, emigration of the correct proportion of capital and labour would create an ideal society free from social, economic, political, or religious problems, and as a result would be a self-sustaining society, prosperous and virtuous and without the problems caused by the poor and impoverished.

Obviously this ideal was completely unsustainable and, almost from the very start, it became clear that this utopian society simply could not exist. As early as 1843 the government passed its first legislation to deal with poverty and a destitute asylum was planned and built.

Far from being a place of aid and compassion, it was more to keep those without money out of sight and, therefore, out of mind of respectable citizens. In 1855, roughly 3,000 men and women lived within its high bluestone walls and grounds, and crimes such as looting, rape, and murder were very much prevalent.

Now the Migration Museum, one can wander around the displays, including a room full of medical devices and surgical tools from the Victorian age. In this room it is said that ghostly activity can often be heard and seen. In addition, the upstairs office of one of the buildings is said to be the site of unusual goings on, including disembodied voices, shadowy figures that lurk in doorways, and even invisible hands that have tried to push people down the stairs. Indeed, one of the museum's graphic designers once reported seeing the ghost of a man in a grey uniform sitting on a staircase. When he spoke it simply disappeared.

Whereas we would expect a place like the Migration Museum, due to its past, to be haunted, what of less obvious places such as our next haunted venue: the Steamtown Heritage Rail Centre in Peterborough?

Steamtown is a historical train museum in Peterborough in South Australia's mid-north. Once South Australia's busiest regional railway hub, the old depot and workshop is now home to the state's most unique and interesting Heritage Railway museum. It is also reputed to be the home of a number of spirits and paranormal activity, the most unusual and most reported sightings being the ghostly figure of a man dressed in overalls, who disappears in the noise, lights, and steam. Who he is no one is sure, but it is suspected that he is an old railway worker or mechanic. Other reports include disembodied voices, ethereal footsteps, and other strange, seemingly paranormal phenomena on Platform 13.

A local supernatural investigation group, while examining the site in 2011, reported that near Platform 13, a member of the group had a sighting of the ghostly man. This sighting was later corroborated by another member of the group, who said she had seen the same male figure earlier in the evening. It must be also noted that, at the time, the site was locked down and there was no way that anyone could enter.

Also in Peterborough is the Capitol Theatre, which opened on 17 May 1926. As was common for the time, the opening was a grand affair and attracted such a large crowd that hundreds were turned away from the opening. Although it is unknown whether the theatre has experienced death or tragedy, it is still considered haunted with numerous reports of spirits roaming the building and associated sites. One spirit is said to be that of a little girl about seven to eight years old and wearing a long white dress with frills at the bottom and who is generally seen near the stage or up in the balcony area.

As well, the apparition of a man is often reported looking down from the balcony near the entrance. He is said to have a long, drawn-out face and may have something to do with a door behind the stage that, although locked every night, is regularly found open again in the morning, even though the door locks only from the inside and has no handles on the outside. In that same area, people have reported hearing the voices of a man and younger female, although when investigated, no one is ever found to be there.

Disembodied footsteps are also often heard walking through the antique store, and full-bodied apparitions have also been reported near the check-outs of the store suggesting that, like the National Museum and Tailem Town Pioneer Village, these spirits could be attached to the actual items rather than the building, although this does not always seem to be the case as in our next site where the spirit is definitely linked to a place.

The Waterfall Gully Restaurant sits in an idyllic setting of scenic winding roads, crisp bubbling streams, lush green hills, and towering century-old trees. Nestled at the base of a spectacular eighteen-metre waterfall, it is a beautifully preserved 100-year-old stone chalet just 10 kilometres from the Adelaide central business district.

Originally constructed as a tea room in 1912, it was designed by Albert Conrad in the style of a Swiss chalet and is now considered Australia's earliest example of a "refreshment room." It is also the home of a ghost, reputed to be that of South Australian Police Foot Constable Thomas Tregoweth.

Tregoweth tragically died while fighting a bushfire that struck Waterfall Gully in 1926 after he lost his footing on one of the gully's cliffs and rolled down a hill where he received terrible and fatal burns and injuries. Since the early 1930s, there have been ongoing reports of his ghost in and around the old chalet as well as in the surrounding bushland and walking trails. Witnesses say the ghostly constable is still dressed in his distinctive period police uniform and greatcoat and many people speculate that he is still keeping watch over the area.

In addition, staff at the chalet often report strange happenings, including mysteriously moving items, clanking keys, footsteps, late-night whistling, and what has been described as "a comforting presence." In one encounter a couple driving to the exit of the gully late one night were shocked to be stopped by a man dressed in a greatcoat and whose face had no distinguishable features who, after a moment, simply melted into the surrounding bush.

But as we have seen previously, it's not just buildings that can be haunted. Indeed, Talia Caves on the rugged and windswept Eyre Peninsula is one such place. Created by weathering and erosion over thousands of years, it appears to hold a dark secret, one that has only come to light with the publication of an exceptionally perplexing photograph.

In 1923, it is alleged that a nurse had become pregnant to a respected local married man who, upon finding out about the pregnancy, lured the woman to the cliffs and pushed her off. A memorial to the murdered woman stands near the cave to this day. However, it was not until 1962 that something seriously strange was noticed when a couple took a photograph of the swirling waves battering the rocks in the small bay. Remarkably, in the photograph, walking upright through the dangerous swell across what appears to be a rock ledge is the undisputed figure of a woman, fully clothed and apparently oblivious to the danger.

When asked about the photograph, the couple stressed that they had seen no one and that the seas were simply too dangerous to be wandering around on the rocks. Besides that, the stance of the woman seems quite unnatural given the waves at the time.

The image was widely circulated in the media and locals began to wonder if this figure was in fact the ghost of the murdered nurse. Photographic experts at the time were equally perplexed, suggesting that double exposure, tricks of light, and optical illusion were highly doubtful.

John Pinkney, in his book *Haunted: The Book of Australia's Ghosts*, states that the current owner of the photograph, a Michael Leyson of Port Lincoln, told him that it was "taken by a friend's parents back in 1962," and that "they swore they'd photographed nothing more than sea pounding on the rocks. But when the prints came back, there was this mist enveloping a woman, whom neither of them had seen at the time, walking through the water. My friend's parents ruled out any theories about a double exposure and the picture has been intriguing people in this area ever since."

Given the tragic demise of the woman, is it possible that somehow, as we have previously seen with the stone tape theory, that her being, or soul, or whatever you want to call it, has somehow become a part of the environment, and in the right circumstances is visible for all to see, or, in this case, to be photographed?

Of course, if one jumps on to the Internet and searches for ghost photos, one will be completely inundated to the point that it is almost a pointless exercise. And yet, throughout history, there are a number of alleged ghost photographs that defy explanation, including the Bungendore photo taken in 1949 at the Royal Hotel. Apart from that, there exists another very famous photograph taken in 1936 by photographers Captain Provand and Indre Shira while shooting for *Country Life* magazine, which appears to show a ghost descending a staircase at England's historic Raynham Hall, known as the "Brown Lady."

The photograph of the Brown Lady is arguably the most famous of all ghost photographs ever taken, and it is believed to be that of Lady Dorothy Townsend, wife of Charles Townshend, the 2nd Viscount of Raynham who lived at Raynham Hall in Norfolk, England, in the early 1700s. It is rumoured that Charles suspected Dorothy of infidelity and had her locked away in a remote area of the house until she died. Her ghost is said to haunt the oak staircase as well as other areas of Raynham Hall and was seen by King George IV. Interestingly, as in the case of the Talia Caves nurse, Provand said he saw nothing although Shira noticed something coming down the stairs before directing Provand to take the shot.

But there exists quite a few more strange photographs that purport to show ghosts, such as that taken by the Reverend R. S. Blance at Corroboree Rock near Alice Springs in 1959. As well, in 1891, Sybil Corbet took an unusual photograph at Combermere Abbey Library, one that clearly shows the figure of a man sitting in a chair, his head, collar, and right arm on the armrest most obvious to the viewer. It is believed that this is the ghost of Lord Combermere, a British cavalry commander in the early 1800s who died after being struck by a horse-drawn carriage in 1891. Strangely, at the time Corbet took the photo, Combermere's funeral was taking place and, although it has been suggested that the photo is a long exposure of a servant who has simply entered the room and sat in the chair, this has been rejected by everyone involved as they were all at the funeral at the time.

Another quite unexplainable photo that one often encounters while investigating the supernatural is that of Airman Freddy Jackson, a wartime mechanic who walked into a propeller and was killed. Remarkably, a few days after his death, in 1919, an official RAF photograph was taken of the men in his squadron who had survived the war. When the photograph was developed it was placed on the squadron bulletin board for people to see and to purchase as a memento of their service. However, on close examination, there was an extra face in the shot: that of Freddie Jackson.

As such, one must ask, did the spirit of the murdered nurse at Talia Caves make itself known to the photographer for some purpose? And if so, then what purpose? Or is it that her energy or life force still exists in the area where she died? Is it possible that, in her death, the emotion of the event was so strong that it still existed in 1962 and was strong enough to be photographed? Likewise, we can ask the same questions of Freddie Jackson. Was his spirit still there at the base with his mates? Is it possible that his soul or life force still remained and as such, turned up for the photo? Or could it be that the collective memory of the men in the photo somehow conjured up an image of Jackson that could be seen in the photo?

Whatever the case, it seems that somehow, and in certain circumstances, ghosts can appear to us, not only as full apparitions, but as unseen images only evident on film. And if we acknowledge this, then what can we make of other anomalies often caught on film or seen in real life? Anomalies such as this can be found in cities such as Melbourne, Ballarat, and Beechworth in the picturesque state of Victoria.

The hangman's noose in Fremantle Gaol. Martha Rendell was the last woman to be hanged in Western Australia in October 1909. A day after she was executed an unusual image appeared on the outside of one of the church windows, and her unhappy ghost is said to haunt the cold stone corridors and rooms. (Photo: Steve Salliard)

Fremantle Gaol (Western Australia). Built beginning in 1851 and the site of forty-four executions, it is not surprising that it is rated as one of Perth's most haunted locations. (Photo: Steve Salliard)

The North Kapunda Hotel (South Australia). Although mainly a hotel, it once served as a brothel and is said to be haunted by a number of spirits, including ex-residents, publicans, prostitutes, and miners. (Photo: Elyse Herrald-Woods)

Adelaide Gaol (South Australia). Operating from 1841 until 1988, it housed approximately 300,000 prisoners during its 147 years of operation. At the time of its closure, it was the longest continuously operating prison in Australia, and a total of forty-five people, including one woman, were hanged inside its walls. (Photo: Marianne Hope)

Adelaide Gaol. Not surprisingly given its gruesome past, many people have reported paranormal activity in the gaol, including full body apparitions, disembodied voices, cold spots, and EVPs. Others have reported being touched, pushed, and scratched, and seeing ghostly apparitions of guards. (Photo: Marianne Hope)

The Exeter (South Australia). A typical Adelaide pub, it is reputed to be haunted by the ghost of a former manager. Her ghost is sometimes seen at the scene of her murder in her old room. On some occasions, her footsteps can be heard pacing along the upstairs corridor. (Photo: Marianne Hope)

Old Melbourne Gaol (Victoria). One of Australia's most haunted sites, its grim bluestone walls have witnessed 136 executions, including notorious bushranger Ned Kelly, who was captured at Glenrowan and executed by hanging in November 1880. (Photo: Michael Montgomery)

The Princess Theatre (Victoria). Completed in 1886, but dating back to the 1850s, it is reputed to be haunted by the ghost of Federici, the stage name of the Italian-born Englishman Frederick Baker who died of a heart attack in March 1888. (Photo: Michael Montgomery)

The State Library of Victoria (Victoria). Established in 1854 and holding over two million books and 16,000 serials, as well as housing the original armour of Ned Kelly, this magnificent heritage building is rumoured to be haunted by up to twenty different ghosts. (Photo: Michael Montgomery)

The Drunken Admiral (Tasmania). Constructed in 1824, the building is one of the oldest in Tasmania and has been used in the past as a granary, an army barracks, an annex to a jam factory, and a warehouse before being converted into a restaurant. Local legend has it that it is haunted by the spirit of an old Chinese man. (Photo: Fiona Levings)

Port Arthur (Tasmania). Renowned for its harsh conditions, Port Arthur is probably Australia's most haunted site. Indeed, it is said that, since the prison's closure in 1877, there have been over 2,000 accounts of ghost sightings and hauntings within the historical precinct. (Photo: Fiona Levings)

Port Arthur (Tasmania). With countless stories of disembodied heads, voices from no-where, apparitions, mysterious lights, odd thumping sounds, and people having their hair pulled, or being shoved in the back, it is a truly frightening place after dark. (Photo: Fiona Levings)

The Separate (Model) Prison at Port Arthur (Tasmania). Even during the day this corridor and the adjoining cells seem to have a menacing feel, and in 2004, the author was lucky enough to hear spinetingling disembodied footsteps on the wooden stairs that lead to the building's chapel. (Photo: Fiona Levings)

Richmond Bridge (Tasmania). The oldest bridge still in use in Australia and constructed using convict labour, it is reputed to be haunted by the ghost of George Grover, who was employed as a gaoler and whose duties included flogging the prisoners. In addition, the ghost of a large black and white dog, sometimes called "Grover's Dog," has also been seen on the bridge. (Photo: Fiona Levings)

Kodak House (Tasmania). A narrow five-story building with a crenelated parapet and bay windows on the upper story, it is allegedly haunted by the ghost of a woman called Beryl. (Photo: Fiona Levings)

Oppsie top: The Theatre Royal (Tasmania). Australia's oldest continually operating theatre, it is said to be haunted by the ghost of a deceased actor and stagehand called Fred, who is believed to be a sailor who was stabbed to death by a prostitute. Australian actress Jacki Weaver, famous for her roles in movies such as *Picnic at Hanging Rock* and *Caddie* is among those who have witnessed his eerie presence. (Photo: Fiona Levings)

Oppsie bottom: Norfolk Island. For all its island paradise looks, this was a horrific place where torture, lashings, murders, rapes, and cruelty were commonplace, and with such a violent past, it is no surprise it is seen by many as one of the world's most haunted islands. (Photo: Mark Hallam)

The Norfolk Island Cemetery. Outside the infamous Port Arthur, Norfolk Island is said by some to be the most haunted place in Australia with more ghosts per square kilometres than any other state or territory. (Photo: Mark Hallam)

CHAPTER SEVEN

Victoria

A Headless Bushranger, a Lunatic Asylum, and a Haunted Air Force base

Victoria is Australia's most densely populated state and its second-most populous state overall with most of its population concentrated in the area surrounding Port Phillip Bay, including the capital Melbourne, which is the country's second largest city. It is a state that features rugged mountain ranges with snow topped peaks, windswept, barren seaside cliffs, beautiful meandering rivers, serene lakes, river-red gums forests along the Murray River, and endless horizons in the desert-like Mallee. It is a place of big city living, wilderness, and culture.

Melbourne is an old city by Australian standards. These days it is dynamic and cosmopolitan and has a reputation for its artiness. Its stately mid- to late-1800s architecture and multicultural makeup reflect the city's history, while high class restaurants, museums, and art galleries give it a contemporary, exciting feel.

Founded in August 1835, and incorporated as a Crown settlement in 1837, it was named Melbourne in honour of the British prime minister of the day, William Lamb, 2nd Viscount Melbourne. In 1847, it was declared a city by Queen Victoria, and became the capital of the newly created Colony of Victoria in 1851. During the Victorian gold rush of the 1850s, it was one of the world's largest and wealthiest cities and, after federation in 1901, even served as the seat of government for Australia until 1927.

And, as one would suspect from a place with such an interesting history, it also appears to have a wealth of ghosts and paranormal events. And so, to start our journey of discovery, we'll start at a very likely site: the Old Melbourne Gaol.

Gaols all over the world, including Australia, have reputations of being haunted. Indeed, except for the most modern of gaols one could confidently say that pretty much all would have their own stories about resident spectres that haunt the lonely corridors and cells of these places of incarceration. And in time, who is not to say that even modern gaols will soon start to tell of stories of strange apparitions, unseen hands that touch people, or unexplained knocking or steps on the hard sterile floors?

Without doubt the Old Melbourne Gaol is one of Australia's most haunted sites. It is situated on the corners of LaTrobe and Russell Streets, and its heavy bluestone walls sit gloomily alongside a major city road that sees traffic twenty-four hours a day, seven days a week. Outside the gaol, the city continues to function much as it has for over 200 years; however, inside the foreboding walls something more sinister appears to be happening, possibly due to the fact that the gaol itself witnessed 136 executions.

The Old Melbourne Gaol was the first extensive gaol complex in Victoria with the first Melbourne Gaol being built in 1839–1840. This gaol was unfortunately found to be too small, and a second, larger gaol was built at the corner of Russell and La Trobe Streets from 1841 until 1844. This second stage was later demolished early in the twentieth century to allow for the building of a new Magistrate's Court.

The building that is left standing today was officially a new wing of the gaol, but in reality was stage one of a third Melbourne Gaol. Built in 1852 to 1854, it was made from bluestone rather than sandstone and was based upon the Pentonville Model Prison in London. At the time, it employed the most modern of prison reform ideology and theories.

In spite of continual refurbishment and extending, the building complex was consistently overcrowded. In 1857, it was extended in two stages and again in 1858 when the boundary wall was also extended. The present north wing, which comprises the entrance buildings, central hall, and chapel was started in 1860, and between 1862 and 1864, a western cell block was built to house female prisoners. The perimeter wall was finally completed in 1864.

In 1870, a review of the penal system recommended that the gaol be closed and the prisoners be moved to a less crowded location. Between 1880 and 1924 the gaol was abandoned, left to the elements, and slowly became derelict. It was finally closed for good in 1929, although it was briefly reopened during the Second World War as a military prison for Australian soldiers. In 1972, the National Trust of Australia took over management of the gaol as a tourist attraction, and as such, it is now protected and conserved for future generations.

The gaol's most infamous prisoner was Ned Kelly, the notorious bushranger who was captured at Glenrowan. He was executed by hanging in November 1880. Bizarrely, his headless body was originally buried within the Old Melbourne Gaol grounds in an unmarked grave, but later removed, under much controversy, to Pentridge Prison. Just as odd, his coffin was discovered and workers stole his bones.

And yet, even with this strange historical event, it should be noted that Ned Kelly's ghost does not appear to haunt the gaol. However, the lack of his ghost is easily made up for by numerous others, including the Woman's Ward, particularly from Cell 16 where there have been numerous reports of cold spots and shadowy figures. As well, there have been reports of voices being heard, and one paranormal team who visited the gaol managed to capture an EVP or Electronic Voice Phenomena, recording of an Irish woman apparently saying "Get out!"

As with many haunted sites, especially prisons, people have reported being touched by ghostly hands and often hear crying and other slightly unintelligible voices in uninhabited areas. In addition, visitors often find they cannot enter some of the cells or get such a strong feeling from them that they refuse to enter. And in a slightly more disturbing encounter, a woman visiting the gaol came across a cell with what appeared to be a distressed-looking mannequin sitting with head in hands at a table. As the woman looked at the mannequin she started to feel uneasy and then got the shock of her life when it lifted its head and stared at her. Quite shaken, she later complained to staff that they should not have such lifelike automated mannequins as they could cause someone to have a heart attack. The staff member replied that the gaol did not possess any automated mannequins.

David Barker, cofounder of Ghostseekers, is another who has had a strange experience while in the complex. Looking down from the second floor, Barker saw a man walking towards the gallows on the ground floor. Naturally, he assumed it was a staff member, in fact, a staff member who he was familiar with. Apparently, he called out to the figure, but as it came closer he realised that it was wearing an old prison uniform and a "silence mask," a cloth facial hood.

Barker recalls that it "just kept walking towards me as I was standing on the landing above. I just stood there and went, 'Oh God.' Then it walked into the last cell below the gallows and just disappeared in front of my eyes."

Although the whole encounter took around twenty seconds, Barker still cannot explain it, especially as the figure looked as if it were a real flesh-and-blood person, something that is often reported in ghost encounters.

But it's not just places of death and mental anguish that seem to entice ghosts. Indeed, from Drury Lane in London to the Princess Theatre in Melbourne, such cultured and benign places as the theatre are often reported as being haunted.

The Princess Theatre in Melbourne is reputed to be haunted by the ghost of Federici, the stage name of Italian-born Englishman Frederick Baker, who died of a massive heart attack at age thirty-eight in March 1888 after a successful performance of the opera *Faust*. When the play resumed after his death, the cast swore that they saw him there with them. In addition, they claimed that two Mephistopheles, Federici's part, stepped forward to take their bows that night. Ernest St. Clair, who was understudy to Federici, swore that every time he stepped forward to take his bow at the end of the performance, invisible hands pushed him backwards.

On another occasion one of the theatre staff reported a strange man sitting in the dress circle during a late-night rehearsal. Wondering how he had got in, he chastised another employee for allowing a visitor into the theatre. The employee swore that he had admitted no one, and a search was made of the theatre, but there was no sign of the strange visitor.

Many actors over the years have claimed Federici's ghost has brushed by them in the corridors behind the stage, and many equipment failures have been blamed on him. In the early 1900s, a new fire alarm system was installed in the theatre, and the resident fireman was required to punch a time clock every hour, triggering a light on a switchboard at a nearby fire station. If he failed to do so, an alarm was raised and a brigade dispatched to the theatre.

One particular night, during a heat wave, no message came through on the hour and the fire brigade was duly dispatched. When they reached the theatre, they were shocked to find their colleague huddled terrified in a corner. Apparently he had opened a sliding section of the roof to allow some cool air in, but when he had done so, moonlight had flooded in illuminating the stage revealing a tall figure with distinguished features, dressed in evening clothes with a long cloak and a top-hat.

Then, in 1917, the theatre's wardrobe mistress was working late to finish costumes for an upcoming production. At about 2:30 in the morning a fireman knocked on her office door and politely asked her if she'd like to see a ghost. Sceptical, the woman said yes, and together the two climbed a set of side stairs to a landing beside the dress circle. At the top the fireman pointed to the apparent figure of Federici, who was sitting in the middle of the second row of the dress circle. The seamstress and the fireman watched for a while before going back to their tasks, apparently quite amazed at what they'd seen.

A few years later, another fireman had a couple of similar experiences when he saw the ghost standing in the same spot on two separate occasions. Many people have since described seeing Federici, and it is now considered good luck if he is seen on opening night.

That Melbourne, like Sydney, has so many ghostly tales is not a surprise. Ghost stories are as much about history as they are about the supernatural, and Melbourne is certainly a place with a rich historical past. And, after all, what is a ghost if not the past intruding on the present?

As we have seen with the Old Melbourne Gaol and the Princess Theatre, the ghosts of Melbourne are generally centred upon colonial and Victorian times. And, although this is not always the case, there is plenty of evidence to suggest that this time in the state's history is somehow conducive to ghosts and hauntings.

Beechworth Lunatic Asylum was originally known as Mayday Hills Lunatic Asylum and is a decommissioned psychiatric hospital that sits quietly at the top of a hill outside Beechworth in northern Victoria. In its day it was one of the three largest psychiatric hospitals in Victoria and operated for 128 years before closing in 1995. Although grand, the building has a foreboding air of menace.

Now owned by La Trobe University, nightly ghost tours are held at the hospital, allowing public access to the most historic buildings in the complex. It is also used as a wedding venue and the gardens, which date to the nineteenth century, cover eleven hectares, and are open to the public most days.

During its operation the asylum was a hellish institution where patients were subject to gruelling and doubtful treatments and, in a time when mental illness was barely understood, many people were condemned to spend their lives in the place, even those with no real reason for being there, given that it took just two signatures to have a person condemned to a psychiatric ward in those days. In all it is believed that up to 9,000 people died in the facility.

There are plenty of supernatural stories about the asylum. Many visitors have reported the ghostly figure of a man who appears near the cellar before vanishing into thin air. As well, Matron Sharpe, who spent most of her working life in the building, has been spotted on more than one occasion. She appears as a grey, hooded figure in period costume. As well, doors swing open by themselves and people report hearing mysterious bloodcurdling screams. Meanwhile, the surrounding gardens are reputed to be haunted by an old man in a green jacket who is believed to be a former groundskeeper. Also, a woman has been seen and photographed standing at the window from which she was reputedly thrown out of by other inmates.

Adam Wynne-Jenkins, who runs a ghost tour of the former asylum, is a historian who, after a trip to Scotland, developed an interest in ghosts. Originally from Beechworth and with a background as a historian, he decided that he could run ghost tours in his hometown, and with the asylum sitting abandoned, realised that this was the perfect place to start. At first he used the supernatural theme as a marketing tool to engage people in what he thought would be largely historical tours. That is, until he actually encountered what he could only describe as a ghost when: "About six weeks after I started running the tour, I saw the ghost of a matron of the asylum. Her name was Matron Sharp. She came out of a bricked-up doorway, came almost right up to me, and then hurried away."

Although slightly distraught, Wynne-Jenkins wasn't actually scared by the strange event and recalls that he was "tingling all over and could hear my heart beating loudly in my ears and I felt static electricity all over me."

Wynne-Jenkins also suggests that, "You don't usually get interaction with a ghost; mostly it seems they are just going about their day as they would when they were alive: the warden at Geelong Gaol checks the doors, the matron is holding her keys, and so on."

Whatever the case, there have been many other sightings and unexplained happenings in the building and surrounding grounds and, whether these tales are true or not, the place has a certain eeriness about it that has one furtively looking over their shoulder and sends chills down the spine.

Wynne-Jenkins is also involved in another ghost tour, this one at the Old Geelong Gaol where he says he has seen dozens of ghostly apparitions since starting the tours, including "the ghost of a little girl sitting on the steps." As the gaol was used as a girl's school from 1865 until 1872, this makes perfect sense as does his report of the ghost of a warder, resplendent in a blue woollen jacket.

The gaol itself was a maximum security prison on the corner of Myers Street and Swanston Street in Geelong. Built by convicts who were housed in ship hulks moored in Corio Bay between 1849 to 1864, its design was based on Pentonville Prison in England and was officially closed in 1991. Since then, little has changed in the gaol although historical exhibits have been added to enhance the visitor experience. Still, even today it is an imposing and dread-inspiring building.

During its life as a prison, the building housed a number of convicts, murderers, and lunatics under extremely harsh conditions. With tiny cells, lack of toilets and facilities, and freezing temperatures, it was a soul-destroying and cruel place where life would have been excruciating. Prisoners were subjected to back-breaking labour, floggings, and general cruelty in a system designed to break their spirits. In all, six men were executed and buried within its wall, and it was the site of numerous murders between prisoners.

It has been reported that the notorious twentieth-century criminal Mark "Chopper" Reid said he never wanted to go back to it. Whether or not this is simply because of the dank, dark, and depressing atmosphere or the rumours of ghosts is unknown; however, if a person such as Reid didn't like it, then it surely must possess something of a malignant nature within its thick stone walls.

Many past inmates have reported hearing plaintive female cries at night, especially in the east wing, the site of the Industrial School for Girls in the late 1860s and early 1870s. Tour guides, such as Adam Wynne-Jenkins, have reported witnessing several strange and unexplainable events, including swirling mists that often appear to take human form, to feelings of being watched and people being struck or touched by invisible hands. Others have reported strange mists, odd sounds, and orbs. Mediums and psychics have reported the presence of various spirits in the gaol, with the old infirmary, cell 45, the gallows, and the external shower block being the most active places.

And while on the subject of gaols, let us now explore another one, also modelled on the Pentonville system, and the site of ten executions over its lifespan.

The Old Castlemaine Gaol was built in the 1850s and operated until 1995, and during its time as a fully functional prison held some of Australia's worst and most violent criminals. Again, like most gaols around the country, it is widely regarded to be one of Australia's most haunted locations.

An impressive building, it stands four storeys high and, since its decommissioning, has served as a school camp, conference centre, and a base for a community radio station. It is also the site for numerous ghost investigations due to the number of executions held at the site, including the 1863 execution of police murderer James Murphy. Visitors to the gaol have experienced cold spots, eerie drafts, shadowy figures, and even ghostly encounters of bodies swinging from the hangman's noose. A ghost named Jack is said to roam some of the cells, although some believe that this is in fact the ghost of John Duffus, the last man to be hanged in old gaol.

David Young is another convict whose spirit is said to wander the prison halls. He was executed in 1865 after being convicted of the murder of Margaret Graham and, although executed for the crime, maintained his innocence to the very end and even asked the audience at his execution, which apparently numbered over 60, to pray for him as he was hanged.

Previously we studied Beechworth Lunatic Asylum which, to be perfectly honest, has all the hallmarks of a haunted building in that it is old, decrepit, impressive, and holds a dark past full of cruelty, loneliness, death, and despair. And so, with this in mind, we can look at some other asylums, namely Kew Mental Asylum and Aradale Mental Hospital, the latter being Australia's largest abandoned lunatic asylum.

Kew Mental Asylum, real name Willsmere, was one of the largest asylums ever built in Australia. It was operational from 1871 to 1988 and sits in between Princess Street and Yarra Boulevard in Kew, a suburb of Melbourne. The first purpose-built asylum in the Colony of Victoria, Kew is an extremely impressive building and is a typical example of the French Empire style, which was popular in Victorian Melbourne. Elegant, attractive, stunning, yet substantial, it was designed to portray Melbourne as a civilised and benign city by avoiding the jail-like appearance of other asylums.

Kew, however, was not without its problems and suffered from overcrowding, mismanagement, lack of resources, poor sanitation, and disease and, although continuing to operate as a psychiatric hospital, treating acute, long-term and geriatric patients, it closed in 1988. The main building and surrounding grounds were sold by the state government and were redeveloped as elegant residential properties. Similar to Beechworth Lunatic Asylum, it also has extensive and quite magnificent gardens and once featured vegetable gardens, farms and cricket ovals, and bowling greens. It is a site of cultural and historic significance, and both the main building and outbuildings were put on the Register of the National Estate in 1978.

Residents these days have reported hearing the sounds of partying in the upper levels of the building but upon inspection have found the place deserted. As well, witnesses have given accounts of ghostly apparitions moving down staircases and corridors, and some have even claimed to have been woken in the middle of the night by ghostly figures standing at the end of their bed staring at them and sometimes gently tugging at their bedclothes. Others have reported knockings, screams, and disembodied running footsteps in empty hallways as well as loud unexplained banging noises.

Similarly, Aradale Mental Hospital, a collection of over sixty buildings amid over a hundred acres on the top of a hill near Ararat, is an equally impressive facility. Australia's largest abandoned lunatic asylum, it was opened in 1867, and over its 130 years of operation housed tens of thousands of people. Being in Ararat, roughly two-and-a-half hours drive northwest of Melbourne, it was far from the prying eyes of gentrified suburban Melbourne and so received the very worst of patients. It is believed that over 13,000 people died in the complex and, as such, it is possible that the place saw more emotional and physical trauma, hardship, and cruelty than any other place in Australia.

And with such a history of torment, despair, and death, one would suspect that, if any place were to be haunted, then Aradale would be it. There have been numerous reports of supernatural activity within the boundaries of the abandoned asylum, including stories of the ghost of Nurse Kerry, who allegedly haunts the women's wing and is said to appear often on ghost tours while in the old men's wing people describe unexplained pains and sense of being touched. The place is also known for unexplained cold winds emanating from the old office of the facility director.

The men's wing isolation cells—old, decrepit, and seemingly full of despair and loneliness—experiences unexplained banging on the walls, as if someone is trying to get out or to alert someone of their presence. Apart from this, there are stories of a ghostly woman called Old Margaret, who was supposedly one of the many patients kicked out in the late '90s when the complex closed and, although she didn't die in the asylum, her spirit remains as it did during most of her life, again suggesting that ghosts are not just the spirit or soul of a dead person, but more so the energy or life force that they somehow, probably unwittingly, projected upon a place. Whatever the case, this bleak reminder of the past seems to hold secrets that we can only guess at.

But Victoria isn't simply a place of haunted gaols and mental asylums. It is a state with a long and distinguished history from convicts to bushrangers to gold rushes. And it is the 1850s gold rush that takes us to our next location.

Bendigo is roughly 150 kilometres northwest of Melbourne and has an urban population of over 80,000, which makes it the fourth-largest inland city in Australia. It is an old city by Australian standards and was at the centre of the 1850s Victorian gold rush, which saw it blossom into a boomtown. These days it is a startlingly beautiful city where grand Victorian buildings sit alongside serene grassy parks and old churches. Everywhere one turns is a reminder of its gold rush past, from its broad and regular boulevards to richly decorated privates homes. It is also reputed to be very haunted with one of the major spots for paranormal activity being Fortuna Villa.

Fortuna Villa, a grand mansion and grounds situated in Chum Street, Bendigo, has been the home of the Army Survey Regiment since 1942 and, as such, has been off limits to the public. Built in 1855 by Theodore Ballerstadt, who opened the first quartz-crushing gold mine in the area, the villa has remained remarkably intact, even though it has served as a workplace for sixty-five years. There is a basement, ground floor, and first floor, bedrooms, bathrooms, a conservatory, a ballroom, a billiard room, a music room, along with a stunning entrance hall, and reception room. It is also decorated with elaborate ceilings, stained glass windows, a grand staircase made from cedar and blackwood, and extensive acid-etched glasswork. By anyone's definition, it is a truly awe inspiring and grand building.

In 1871, Theodore Ballerstadt sold the villa to George Lansell who immediately expanded the villa before moving in with his family, and although he died in 1906, his widow Edith continued to renovate the house. During the Second World War the house was used by the Australian Army as a mapping survey centre and later became a listed Heritage site.

There are many reported ghost sightings at Fortuna Villa, including two shadowy, grey-coloured figures that appear in the main passageways of the mansion. As well, an elegant woman in a ball gown has been seen floating around a fountain and front gardens, and a well-spoken ghostly teenage girl has sometimes appeared and asked visitors to leave. George Lansell's spirit has also been seen, an old bearded figure in a white jacket holding a walking cane. In addition, people have witnessed figures floating through the buildings, eerie orbs, disembodied voices, unexplained smells, as well as strange feelings of being watched or as if things are not quite as they should be.

Others claim to have heard Bedilia, Lansell's first wife, who died in indeterminate circumstances. Military personnel stationed in the mapping survey centre have also reported that locked doors are often found open and oddly, a ghostly boy in a sailor suit was reputed to have appeared in front of a female soldier before disappearing when she called out for help.

Patrick Thwaites was working as head of security at Fortuna Villa one summer day in the late 1980s when he encountered a particularly strange incident. According to his account he was alone apart for guards at the front gate, on the top floor of the villa on a very hot, windless day and that he "had to keep the windows and doors closed because there were flies everywhere and we didn't have fly screens. Then, all of a sudden, there was a waft of air as if someone had fluffed a blanket. With it I got a very strong smell of perfume."

With the smell being so strong, Thwaites got up and went out into the hallway to see who was outside. Puzzling, however, it was empty, although the smell stayed around for at least five minutes, and though Thwaites stated that he didn't believe in ghosts, he acknowledged that this was one of a number of experiences at Fortuna Villa that he and others couldn't explain. In fact, he suggested that it could have been the spirit of a former governess, named the "perfume ghost," who lived on the top floor with the Lansell children and who has been reported by others at the facility.

Thwaites also recalled that there was something "called the Ghost Book where we recorded all the sightings. It had absolutely everything for probably about 25 years, but it has disappeared; it's been souvenired." Included in the records, according to Thwaites, was a sighting from cartographer and resident Fortuna ghost hunter Richard Arman, who reported seeing a man's head and torso pass through the banister of the main staircase in 1986.

Arman apparently kept his own list of other reported sightings. This included a disembodied voice of a young woman who, in the former security office of the main building, would tell staff to leave. Apparently she was never seen but would whisper into people's ears speaking softly and asking, "Who are you? What do you want? Please leave."

He also noted that: "Numerous sergeants over the years, when on piquet duty of a night time, would experience such an encounter and in the old days it happened quite regularly. While some got used to it after a while, others never did, and the indoor security check of the building ceased to be mandatory after a number of complaints by duty staff."

A female soldier once reported that she had woken up to find the ghastly apparition of a young soldier hanging by a rope at the end of her bed, although later checks of records could never find details of any soldier who had hanged himself in the facility. As well, George Lansell himself would often appear. However, Arman noted that "the last recorded time was in 2006 when a member of staff working the night shift was taking a task up to the reproduction section for processing. As he climbed the stairs to the stables he looked up; standing in the doorway of the stables was the faded, bearded figure of George Lansell dressed in a white jacket and straw boater holding his walking stick."

Whereas many people truly believe in ghosts and supernatural activity, many don't and simply write it off as the delusional rantings of someone who has, in their eyes, either a screw loose or has misinterpreted what is a natural or normal event or occurrence. However, in light of this, one can still confidentially say that, while some have experiences that can be explained, there are others that simply defy any rational explanation. So far in this book we have seen that ghosts and the supernatural seem to be commonplace and that a large percentage of people not only believe in ghosts but have also experienced something that they believe is of a supernatural origin. Indeed, many people have reported the same supernatural occurrence happening at a specific place over a number of years thus legitimising their experiences, even though they have had no contact with others who may have seen, or heard, or experienced the same thing.

Can all these people be wrong? Are they simply deluded? Have they misinterpreted what they have experienced? In many cases, yes. And yet, as we previously mentioned, there are still cases that simply defy explanation.

Bendigo, one must remember, is a city of hundreds of historic buildings and homes, each and every one with a history of its own and all here long before any of their current residents. Whether you believe in ghosts and the supernatural or not, there's no denying that the city has some interesting stories when it comes to the paranormal.

Her Majesty's Prison Bendigo, commonly known as the Old Bendigo Gaol, is another such place. A medium security prison facility, it provided accommodation for prisoners assessed as suitable for treatment in the area of substance abuse. The prison opened in 1863 and was officially closed in January 2006. However, although being a medium security prison, it did see three executions over its long life, from Edward Hunter in 1885 to Charles John Hall, who murdered his wife, in 1897.

Jim Evans, president of the local historical society, believes the gaol is haunted noting that: "There's been various sightings by wardens and presumably prisoners, too," and that a figure has been seen "standing in the central part of the jail where the wings meet."

Interestingly, there have also been reports of a ghost haunting a cell below where the gallows used to be. Whether or not this is the spirit of one of the executed men is unknown, but it is believed all are buried within the walls of the prison.

Continuing on our journey through this quaint gold rush city we find the Bendigo Cemetery, which sits on the corners of Victoria Street and Grenfell Avenue , where people have also reported strange incidents, such as lights, orbs, and shadows, and even the ghost of a small child of undetermined gender.

And while on the subject of haunted gold towns, we would be remiss if we were not to visit Ballarat on the Yarrowee River, roughly 105 kilometres northwest of Melbourne and the state's third most populated inland settlement.

Named by Scottish squatter Archibald Yuille, who established the first settlement in the area in 1837, and derived from the local Wathaurong Aboriginal words for the area, *balla arat*, thought to mean "resting place," it was proclaimed a city in 1871 and is one of the most significant Victorian era boomtowns in Australia. Apart from that, it was also the setting, in December 1854, for the Eureka Rebellion, the only armed rebellion in Australian history. It is also the site of the Eastern Station Hotel, which is reputed to be haunted by a number of ghosts.

Currently being restored to its original 1862 style with added industrial style flourishes, the pub has featured in Ballarat's daily life for over 150 years and will, in time, incorporate original Beechworth Gaol doors, including the one belonging to Ned Kelly's cell and another from the death row cell. It is believed to be haunted by a number of ghosts, including two-year-old James Nunn, who drowned in December 1863 after falling into a waterhole. Subsequently, his body was kept in the hotel cellar until his autopsy and burial. His ghost has been seen in the hotel wearing a brown vest, brown three-quarter-length pants with socks, and a brown pullover hat.

As well, Thomas Hunt, the original owner of the hotel, has been regularly seen standing near the bar and in the cellar, generally wearing a black top hat, and is always preceded and then accompanied by a strong smell of pipe tobacco. And in a quaint tradition, a pint of beer has been left out on the bar's open fire mantelpiece for Hunt's spirit, and it is slowly but surely disappearing—most probably due to evaporation rather than any ghostly drinking. Having said this, manager Christine Crawshaw said she has often gone to serve a customer, only to discover that it was Hunt's ghost and that she often finds the kitchen particularly chilling due to it being the place where the murder of the former soldier took place.

This murder was in fact of an ex-World War I Irish soldier who is now said to haunt the kitchen. He was stabbed in the back by a fellow staff member and love rival, and his spirit, wearing moleskin pants and a pale grandpa shirt, is seen in the kitchen, the original ballroom, and sometimes walking through a wall where a door used to be.

It is believed that an English mother and daughter, Maggie, aged thirty-five, and Sarah, aged twelve, haunt an upstairs room of the pub. They apparently arrived at the Eastern Station Hotel by train straight off the boat where they went to their room and then died from yellow fever, caught on the long journey from England. They are mainly seen in the upstairs hallway and staircase, with Maggie wearing a red dress and Sarah a light brown one. Both have been reported as having long beautiful hair.

And to round it up, the pub also boasts the spirits of two bearded Indigenous caretakers who have been seen around the lower levels of the hotel. One of them is said to be much older than the other, but apart from this, no one really knows much more about them.

And while on the subject of haunted pubs, which we have seen to be fairly commonplace, Craig's Royal Hotel also provides us with a hint of the supernatural.

Located on Lydiard Street in the centre of Ballarat, the hotel opened in 1853 and is your stereotypical gold rush era grand hotel. Over its 150 year history it has played host to poets, princes, and prime ministers, and is a true icon of the Victorian and gold rush period.

Recently refurbished, the hotel is famous for having Dame Nellie Melba sing from the balcony, as well as playing host to such luminaries as Mark Twain, Sir Donald Bradman, and no fewer than seven various royals. However, this is not why we are interested in the place; indeed, we are more interested in its nineteenth-century owner, Walter Craig.

In 1870, Craig was puzzled by a strange dream he had in which he envisioned his horse, ridden by a jockey wearing a black armband, winning the prestigious Melbourne Cup. Sadly for Craig, he died shortly after, but bizarrely, his premonition came true and his horse, ridden by a jockey wearing a black armband in tribute to Craig, won the Melbourne Cup.

These days visitors can have a drink at the hotel and view a portrait of Craig, whose ghost has been seen on a number of occasions, once when a businessman was apparently woken in the dead of night to find the spectral figure of a man in the room, its mouth moving as though trying to speak. Shaken, but not too perturbed, the man managed to get back to sleep. However, once again he was woken. This time a portrait of the same man's face on the wall seemingly had come to life, and again, its mouth was moving noiselessly. Now thoroughly spooked, the man left the room for the night. The portrait, which now hangs in the foyer, was that of Walter Craig, a man who apparently foresaw his own death in a dream.

Nathaniel Buchanan, who runs Ballarat Ghost Tours, says of Craig's ghost: "People have seen the figure of a man in old Victorian garb coming down the corridors. He'll either walk straight through a door or just stand there."

But it's not just pubs that are haunted in this elegant mid-1800s city as, among Ballarat's supposedly haunted buildings, are the St. John's Anglican Church at Soldier's Hill in North Ballarat and the nearby old vicarage where people believe that the spirits of former ministers are responsible for numerous paranormal incidents, including strange apparitions and lights, slamming doors, and eerie footsteps at night.

Canon Denys Tonks, who spent twelve years in the old vicarage, had heard stories of the residence being haunted, but, as a rational-minded person kept an open mind to the subject of ghosts. That is, until he experienced a number late-night disturbances that he could not explain, including "scratching every morning at about three o'clock. It sounded like a crab on the floor."

As well, he and his family experienced otherworldly footsteps, a doorbell that constantly chimed, knocks and rapping, and doors that opened and closed seemingly of their own accord. His children apparently became so annoyed with the disruptions that they demanded he sprinkle holy water around the house in an attempt to stop whatever it was. Surprisingly, after doing this the activity ceased.

Intriguingly, a previous resident reported seeing the ghost of Canon Rigby Johnson Mercer in the vicarage, identifying him by an old photo in church records. Mercer, it was said, was a tireless worker for the church with a strong Protestant work ethic and served as vicar from 1875 to 1892. Tonks now believes that the old vicar was still hanging around when he lived there, and there is some thought that Mercer, who in life requested that a memorial to himself be installed in the church after his death, may have regretted the decision, leading to the poltergeist-like activity that was experienced.

Lake Gardens housing estate, formerly the site of Lakeside Mental Hospital, is also said to be haunted, as is Her Majesty's Theatre, which is reputedly haunted by the spirit of a young actress who, after a bad review, killed herself. Built in 1858, the theatre hosts the ghost of Gloria, who was sixteen years old at the time of her death. She appears in a white evening dress in a side box in the dress circle. She is also associated with disembodied whispers and banging seats.

Bailey's Mansion, another superb Ballarat boom-time building, is said to be haunted by the ghost of gold tycoon William Bailey, which tends to encourage the idea that Ballarat is one of the more haunted places in Victoria.

And yet it's not just Ballarat that has a mortgage on gold rush ghosts and hauntings as the Coaches and Horses Inn at Clarkesville, a simple forty minute or so drive from Melbourne, has a long history of murder, robbery, and shootings and, as a result, is believed to be haunted by a number of ghostly entities.

Built in 1857, the hotel once served as the first Cobb and Co. coaching stop outside Melbourne on the way to the gold fields. The two-storey bluestone building is a lovely example of provincial hotel architecture and the stone construction and the intact nature of the whole site is significant. Sadly there is little left of Clarkesville these days except for the pub.

There have been reported sightings of at least three ghostly presences with the most tragic being that of a ten-year-old autistic girl who was reputedly beaten to death by her father around the turn of the century. According to local folklore the girl witnessed a violent argument between her mother and father where the husband began to savagely beat the wife. The girl tried to intervene, and the father was so incensed that he beat her as well, leading to her death. Fearing retribution, he is supposed to have dumped her body into a well at the back of the hotel and then filled it in with dirt. Later his wife left him and alerted authorities to the murder, but the girl's body was never recovered. It is said that she now haunts the upstairs part of the hotel, knocking on doors and crying. The father, who died soon after, most probably from suicide, is also said to haunt the building, and his presence is often felt in the ladies' toilet and the back dining room.

There is also the ghost of a Chinese man who was either murdered in his room when robbers found that he had struck it rich on the goldfields or, alternatively, committed suicide in the stables. As this hotel was near one of the first Victorian gold fields there are many reports of murders in and around the hotel grounds by thieves who robbed gold miners of their gold.

Visitors and staff have reported hearing footsteps in the hotel in the middle of the night, glasses smashing for no apparent reason, and paintings flying around of their own accord. As well, the ghost of the Irish seaman has been seen running down the stairs, and a woman, who broke her neck when pushed down the staircase, is also said to appear on occasions. Staff has reported shadowy figures, and, in one case, in the women's toilets, a girl reported seeing a ghostly face in a window that rushed towards her.

The Coaches and Horses Inn is not the only haunted pub in Victoria, and as we have seen the country over, pubs seem to be a conduit of all sorts for paranormal activity. And so it is for another elegant bluestone building: the Elephant Bridge Hotel in Darlington, roughly 190 kilometres from Melbourne and built in 1842, which possibly makes it the oldest pub in Victoria. It is said to be haunted by at least four ghosts, including a young woman, a man in his thirties, and another child who drowned on the property. However, it is most famous for the ghost of Adeline Eliza Satchwell, the hotel's longest serving publican, who died in 1943 at the age of eighty-three.

Born in 1861, married twice with ten children, Adeline inherited the pub from her father in 1889 and went on to become Australia's oldest licensee after running the pub for fifty-four years. Her spirit is often reported sitting at a front corner window dressed in turn-of-the-century clothes. To some it appears that she never really left the pub, and her spirit remains keeping a constant watch of her previous business.

A previous owner, Leone de Ferranti, who took over the Elephant Bridge Hotel in 2004, explained how she first encountered Adeline's spirit when she "walked into 'her corner' and she let me know she was here. You know that feeling when you get shivers down the back of your spine? I was pulling the blinds down and I shivered and took two steps back. It was as if she was saying hello, I'm here. I told her (that) I'm just looking after the pub for you."

Perhaps the strangest story about the Elephant Bridge Hotel comes from Geoff Risbey, another former owner who recalled the day that a group of men had an encounter while staying at the pub in May on their way to some horse races. "One of them came back from his room as white as a sheet and said, I can't go in there; there's a ghost in there." Risbey recalled that the man had "walked in and the ghost was standing in the middle of the room crying."

A clairvoyant called to check the hotel later and drew pictures of four ghosts, including one that was identified as Adeline. As de Ferranti stated: "Adeline was quite clearly one and two others were identified, but there was another one that no one knew."

Another reputedly haunted pub is the Criterion Hotel in Rushworth, which was built in 1856. Downstairs the place seems like a regular country pub with a bistro, a few poker machines discreetly tucked away in the corner, an old pool table, and a few stools that hold locals slowly sipping cold beers and talking about horse racing. However, upstairs is a different story, for it is here where the spirits seem to reside.

An old staircase leads to the upstairs section of the hotel where small rooms run off a thin, dark corridor. The floor is wooden and creaks and groans under foot while the rooms are furnished modestly: an old bed, a chest of drawers, and a chair. It is a place where one could begin to believe in ghosts, especially at night. Owner Cath Cornford, who lives in the hotel with husband Phil, says she first noticed strange, unexplainable noises in the building after they moved in explaining that: "There was one night my kids had some friends over and they were all upstairs, and they heard noises in the kitchen that sounded like doors slamming and things being thrown around. They were terrified and thought somebody was up there."

Upon inspecting the kitchen, Cornford found that it was as it should be with everything neatly put away and in its place. What made the noise was no longer there and, as such, she put it down to a supernatural incident saying: "There was no explanation for it, so we put it down to ghosts."

Likewise, legend has it that the ghostly figure of a prostitute used to haunt the cobblestone streets outside the Young & Jackson Hotel in Melbourne's CBD. Situated on the corner of Swanston and Flinders Streets, it is listed on the Victorian Heritage Register and originally opened as the Princes Bridge Hotel in 1861 before, in 1875, being taken over by Irish diggers Henry Young and Thomas Jackson and renamed the Young and Jackson.

The hotel is well known for a nude painting by French artist Jules Joseph Lefebvre in 1875. Painted in oil on canvas and life sized, Chloe was purchased by a Dr. Thomas Fitzgerald and hung in the National Gallery of Victoria for three weeks in 1883 until withdrawn because of its subject. In 1908 it was bought by the hotel and has been exhibited ever since. The model for the painting was a girl by the name of Marie who, sadly two years after the completion of the work, committed suicide by boiling up a poisonous brew and drinking it.

However, it's not the painting that interests us in this case but a legend from the hotel's gold-mining days. And, as the legend goes, outside the hotel late at night, when other establishments have closed, young miners would often see a young prostitute with a pink parasol walking the street. However, as the witness got closer to the woman her face would change, looking older and more haggard until, when close enough to clearly see her features, her skin would be peeling off. Then, terrifyingly, she would pull down her dress revealing a gash across her throat before letting out a horrifying scream and disappearing.

Ross Daniels, the host of Lantern Ghost Tours in Melbourne notes that, although the ghost has not been seen too often, she might have been the spirit of a murdered prostitute and adds that, "unfortunately in those times murdered sex workers would go largely unnoticed, and danger was seen as part of the profession."

Having said that, others believe it to be the ghost of Chloe or possibly the woman who modelled for the painting. However, given that Chloe was fictional and the model Marie, died from poisoning, this is doubtful. Who the ghost is, or was, is a complete mystery.

Not surprisingly, it's not just pubs that are haunted in this part of the city. Queen Victoria Market, built in the late 1800s, was built on the site of the Old Melbourne Cemetery, which contained the bodies of up to 10,000 early Victorian settlers. Having said that, it's hard to imagine the markets being a spooky place, certainly not during the day when crowds of people swarm through the place eager for bargains. At night, however, it's a different story. The silence of the place is all pervading and the old building appears to retain its secrets from long ago. Rumour has it that the ghosts of two long-dead bushrangers haunt the area and others have commented on seeing shadowy, furtive figures amongst the stalls. Still, in 2013 a redevelopment plan for the market had to be changed so that the bodies that lay beneath the building were not disturbed. Maybe this has kept the spirits happy?

Lalor House in Richmond was built in 1888 for a local doctor, Joseph P. Lalor, son of the celebrated Eureka Stockade leader and politician Peter Lalor. The arcaded, two-storey brick and stucco residence and surgery was designed in an original and exaggerated boom classicism style and was, in later years, also the home of Peter Lalor. Born in Ireland and the only outlaw to make it to parliament, he and his wife both died of natural causes in the house at 293 Church Street. However, both his children committed suicide in the house, his daughter jumped to her death off the balcony, and his son, the doctor, hanged himself in the downstairs surgery. The house is now blamed for a number of seemingly strange incidents that have occurred on the property. Indeed, local children are said to cross the road so as not to pass the "haunted house."

The mansion was a boarding house in 1962 when it was purchased by the Morton family. Margaret Morton, who lived there with her family, recalls that her sister, now deceased, claimed to have been grabbed by a ghost when "somebody grabbed her ankle when she was sitting in the hall on a rocker. She reckoned it was her husband having a joke on her, but he said: 'Look, there's no way I could put my hand under a rocking chair.' She also used to hear the tinkle of bells. She wasn't scared; she said it was a friendly ghost."

As previously stated, Melbourne's ghosts almost always seem to focus on the convict or colonial era, the latter being quite understandable given that this was the boom time for this great city. However, this is not always the case as we shall see with our next location, which although not in Melbourne, could be considered part of greater Melbourne itself.

Point Cook was purchased in 1912 by the commonwealth government for the then predecessor of the Royal Australian Air Force (RAAF), the Australian Flying Corps. It was the RAAF's only base until 1925 and is considered to be the spiritual home of the Australian Air Force containing a memorial parade ground that dates from the 1920s. Although it still has an operational airfield, the base now almost solely caters for the RAAF Museum. Significantly, it is the longest continuously operating military airfield in the world.

But history aside, Point Cook is widely regarded as the Air Force's most haunted base with numerous ghost stories having arisen over the years, encompassing most of the heritage buildings in the area.

As with most alleged hauntings, some of the occurrences can easily be explained by old and creaking buildings, rusted or partially blocked plumbing, worn door hinges and locks, animals, and other perfectly normal events that would occur in any old buildings or sites. And yet some occurrences cannot be so easily explained. For instance, a heater sealed behind a false display wall in the museum once, for no apparent reason, turned itself on. Comically, it was reported that staff literally had to demolish the wall to turn it off before it burnt the place to the ground.

In addition, staff at the museum have complained that reference books often move around and are found in places where they shouldn't be, something that is perfectly explainable in a university or school library, but totally inexplicable within a military environment. And yet as interesting as this is, it is other more frightening stories that command attention.

On one occasion, in 1989, a RAAF fireman was asleep in the twenty-four-hour manned fire station when he felt unseen hands pushing on his legs and shoulders. Although fit and strong, the fireman was unable to raise himself from the bed. After this happened two more times he understandably refused to work the night shift any longer. Others at the fire section have reported objects moving or going missing, doors mysteriously opening and closing apparently of their own accord, rattling cups, and footsteps on wooden floor boards. Apart from that some claim to have heard distinct voices that have come from no apparent source.

A RAAF dog handler also may have come across one of Point Cook's ghostly residents one night when he challenged a figure in uniform walking through the base. While the guard dog barked incessantly the figure appeared not to notice and simply continued on its way, disappearing in front of the disbelieving guard's eyes. Add to this a dim ghostly figure that has been seen hanging from the now demolished air control tower, and you have all the ingredients for a truly haunted site.

Do the ghosts of long-dead airmen haunt these old hangars and grounds where they once worked and lived? Have the spirits of airmen killed overseas in the combat of two world wars returned to where they learned their trade? And if so, then one must ask why? And how? Can ghosts find their way back to a place even though their earthly bodies may have died elsewhere? Or is it possible that these spirits remained as a collective but intense memory long after the living people had departed. After all, a military base will always be a place full of sad memories and tragic reminders of the futileness of war. Who is to say that the place itself, the very site, cannot retain these memories, emotions, and feelings?

But what are we to make of these hauntings? Not surprisingly servicemen and women are not the types to be easily spooked, nor to make up fanciful stories of unnatural occurrences. And yet these airmen and women, and officers, are adamant that something strange is afoot in this historic airbase.

But if Point Cook is haunted, then why not other sites where military accidents have happened? In August 1962, four RAAF Vampire jet trainer aircraft crashed near RAAF Base East Sale killing six air crew. They had been practicing for a RAAF Open Day display, and all four aircraft struck the ground almost simultaneously in the final stages of completing a low-level barrel roll. The oval at RAAF East Sale is now named after Peter Hearnden, apparently a brilliant sportsman and one of those killed.

Is the site of this tragic accident haunted? And if not, then why not as it has all the hallmarks of what would be considered a classic haunting. For instance, the Air Disaster Memorial in Canberra where, in August 1940, a Lockheed Hudson bomber crashed into the mountain killing three cabinet ministers, the chief of the General Staff, and another six RAAF crew members, is considered exceptionally haunted.

RAAF East Sale sits just south of the Gippsland city of Sale. It is a pretty place for a military base, surrounded by creeks, canals, trees, and miles and miles of farmland and lakes. It also has old buildings dating back to around the Second World War, air raid shelters, and a large water-filled pit that was reputed to have the remains of a Hudson bomber laying in its depths. But as pretty as it is, in the dead of night it can be a bleak, spooky place with a thick fog shrouding dim street lights.

During the Second World War, RAAF East Sale was a bomber training base and many airmen based there died in horrific aircraft crashes. Most met their end in the icy depths of the numerous lakes in the region. Others died on the runway that stretches out like a black ribbon into the distant grassy fields.

How many of these lost souls still fly over the base searching in vain for the airstrip, fated to fly endless figure-eight patterns as they wait for the signal to land, something that can never happen? How many spirits still wait on the ground, searching the skies for long-departed loved ones, now dead in icy lakes?

But whereas this RAAF base doesn't appear to be as haunted as one would expect, where else in the state can we travel to find more evidence of this supposed supernatural world?

Overnewton Castle in Keilor was built by William Taylor in 1849 and is a miniature Scottish Baronial Castle complete with rough textured masonry, steeped pitched roofs, and overhanging battlement corner turrets. Inspired by sixteenth-century English and Scottish architecture, the homestead consists of over thirty-five rooms and outbuildings, including a dairy, lamp room, a coachhouse, stables, woolshed, shearing sheds, and a machine shed. It also has a reputation of being haunted.

Local folklore suggests that a fifteen-year-old boy once died in the house after tripping and falling down the stairs, breaking his neck. Apparently the dead boy attended a school that was opposite the castle and was visiting a library on the top floor. Since then other children have continually reported seeing a boy standing at the top of the spiral staircase, and this event actually led to the school ceasing using it as a library.

A number of witnesses have reported this phenomena, and it is also said that the main gate closes itself and lights flash on and off when the place is empty. As well, passersby often report seeing apparitions in the windows of the upper reaches of the building. These days the place is a functions centre and hosts numerous weddings; however, the spiral staircase, it seems, is now off limits to everyone.

Methodist Ladies' College, which was founded in 1882 as a "modern school of the first order," is in Kew in the eastern suburbs of Melbourne. A wonderful ivy-covered building with a neo-Gothic tower, it is reputed to be haunted by the ghost of a former student, Nellie Fitchett, who died of meningitis in December 1897.

The youngest daughter of the school's founding principal, the Reverend Dr. William Henry Fitchett, she was only eighteen months old when her father became principal in 1882. At school she excelled as a student, sportswoman, and pianist and, in 1896, achieved top ranking among the piano students, as well as receiving the school's senior tennis prize. A well-liked and friendly girl, her death greatly affected the students and staff at the school.

A number of students these days claim to have seen her ghost wandering the corridors of the school or standing outside her former room. Is it possible that this spirit, so loved by everyone at the time, is unable to move from the place she lived and loved all her life?

Whatever the case, a stained glass window on the east wall of Fitchett Hall was given to the school by Rev. Dr. Fitchett to honour her memory. The window depicts a young woman with a book in one hand and an uplifted torch in the other, symbolising knowledge. As such, however you choose to see the story, Nellie Fitchett will forever remain immortalised at the school, as a ghost or otherwise.

The Milanos Restaurant first opened in the 1840s as the Royal Terminus Hotel and is one of Brighton's oldest landmarks, offering spectacular views across Port Phillip Bay. And it is another place apparently haunted by the ghost of a young girl who allegedly was raped and murdered by the original owners, and although details are scant, it appears that she is hostile towards males, something that is not unheard of as, at the Red Lion in Avebury in England, the resident ghost, Florie, is said to target men with beards.

It is said that Florie lived in the building in the 1600s during the Civil War. When her husband, a soldier went off to fight, she took up a lover. However, unbeknown to the two, the husband unexpectedly returned and in a fit of rage shot the lover dead before stabbing his wife to death after which he threw her body down the village well. What happened to the shot lover is unrecorded. Maybe he is now one of the nondescript ghosts that wander the corridors of the pub.

The well is now a part of the pub, indeed, it now has a glass top and serves as a table. However, Florie's ghost has reputedly been seen on numerous occasions rising from the well or, surprisingly, in the ladies' toilets. Salt and pepper shakers are said to be thrown across the room and men with beards hit with flying objects in scenes similar to poltergeist activity.

Likewise, the Arts Library within the State Library of Victoria is reputed to be haunted by a ghost that has been described as a female dressed in white clothing from the nineteenth century. Recently some night-shift workers heard a note struck on a piano and stated that they saw a shadowy figure in the Arts Library. A security guard saw a chandelier in the same area swinging one night, even though all the windows were closed and there was no one in the room.

The State Library of Victoria was established in 1854 and holds over two million books and 16,000 serials, as well as housing the original armour of Ned

Kelly. It is a magnificent building with some of the city's most beautiful heritage interiors, including a majestic domed ceiling over the La Trobe Reading Room. Situated in the Melbourne CBD and not far from the Old Melbourne Gaol, it is rumoured to be haunted by up to twenty different ghosts.

Drew Sinton, owner of the Haunted Bookshop runs Melbourne's oldest ghost tours and has long been fascinated by ghosts and the supernatural. After spending six months researching the history of the State Library he is convinced it is haunted and includes a woman in white who patrols the children's book section, as well as a ghostly woman in a red dress.

Linda McConnell, who worked as a trainee library technician at the State Library in 1977 recalled how she would go "every afternoon with my slips in my hand up the scary spiral staircase and into the stacks. As I remember it each row had its own light, which you had to turn on and then off. Once you had turned off one light it was fairly dark, and on a winter's afternoon it was a spooky place. I never saw the ghost that some of my older colleagues insisted lived up there, but given the atmosphere I could well believe there was one."

Although McConnell never experienced the ghosts of the place, others have regularly reported strange figures and activity, including a ghostly librarian and small child who have been seen in the oldest part of the library, Queens Hall. Interestingly, although there have been no recorded deaths at the library itself, it is opposite the emergency rooms of the old Queen Victoria Hospital and some have theorised that the ghosts seen in the library may have drifted across from the now demolished hospital.

Previously we looked at the Old Melbourne Gaol and its numerous ghosts; however, we have thus far neglected to look at another important gaol in the Melbourne area: the infamous Pentridge Prison in Coburg, a place that was home to Australia's hardest and longest-serving prisoners, including Chopper Read and Squizzy Taylor, as well as being the site of the very last state sanctioned execution in Australia's history, that of Ronald Ryan in January 1967.

Built in 1850, the prison first saw prisoners in the following year and continued to be operational until May 1997. Colloquially known as "The Bluestone College" or the "Coburg College," it has now been partly demolished to make way for a housing development. The grave site of Ned Kelly was formerly within the walls of the prison even though he was hanged at the Old Melbourne Gaol in 1880 and his remains moved to Pentridge Prison in 1929. In 2011, his remains were once again exhumed and returned to his surviving descendants for a proper family burial. In all, forty-four burials took place within the bluestone walls.

The prison was the site of eleven executions, including, as we have seen, that of Ronald Ryan, who was executed after being convicted of the shooting death of a prison officer during a botched escape from the same prison. And with a history as such, it is not surprising that many believe it to be haunted.

The building itself is a dark and foreboding place with imposing grey walls and parapeted guard towers that look down upon the yards in which the prisoners exercised. Dozens of prison wardens have reported seeing a fog that looks like a woman's form, and more recently a security guard was patrolling with his dog and noticed a silhouette. When he approached the ghostly figure, the dog recoiled and whimpered. Others have reported unexplained noises, cold spots, and drafts. And yet, this is not the strangest of reports coming from this grim place.

Mark "Chopper" Read died in 2013 at the age of fifty-three and spent most of his adult life behind bars, including a stint at Pentridge. It is believed that his ghost now haunts the cell he used to stay in. According to witnesses, the large figure of a man has been seen with arms crossed, leaning against a wall, sometimes smoking a cigarette and watching silently as visitors pass by. It then disappears into Cell 16, Read's old cell.

Recently, a ghost tour guide, Jeremy Kewley, was leading the group of lawyers around the forbidding historic prison when they heard the loud yell of a man near Read's cell in D-Division of the prison. Startled, the group initially thought it was a prank until, according to Kewley, "Suddenly came this incredibly loud and aggressive male voice basically screaming 'get out!'"

The group, thoroughly spooked, apparently froze as the voice continued to yell. The cell at the time was deserted and a later police search of the area found no one and could not determine where the angry-sounding voice had come from. Kewley is adamant that the voice was that of Read.

As we have seen, hauntings are not always limited to buildings and sometimes appear to be attached to objects or artefacts, including, it would seem, pieces of furniture or decorations. And so it is for the historical Black Rock House, which was built in 1856 as a holiday house for Victoria's first Auditor-General Charles Hotson Ebden.

Black Rock House is a unique property consisting of a T-shaped brick-and-timber house with a cellar and joined by a covered walkway to a castellated stone courtyard and stables. Over the years the house has been used as a guest house, a private residence, and was for a decade converted into four flats, and while it does not appear to have a particularly nasty past, it does seem to be haunted by a number of spirits.

Carolyn Brown, president of the Friends of Black Rock House, has indicated that two vigils held by ghost-hunter groups had identified twelve distinct spirits who either had connections to the house or to items of furniture, such as the piano stool, and that she believed they were friendly and "not restricted to a certain period of time either."

Brown suggests that a person who died in a recent crash on Beach Road, where the house is located, made contact with the group one night during a vigil. In addition, she noted that there "has been a sighting of someone falling off the roof and as it turned out, there was a viewing tower up there." And that:

"There was a group of people seen fighting under the fig tree and it transpired that it had once been the site of an illegal fist fight."

David Dodds, also from the Friends of Black Rock House, said that visitors to the house were often unnerved, and that some "have had some strange experiences, like seeing shadows and feeling things moving."

And so it is for another mid-1800s building, the Altona Homestead, built by Alfred and Sarah Langhorne as their principal place of residence and the first homestead built on the foreshore of Port Phillip Bay. It is said to be haunted by the ghost of Edward John Goodson, a homeless man also known as the Cat Man, who was found murdered at the front of the property in 1909. He was nicknamed the "Cat Man" because he spent a lot of time catching fish and keeping them, even after long dead, which attracted cats. Ross Daniels of Lantern Ghost Tours explained that people say that "when you sit down on the toilet outside the homestead, people feel like a cat is stroking their feet. It's the Cat Man. They say his ghost haunts the park area of the homestead."

But this is not the only strange happening witnessed by Daniels as one time, when he was taking a group of people on a tour, a tea trolley started to rattle and shake and, according to him, "moved about a metre. Then it moved a metre back. Part of me wants to think there is a logical explanation, but there is another part of me thinking it's strange it has rolled by itself."

The homestead is thought to be haunted by at least eleven ghosts, one of these being the original owner Sarah Langhorne. She married Alfred at the young age of sixteen and lived a lonely life at the then remote homestead. People have reported her walking past the veranda and peering in the window. In addition, it is believed that she interferes with the building's alarm system, setting it off at strange hours of the night. Other strange incidents include the drawers of a heavy wooden chest being found open, even though no one was in the room at the time, and a security guard who once reported seeing a woman in old-fashioned clothes standing in a window.

Of course, not all ghosts are benign and, as we have also seen, Victoria appears to have a large number of haunted former mental hospitals. And so it is with Larundel Hospital on Plenty Road in Bundoora.

First conceived in 1938 by the Victoria State Government to replace the aging Kew Mental Hospital, Larundel's construction phase was stalled by the outbreak of World War II. By 1946, however, it was given to the Victorian Department of Housing for emergency accommodation, and the wards were hastily converted to flats. The site continued as housing until 1949 when patients from Beechworth Lunatic Asylum were introduced. Then, in 1953, it was officially declared a metal hospital. At this stage, it had just under 400 patients, and this capacity was increased further with an additional two wards being added over the next couple of years.

Larundel continued to operate until the late 1990s when the government moved away from institutionalised care of patients and instead tried to integrate them back into society. The remaining buildings soon became derelict and vandalised with no access to the general public.

Today it is to be redeveloped although, for the past fifteen or so years, the building has been of interest to paranormal groups who have illegally entered the property in search of evidence of the supernatural. People who have explored the building have reported loud banging on the walls, odd smells, and the sound of crying children. As well, it is rumoured that a young girl who had a particular love for a music box that she owned, died on the third floor and that some have heard the distinct chimes of the music box.

There are numerous stories of supernatural phenomena occurring within the walls of the rundown old building and the complex itself is vast and spooky enough to scare the most intrepid of explorers, even without ghosts and unexplained manifestations. Could it be that Larundel is haunted, or is it simply the eeriness of the site that scares us? And as such, do we create the ghosts in our own minds through a heightened sense of suggestion and awareness whereby a breath of wind becomes the touch of a ghostly hand, and the vague scratching of a mouse take on a more sinister tone?

Maybe we will never know; however, our next destination is a place where one can truly believe in ghosts and, if we were to be honest, it could rightly call itself the most haunted place in Australia. However, to get there, first we must travel across the treacherous waters of Bass Strait.

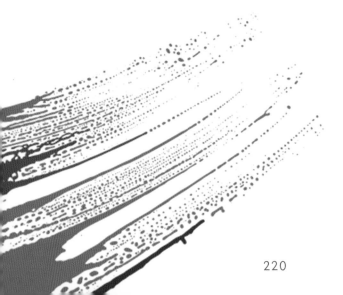

CHAPTER EIGHT

Tasmania

Hell on Earth, a Haunted Bridge, and a Gibbetted Bushranger

Tasmania, previously known as Van Diemen's Land, was first settled as a part of the British colony in 1803, only fifteen years after the arrival of the first fleet on the shores of mainland Australia. And like those in early Sydney, the early arrivals to Tasmanian shores were predominantly convicts and their guards and were tasked with developing agriculture and other industries on the island. Resistance by local Indigenous people was fierce, and death and injury were commonplace.

The first reported sighting of the island by a European was in November 1642 by the Dutch explorer Abel Tasman. He named this densely wooded island Anthoonij van Diemenslandt, after his sponsor, the governor of the Dutch East Indies. In time, however, it was shortened to Van Diemen's Land by the British.

The first settlement was at Risdon Cove on the eastern bank of the Derwent estuary by a small party from Sydney under the command of a Lieutenant John Bowen. In 1804, another settlement was soon established by Captain David Collins some five kilometres to the south at Sullivans Cove on the western side of the Derwent due to a plentiful supply of fresh water. This settlement was later to become what we now know as Hobart.

Named after the British colonial secretary of the time, Lord Hobart, the city was known for its convict past and is the second oldest Australian city. Indeed, a historian once wrote of Hobart: "Such a hard and inhospitable place inevitably attracted a certain kind of person. By the 1820s, the flotsam and jetsam of the world, men seeking refuge from the law or seeking isolation from other human beings, has been drawn to the shores of the island. Some of the men came as convicts and were emancipated, some came as convicts and fled into the bush, and some walked off boats and ships in Hobart Town or Launceston and became sealers, whalers, farm hands, or drifters. They were rough frontiersmen. Not frontiersmen in the sense of opening up new land, frontiersmen in the sense that they despoiled and exploited everything and everyone they saw."

These days Hobart is widely recognised as one of Australia's most beautiful cities with its idyllic location on the Derwent River and its distinctive old world charm consisting of its docklands and port and historic buildings. In his book *Following the Equator*, Mark Twain wrote: "How beautiful is the whole region, for form, and grouping, and opulence, and freshness of foliage, and variety of colour, and grace and shapeliness of the hills, the capes, the promontories; and then, the splendour of the sunlight, the dim, rich distances, the charm of the water-glimpses!"

However, beauty or not, Hobart's convict past, much like Sydney, has a grim and cruel penal past, and a long history of ghosts and haunted buildings.

The Theatre Royal, on Campbell Street is Australia's oldest continually operating theatre and is said to have been haunted for many years by the ghost of a deceased actor and stagehand called Fred, who is often seen both backstage and in the audience. In 1984, a fire started after hours in the empty theatre and amazingly the fire curtain was mysteriously lowered, dowsing the flames and saving the theatre from burning down. Many believe it was Fred's ghost who lowered the curtain and saved the theatre.

Although there is some doubt as to Fred's real identity, some believe he was a sailor who was stabbed to death by a prostitute; there is little doubt in the local theatre community that he exists. One night, a wardrobe mistress was working late one night on stage when she suddenly felt afraid, as if she was being watched. Although the theatre was securely locked and nobody could get in, she distinctly felt as if someone was in there with her. She then felt a chill and looking up, saw a young man walk through the doors at the back of the room while singing. He walked up an isle and sat in a chair then simply disappeared. The wardrobe mistress fled but in hindsight realised that she had witnessed Fred's ghost. Another to have witnessed his ghost is none other than Australian actress Jacki Weaver, famous for her roles in movies such as *Picnic at Hanging Rock* and *Caddie.*

Only a short walk from the Theatre Royal is Her Majesty's Gaol Hobart or the Campbell Street Gaol. Built by convict labour, the gaol operated between 1821 until the early 1960s and housed both males and females. Now managed by the National Trust of Australia (Tasmania) as a historic site known as the Penitentiary Chapel historic site, it has long been considered haunted.

The chapel building, which remains at the site, was once part of the Hobart Penitentiary even though the prison walls were demolished long ago. A T-shaped structure, it was designed so that free settlers and convicts could share the same church but sit in different wings. Over time, two of the three wings were converted into court rooms where a number of prisoners received death sentences.

Staff and visitors at the site have long been aware of what appears to be the spirit of a woman, and she is commonly referred to by staff as Ivy, although research suggests that her name may have been Sarah. And, as is the case with a number of hauntings, she is more often smelt than seen, manifesting as a subtle hint of lavender perfume that drifts through parts of the building. As well as the faint lingering scent of perfume, she is also believed to open and close doors, and some have reported hearing the sound of a dress swishing in the hallways. Whatever the case, her presence is generally regarded as benign;

although, in one room, called Ivy's Room, which now houses display cases of historic artefacts and a couch, a woman resting on the antique couch was once told by an angry disembodied female voice to "get out!"

It would seem, however, that not all ghosts are sweet smelling and benign. The Drunken Admiral on the waterfront on Hunter Street is better known for its seafood than its resident ghosts with a mysterious death from the nineteenth century seemingly having inflicted the restaurant with a bad tempered entity.

Constructed in 1824, the building is one of the oldest in Tasmania and has been used in the past as a granary, army barracks, annex to a jam factory, and a warehouse before being converted into a restaurant. Local legend has it that a Chinese man was once found hanged in the courtyard behind the building in the 1880s, and although thoroughly investigated, no one is sure whether he was murdered or committed suicide.

In the years since, there have been several sightings of a ghostly Chinese man who walks through the courtyard before vanishing into a wall. Interestingly, and quite scarily, this wall is the back of the restaurant's toilets, which has led to some chilling moments for those using the ladies' restroom. Indeed, women using the toilet have occasionally reported the sensation of someone trying to strangle them, almost as if they have a rope around their necks.

Owner Craig Godfrey, in an interview on ABC radio in 2006 commented that: "This would have to be the most haunted toilet in Hobart. We've had customers on several occasions, women, run from this bathroom, completely upset. They've come in here, they've been minding their own business, they've sat here, they've been asphyxiated. They've had this horrible strangling feeling around their neck. And we do know that a Chinaman was found hanging in the 1880s in the back courtyard here. As recently as 1960 someone saw an apparition of a Chinaman drifting across the courtyard. So he seems to hang out in this toilet, and only the ladies' toilet, and it can't be ignored."

In addition, the restaurant has seen glasses exploding in patron's hands and bottles of wine mysteriously sliding off shelves and smashing on the bar floor. Godfrey also recalls a time when "we had a customer sitting on table 23, just sitting there minding their own business; her partner had gone to the loo and the ice bucket just mysteriously slid along the counter, right in front of her; it just moved for several inches."

Elsewhere in Hobart is Kodak House in the Elizabeth Street Mall. It is a narrow five-storey building with a crenelated parapet and bay windows on the upper storey. The ghost of a female named Beryl is said to haunt the top two stories of the building, although, on occasions, she is said to come down to other floors where she knocks over displays. Over the years many visitors and staff have glimpsed her ghost.

But as haunted as Hobart appears to be, our next destination probably has the right to call itself the most haunted place in Australia, and to be honest, it's probably up there with the most haunted places in the world.

Port Arthur was a convict settlement that began life as a sleepy timber station in 1830 but soon developed into one of the most, if not the most, important convict prison within the penal system of the colonies. By 1848, the first stones of a separate prison were laid, which bought about a shift in punishment philosophy of the time, that from physical to mental subjugation. By 1857, an old flour mill and granary were converted into a penitentiary, and in 1864, an asylum added. Indeed, one of Australia's great novels *For the Term of His Natural Life* was partly based on the convict experience at Port Arthur.

Port Arthur was renowned for its harsh conditions. Many convicts died, and many went insane. By the time the penitentiary closed in the 1870s, the remaining convicts were too old, too infirm, or too insane to be of any use to anyone, and they presumably stayed there until their deaths. It was described by the men who lived and worked there as hell on earth.

It is not surprising that the place is considered Australia's most haunted site. Most of the buildings have a history of ghosts and supernatural activity with some stories going back as far as 1870. It is said that, since the prison's closure in 1877, there have been over 2,000 accounts of ghost sightings and hauntings within the historical precinct.

In 2004, I visited the site with my partner, Kirsten. Today, it is a thriving tourist destination and its superb ruins and colonial-style houses and buildings are wonderful to see and explore, even if one has no interest in the paranormal. However, as this is a subject that has intrigued me for decades, I booked us on the Port Arthur Ghost Tour.

So far in this book we have looked at a number of ghost tours around the country, and although I tend to view ghost tours more as entertainment than actual research, I cannot say the same for Port Arthur.

And so that night, as a group of tourists milled around the visitors' centre watching videos and buying tourist books, our guide introduced himself. He was a tall, gaunt man with long black hair, a large black coat, and an impeccable speaking voice by the name of Todd Darling. We followed him outside while he regaled us with stories of disembodied heads, voices from no-where, apparitions that have appeared to people, mysterious lights, odd thumping sounds, and possibly the most frightening of all, people having their hair pulled, or being shoved in the back, or being touched by unseen hands.

As we stood outside the visitors' centre in the drizzle on this dark night, Todd mused out loud. "You have to wonder how it is that people who don't know each other and don't know about this place have seen the same thing ten years apart." Indeed. How could so many people with no previous knowledge of Port Arthur and its ghostly ways continue to report the exact same ghostly events, even though the events may have happened years apart?

He then went on to explain that he has worked at Port Arthur for five years, has conducted nearly 1,000 tours, and that in that time he's seen three ghosts and had about a dozen strange occurrences. As we wandered out into the gloomy night to visit the actual buildings, no one doubted his word.

We visited the parsonage, which was the Reverend's house when the place was a prison. It is thought to have as many as seven different ghosts, the most famous of which is the Reverend George Eastman who died in an upstairs bedroom in the mid-1800s. Apparently, the ghostly activity began soon after his death. Darling suggested that this building was probably the most haunted on the whole site and that Eastman, apparently a huge and obese man known for his loud and frightening sermons, has been seen in the upstairs windows of the old building.

Visitors since the 1800s have reported a range of strange phenomena in the house, including the smell of rotting flesh, strange lights, moaning noises, and ghostly apparitions. In one case, a woman in a blue period dress was seen wandering the building. Darling, in an ABC interview with George Negus in 2004 suggested that the lady in blue "is a young woman, probably a teenager," and that "she died in childbirth and so she's often very sad, she's often crying, and sometimes she talks to kids."

Interestingly, while at university studying cultural heritage, my lecturer, who was the heritage supervisor during the restoration of the Port Arthur site, once told the class an interesting story regarding the parsonage and its heritage restoration. According to him, in the 1980s, a group of tradesmen staying in the parsonage while doing renovations were driven from the building after a terrifying night of strange and seemingly supernatural events, including unexplained bangs and bumps and one tradesman being pinned down on his bed by an invisible entity. Another worker reported seeing a woman dressed in white who was accompanied by a sudden drop in temperature and billowing curtains.

But stories like the previous are not new to Port Arthur as the history of ghostly sightings goes back to the late 1800s when the writer George Gruncell wrote about a number of strange events that occurred at the parsonage in the 1870s. According to his account, the Hayward family were visiting Melbourne while the Reverend Hayward returned to Port Arthur, leaving his family to follow. One night after his return, the doctor at the settlement saw lights in the upstairs rooms and quite rightly assumed that the parson's wife and children had returned. When he went to welcome them home he found the house only occupied by Hayward and a servant who swore that they had not been upstairs. The rooms were then checked, but no one was found. Others at the settlement who saw the lights, also presumed that the family had returned.

But it's not just the parsonage that is haunted in this isolated corner of the state as the commandant's cottage, the separate (model) prison, visiting magistrates house, and the chapel all have their own ghosts and ghostly incidents. At the chapel my partner, Kirsten, took a photo and, although the digital camera had been functioning perfectly while we had travelled around Tasmania, it came out blurred and with a strange flash of light running across the frame. Sadly, at the time of writing, I cannot locate this photograph.

After a while we left the chapel, and I looked back at the dark opening in the ruined buildings' tower. For a second I imagined that I saw a flash of light. Could it be that I had just seen a ghost? Or had the experience influenced my mind in a way that conditioned me to see something? I asked Kirsten, who said that she thought she saw something as well but could not be sure. Maybe the atmosphere caused us both to think we saw something odd in the darkness?

We walked along a winding gravel path towards the surgeon's house, a place reputed to house the ghost of a man who delighted in cutting up convicts for research. I was definitely more apprehensive, and the house loomed out of the dark with a seemingly menacing feeling. The atmosphere had become quite heavy and gloomy and almost threatening in an unexplainable way. The house also had a reputation for ghostly faces popping out of a hole in the wall, only to disappear moments later. This hole was where the servants use to scrape the ashes from the fireplace down into the dissection room to soak up the blood.

In the surgeon's house our guide told us more stories of ghostly encounters and the group looked nervously around the room. It was dark, cold, and eerie and I felt slightly sick. I made sure that my back was not towards a window or a door as I was not taking any chances, except it then occurred to me that we were talking about ghosts and ghosts usually don't worry about insignificant things like doors, windows, or walls.

Apparitions have also been reported in the junior medical officer's residence. Originally built in 1848 for the Commissariat Officer Thomas J. Lempriere, it is believed ghostly children are responsible for footsteps, moving furniture, and rattling windows. Darling, in his ABC interview, relates how the floors in the junior medical officer's house "were re-sanded and revarnished. The builders closed the doors behind them that night, and the next morning they came back and in front of the fireplace they found some imprints of footprints. No one had been in the house, and yet we see a large adult footprint right there, a harder to see one, a child's footprint in front of it." As well, a ghost investigation team once sprinkled flour in the attic of the building and left it overnight hoping for some sign of disturbance. In the morning they were astounded to find barefoot marks across the floor, those of a child.

The commandant's house, originally built as a simple wooden cottage, is now a substantial structure befitting the rank of the Port Arthur's most senior official and was erected on high ground on the fringe of settlement in 1833. It has commanding views over the rest of the settlement and evolved over the years to become a many-roomed complex fringed by ornate gardens and pathways and was separated from the rest of the settlement by high brick walls. Later in its life it also served as hotel and a guest house, which operated until the 1930s.

Inside the building sits a rocking chair known as the "Nanny Chair," which some believe is haunted. Witnesses have reported seeing it rock on its own, and others who have sat on the chair have reported being touched by invisible hands. And, as for much of the site, often those who try to photograph the chair experience equipment failure. Sadly, when I visited the building there was nothing amiss to report; however, one could say that the room felt somewhat "charged" as if there was someone else in there, someone unseen.

However, for sheer terror, the separate (model) prison stands alone. In this gloomy sandstone building visitors have heard the screams of a ghostly boy and dark, ghostly figures have been seen skulking by cell doorways. Mysterious lights have been spotted in the dark cells where prisoners used to be confined for long periods of time in total darkness and silence. Such was the cruelty and isolation of Port Arthur, prisoners often committed suicide and such was the case for William Carter, who committed suicide by hanging. These days people report feeling anxious or depressed when alone in his former cell.

Many years after visiting Port Arthur, I was talking to a friend when he casually mentioned that he did not believe in ghosts until he'd visited Port Arthur. Like me, he had entered one of the small cells in the model prison. According to him, the day was warm and sunny, and yet the prison cell, in his own words, was "freezing, icy cold," and not only that, something pushed him in the chest. The cell was later pointed out to be one where Carter committed suicide.

Apart from this, it is quite literally spine-tingling as the prison is a large building with one wide corridor that stretches into the darkness. From this corridor, dark recesses run into small, dank prison cells. The air is still and heavy and the night almost completely silent. It feels as if someone is standing right behind you, but when you turn to look, there is nothing but endless darkness stretching off into the distance. Standing in the gloom only lit by lanterns a person could easily believe in ghosts.

As we stand there in the darkness Darling recalled a time when he had been in the building alone late one night after a tour. After locking a door at one end, he'd proceeded to walk down the corridor when he heard footsteps following him. He stopped and looked around but saw nothing, noting that the footsteps had also stopped. Feeling somewhat apprehensive, he continued on—as did the footsteps, which were apparently getting louder and closer. Quickening his pace he realised that the footsteps did the same. Slightly panicking he ran to the nearest exit and went outside. The footsteps stopped. The night was quiet except for the beating of his heart.

Interestingly, while listening to the story, I became aware of a creaking noise behind me. At first I was not sure what it was until, suddenly it became clear: the creaking noise was footsteps on the wooden stairs that led to the chapel. They became louder and sounded as if they were coming down the stairs towards us. I glanced at the stairs but saw nothing. A few other people also looked nervously that way. By now I'd had enough of this place. It was frightening, gloomy, and intense with an atmosphere of complete despair and hopelessness. I was literally terrified. We exited the building and headed back to the visitors' centre.

Later, I asked Kirsten about the footsteps and she confirmed that she'd also heard them. I also asked the others in our group and they too confirmed the sounds. Is it possible we were lucky enough to hear the footsteps of one of Port Arthur's many ghosts? Or was it simply a heightened sense of awareness brought on by the environment? Who can say; however, if I were to pick one reason, it would be the former.

Given its grisly past, not just the buildings at Port Arthur that are haunted as people have reported seeing the figure of a man with straight black hair and wearing a ruffled white shirt on the jetty as well as sitting on the front steps of the commandant's cottage. This apparition, which once appeared at the foot of a guest's bed, is believed to be Private Robert Young, who drowned near the jetty in 1840.

About a kilometre off shore and accessible via a ferry, is the Isle of the Dead, an uninhabited and eerie place that was used as the cemetery for the convict settlement from 1830 to 1877. It is believed that 1,769 prisoners were buried here as well as 180 free people, and was the home of the resident gravedigger Mark Jeffrey, an Irish convict serving a sentence for manslaughter who lived in a small hut on the island.

It is reported that, one mid-week morning, authorities spotted a signal fire from the island and sent a boat over to investigate. When they arrived, they found Jeffrey in a severely distressed condition, begging to be taken off the island. He told them that the previous night his hut had been shaken and rocked by an invisible force, and a red glow had lit up the walls and surrounding ground. When he went to investigate, he was confronted by His Satanic Majesty, complete with smouldering eyes, erect horns, and encircled by sulphurous smoke.

Not surprisingly, no one took his experience seriously, but visitors have felt an oppressive atmosphere on the Island of the Dead, and I can confirm it is an eerie place to visit—which is not surprising considering how many people are buried there.

Sadly, and tragically, I must add that on April 28, 1996, the small community was devastated when a lone gunman opened fire at the site and at other nearby places killing thirty-five people and wounding thirty-seven others. The site of their memorial is a poignant reminder that we have far more to fear from the living than we do the dead.

But if Port Arthur is widely regarded as Tasmania's most haunted place, what of other parts of the state?

In the 1990s, in Perth, roughly 20 kilometres south of Launceston and first major town out of Launceston on the route to Hobart, a family suffered what appeared to be an attack by a ghostly entity shrouded in white mist. Perth itself, one must realise, is a historic town with many buildings dating back to the early 1800s.

In his book *Haunted: The Book of Australian Ghosts*, John Pinkney recalls a story relayed to him by Michelle Wilkins, whose family endured the attacks.

According to Wilkins, her mother came to breakfast one morning looking pale and ill and, after some coaxing, revealed that the previous night she had "woken up feeling bitterly cold. Just as she was getting up to find an extra blanket, she saw a man, surrounded by a white fog standing in the corner of the bedroom."

Apparently, she'd tried to scream but found that she couldn't make a sound. Then as she stood there in horror watching the figure, she realised that only half of the man was visible. Then he started fading away and the temperature returned to normal. However, this prompted Wilkins' fifteen-year-old brother to admit that he too had seen the ghost and that it was gleaming white and had been sitting on the end of his bed. He also recalled feeling paralysed, and that he was horrified to see that it had no facial features.

But things were to get worse for Wilkins as, a few days later, the apparition began to visit her room. She recalled that "I saw nothing at first, but I'd be woken by something invisible jumping on my bed. Then I'd feel a series of stinging slaps on my cheeks. One night I opened my eyes to find a ball of bright light floating in my room. As I lay there trying to work out what it could be, my blankets were ripped off and dumped on the floor."

Fortunately for the family, the attacks and sightings soon petered out. Two weeks later, a neighbour informed them that an elderly man had died in the house, and that his grieving widow had kept the body for a week before informing authorities. The room in which the dead man laid was Wilkins' bedroom.

Interestingly, in 1837, five years after the practice ceased in England, the body of John McKay was gibbetted near the spot where he murdered Joseph Wilson, just outside the town of Perth. *Gibbetting* was a particularly cruel and horrid punishment where the dead or dying body of an executed criminal was hanged on a gallows-like structure on public display so as to deter other potential criminals. Not surprising, there was a great outcry, but the body was not removed until an acquaintance of Wilson saw his decaying body and pleaded with the authorities to remove it.

Today, McKay's ghost is said to haunt the site where his body was so brutally displayed and, as if to be a reminder of the past, the place where McKay's body hung is now called Gibbet Hill.

Garth Homestead in the Fingal Valley in the state's northeast is known for its tales of tragedy and death. Located along the Esk Highway, just north east of the town of Avoca, the homestead was once a solid two-storey sandstone building located on a hill looking out across the South Esk River. Sadly, these days it is nothing more than a crumbling ruin. During the day the site is tranquil and offers splendid views of the beautiful valley; however, at night, this serenity evaporates, and the place takes on a more sinister nature.

The building itself came about in the 1830s when an Englishman, who was granted a plot of land, travelled to Tasmania where he began constructing the sandstone building. Previously he had left the woman he loved back in England promising to come back and get her once the building was liveable. Now, with the walls finished and the house nearly complete, he travelled back to England only to find that, in his absence, she had married someone else. In despair, he returned to the homestead and committed suicide in the courtyard.

Not long after, new owners moved into the house along with their young daughter and her supposedly strict nanny who would threaten to throw the girl down the well if she didn't behave. The girl took the nanny's threats seriously and one day, after misbehaving, threw herself into the well. The nanny, upon seeing this tragedy, was guilt ridden and tried to retrieve the girl's body, but in doing so, fell in and died as well.

Sadly, this was not the last death the homestead would see as soon after a Scotsman by the name of Charles Peters was granted some nearby land and took over the lands containing the Garth homestead. As the building was in excellent condition he moved in with his family. Tragically though, in September 1840, Ann, his two-year-old daughter, died after her clothes caught on fire while watching one of the servants make jam over an oven. Her grave now sits a short distance from the ruins.

Charles Peters and his wife left the homestead in 1845 and built the historic Fingal Hotel. The homestead was given to his eldest son who leased it out; however, it suffered a great deal of damage from a fire. Another of the sons moved in and restored it to its past glory, but another devastating fire burnt it to the ground.

Although the building stayed in the Peters family until 1922, it remained empty since the start of the 1900s, and it was said that those who moved in never lasted long due to the incessant disembodied screams and moans, as well as sensations of being watched or touched. Some people consider that the remains of Garth Homestead are the most haunted ruins in Tasmania and it is said that cattle avoid the area.

Bona Vista, a once elegant homestead also in the Fingal Valley near Avoca, like Garth, has a ghostly reputation. Built for Simeon Lord, it is unusual in that under the ballroom in the East Wing are a number of dungeons where the convict servants were confined at night. In 1853, two convicts, Andrew Dalton and James Kelly, escaped and later returned intending to steal money and property. After tying up the other servants, they proceeded to smash the interior of the house in revenge; however, when four policemen arrived from Avoca, a shootout occurred. One of them, Constable Thomas Buckmaster, was tragically shot dead on the front step, and it is said that a bloodstain on the sandstone step cannot be removed, no matter how much it is scrubbed.

In 1862, the child of a German couple was murdered at the property, and in 1898, a young man is said to have been murdered on the woodheap. A ghost investigation team once decided to sleep in the cells below the ballroom but, after drifting off to sleep, were suddenly awoken by murmuring voices. Thinking nothing of it, they soon went back to sleep only to be wakend again by more voices. This time they decided to leave the ghosts to their cells and left rapidly.

Nearby, in the quaint town of Avoca, sits a family home on the banks of the St. Paul's River. Built in 1832 by convicts as a police barracks, it is now the home of Mark and Judi Money who, after moving in, found that they were not alone, with the couple experiencing a number of unexplained events, including knockings on the door, lights being turned on and off, and things being moved around the house. On one occasion Judi felt as if someone pushed her while outside in the garden recalling that it "was such a strong force, like a gust of wind."

Some 80 kilometres northwest of Avoca is Launceston, the second largest city in Tasmania after Hobart. Settled in March 1806, it is one of Australia's oldest cities and contains a large number of historic buildings, including the Royal Oak Hotel, which is on the corner of Tamar and Brisbane Streets and was first licenced in 1851 making it one of the oldest pubs in Tasmania. It has a reputation for being haunted, and many patrons and staff have complained of freezing spots in the hotel, something playing with their hair, and being prodded.

On occasions these interactions are somewhat more hostile as recently a girl on a tour was smashed in the back of the head with an empty wine bottle. Another ghost, known as Cyril, is apparently notorious for pinching people, especially men's buttocks.

Glenn Shipp of the Launceston City Ghost Tour suggests that Cyril "had a nasty accident one night. He went out to meet his loved one, but his horses were spooked, and the cart fell on top of him, and he was decapitated. Now his ghost appears in the basement of the hotel."

Nearly every place in Launceston seems to have a ghost story or two with the Princess Theatre supposedly haunted by the Lavender Lady, an actress who starred in *The Merry Widow* and slipped off the stage into the orchestra pit one evening, fatally breaking her neck. As well, the theatre is haunted by Max Oldaker, an actor who died in 1972 and known as the "ladies ghost" and who is generally witnessed by female patrons. He appears well dressed, often bowing and removing his top hat, or waving to the ladies. Apart from this apparition, heavy disembodied footsteps are often heard as is a piano.

Franklin House on the outskirts of Launceston is another place with a wealth of history and is currently preserved by the National Trust. Built by a former convict and later successful businessman Britton Jones, the building is notable for its use of red cedar. From 1842 until 1866, it operated as a private school, and in 1960, became the birthplace of the National Trust in Tasmania. Today, it survives with stables and gardens and is a regular tourist destination, as well as a beacon for ghost investigation groups.

National Trust volunteer Leonie Ingram is one of several staff members who have experienced strange incidents while working there, and during her time at the house has "noticed a few things move around and it could just be somebody else doing it, just enough to make me notice that it was a bit unusual that it kept happening."

Investigator Simon Coleman from the Tasmanian Ghost Hunting Society suggests that people "can be physically interacted with by the paranormal where they can be scratched or harmed, they can also hear screams and noises and shouts, and objects can move," and that "he has captured some light anomalies with still shots on door frames and things like that, which shouldn't happen."

Other strange occurrences within the walls of this grand historic building include a beam of light that seems to travel up and down the main staircase before disappearing. And apart from that, some believe that they have recorded the voice of a ghost, or ghosts, via EVP.

Electronic Voice Projection, or EVP, is the phenomena where sounds found on electronic recordings are interpreted as spirit voices that have been either unintentionally recorded or intentionally requested and recorded. Enthusiasts consider EVP to be a form of paranormal phenomena often found in recordings with static, white noise, or other background noise; however, psychologists regard EVP as a form of auditory pareidolia, that is, interpreting random sounds as voices in one's own language.

Whatever the case, EVP does sometimes turn up some remarkable results, and in the case of Franklin House this seems to be the case as, in the long reception room at the top of the stairs that was used as the boys' dormitory, groups have claimed to have picked up the names of both a female and male ghost.

When asked its name, the reply apparently came back with the name Will and although Franklin House coordinator Hilary Keeley wasn't too sure about the name at first, the more she listened to it, the more she thought it noting that a number of boys who attended the school were called Will including William Keeler Hawkes who was "buried in the old church yard over the road but maybe he had a conscience that didn't quite move on."

Another response Keeley heard after the question "If you are a female, what is your name?" was a female voice, and she recalls that the response was "a quite definite 'Rachael,'" and that the "only thing we can think of, because she wasn't someone who lived here, is she could have been a servant, or a maid."

Another response, this time to the question "Are you happy here?" turned up a male voice saying "no" and a "definite yes from a woman's voice."

Volunteer house guide Pam Attwood said she was upstairs once and heard a woman call her name recalling that: "I didn't feel anything creepy, but it was a really clear call." After hearing this, she apparently leaned over the banister and replied, but no one answered. Puzzled, she then went downstairs to ask who had called her, but no one had.

As haunted as the stately Franklin House is, other places in Launceton, including the old courts, are equally haunted. Indeed, at the Old Courts where a number of people were hung, one particular cell has a reputation for ghostly activity, even though the place is now a TAFE college. A woman, who was apparently quite violent in life, was found dead in her cell, and her spirit is said to remain, so much so that other prisoners would beg to be removed from that cell.

At O'Keefe's pub on George Street, established in 1836 as the Union Club Hotel, a ghost by the name of Sarah has been seen throughout the pub. As well, lights flicker, and a number of small things have been seen to move around. At Chalmers Church, now a private business, there is a figure of a woman that floats around the building, while a white mist has been observed floating around the steeple.

South of Launceston, along the Midland Highway, is Cleveland, and it is here that we find St. Andrews Inn, a former coaching inn built in 1835 and restored in 1972. And like most self-respecting mid-1800s pubs, it has its own resident ghost.

Lucy, as she is known, is reputed to waylay unwary men on the stairway and rob them of their clothes, folding them neatly and leaving them on the stairs. Whereas owner Greg Wallis has yet to see evidence of this, or the ghost itself, he has heard stories from visitors about ghostly encounters, as well as having heard "voices of people just gently speaking downstairs. It sounds like half a dozen people."

Other colonial places that boast ghostly stories include Rokeby House near Campbell Town and, in Derby, a small town north of Launceston, people have reported seeing a dozen or so ghosts in a room crying, all supposedly victims of a burst dam that killed fourteen people in April 1929.

Of course, it's not just buildings that seem to be haunted as, at Richmond, some 25 kilometres north of Hobart, the ghost of George Grover is supposed to haunt the heritage-listed arch bridge that crosses the Coal River. The oldest bridge still in use in Australia, its foundation stone was laid on 11 December 1823, and construction continued using convict labour until its completion in 1825. In 2005, the bridge was added to the Australian National Heritage List.

George Grover, who was employed as a gaoler and whose duties including flogging the prisoners, was thrown off the bridge by the convicts he had previously tortured during the construction of the bridge. Grover himself was transported to Van Diemen's Land in 1825 for stealing, although by 1829, he was employed as the flagellator at Richmond. His death in early March 1832 resulted in an inquest, which concluded that he had lain down whilst drunk and had fallen or was pushed off the bridge. His ghost is now said to appear on the bridge at certain times as a shadowy figure walking across or standing by the bridge staring at people. Some have reported his figure trying to clamber up the slippery sides of the bridge. The ghost is also said to sometimes become aggressive towards people and has even been known to follow people home and haunt their houses for a while.

In addition, the ghost of a large black and white dog, sometimes called "Grover's Dog," is also seen on the bridge. One lady reported it appearing at her side on several occasions as she walked the bridge at night. It would walk alongside her from one end to the other and then disappear as quickly as it had come, much like the "Devil Dogs" in English folklore. This entity is said to be benign, even friendly, and is usually only seen by women and children.

Phantom dogs, while rare in Australia, have been reported in the British Isles for centuries. Generally they are said to be a spectral being primarily mentioned in folklore and usually associated with the Devil. They are also known as devil dogs, black dogs, or in the case of Essex and Suffolk, Black Shuck.

The phantom dog is essentially a nocturnal spectre and its appearance is often regarded as a portent of death. In general, it is much larger than a physical dog and is quite often reported as having large, glowing eyes and a silent gait. According to some legends, to see it three times will result in the witness dying an untimely and suspicious death.

Given this, not all phantom dogs are bringers of death and bad luck, some being quite benevolent at times. Augustus Hare recalls a tale in his book *In My Solitary Life* about a man called Greenwood from Swancliffe in England who had to ride for a mile through a wood in darkness to reach his destination. As he entered the woods he was joined by a huge black dog that pattered alongside him until he emerged from the trees, where it promptly and mysteriously disappeared.

On the return journey he was again surprised when the dog reappeared and once again mysteriously disappeared. It emerged some years later that two prisoners about to be hanged confessed that they were going to rob and murder Greenwood that night in the wood, but the presence of a large black dog had stopped them. Is it possible that the Richmond Bridge dog acts in very much the same way, protecting and guiding people across this most haunted bridge?

As well as the ghostly dog and Grover, a well-dressed apparition wearing a straw bowler hat and carrying a cane has also been seen walking across the bridge. He is believed to be a convict who jumped to his death, although no one has any idea as to his identity.

Grover's ghost is also said to appear on occasion at the Richmond Gaol where he mercilessly flogged convicts. A small boy who visited the gaol with his grandmother once became distressed and when asked why pointed to an empty space and complained about "the horrible man with the bloody face."

Richard Davis, in his most excellent book *Great Australian Ghost Stories*, recounts a tale of a young curate who was a stranger to the area and encountered Grover's frightening spirit. Apparently, the curate was crossing the bridge when he heard a strange scratching sound from under the bridge. Pausing to listen, he then made out cries for help and so peered over the edge of the parapet. All he could see, however, was white swirling mist, and so he looked over the other side only to find a pair of large hairy hands gripping the stone parapet. Thinking that it was someone who had fallen off the bridge, he grabbed the wrists in an attempt to pull whoever it was up and out of danger.

To his utter surprise, the figure apparently weighed nothing and glided effortlessly upwards until the curate came face to face with a hideous figure. However, the face was not that of a human, well, not that of one alive anyway. The curate later described the face as that of a demon from hell, "living, yet not living."

The curate immediately let go of the figure and ran for his life. Looking back, he noticed the figure was still there, floating above the bridge laughing demonically. The curate then managed to reach a house before collapsing on the doorstep and was later taken to hospital in Hobart where he took many weeks to recover.

New Norfolk is a town on the Derwent River in the southeast of Tasmania roughly 32 kilometres northwest of Hobart on the Lyell Highway. It is a modern regional centre but still retains a great deal of its pioneering past, including Tasmania's oldest Anglican Church, St. Matthews, which was built in 1823 and one of Australia's oldest hotels, The Bush Inn. Numerous private homes from the 1820s have also survived. However, as old as these are, it is another building that we are interested in.

Willow Court is part of the former Royal Derwent Hospital and is the oldest mental hospital in Australia on its original site. Originally the New Norfolk Insane Asylum and later called Lachlan Park, it was built in 1827 to house mentally ill and mentally handicapped persons. In March 1968 it was officially called the Royal Derwent Hospital and, after being open for close to 170 years, finally closed in November 2000.

Willow Court, named thus because Lady Franklin planted a willow in the courtyard, has since become notorious for supposed supernatural incidents and ghost sightings since it shut down, so much so that, in February 2011, the Derwent Valley Council agreed to a paranormal investigation.

These days it is open to the public, and walking through the grounds and buildings is like stepping back in time. There is a public road and footpath that winds its way through Willow Court and Royal Derwent, so you are able to see most of the buildings. Some of the old wards are now in private ownership, have been reused, and are open to the public with one former ward holding an antique shop, while others have been converted into a motel and a restaurant. The old church is now a café, and the nurses' quarters is home to numerous boutique businesses. But even with all its apparent normality, strange things have been reported.

Staff at the former psychiatric hospital often reported being attacked by invisible hands, and even today, there are regular reports of doors slamming and electronic equipment refusing to work. It has also been described as having a particularly malevolent atmosphere as well as the occasional apparition as described by Nick Jarvis from the Australian Paranormal Investigation Unit, who stated that he was "driving down the main avenue here at Willow Court, I was driving over some of the speed humps and the headlights shone on a white apparition figure."

As recently as 2008, investigators from Research and Investigate the Paranormal Australia spent an afternoon and a night inside Willow Court filming for a television program and managed to record a number of strange occurrences, especially in Ward C of the building where, after setting up a video camera and recording equipment, they found the door out had mysteriously locked itself.

After phoning their project manager, Ian Brown, for assistance, producer Jo Jumper half-jokingly passed on Brown's message that the trapped ghost-hunters would soon get their "governor's pardon" when the keys arrived. Apparently, as soon as Jumper uttered those words, the door unlocked and swung open.

Later that same afternoon, three team members went to one of the cells to ask if there was any entity present that wanted to make itself known. Either by huge coincidence or not, at that precise moment the hinges of one of the cell doors from the corridor was heard to squeal before the door slammed closed. This was apparently recorded on audio tape. Brown said slamming doors were a regular occurrence, and that people "regularly report rooms suddenly feeling very cold, doors slamming, otherwise reliable cameras not functioning, and then starting again quite happily as soon as they leave."

Indeed, the photographer for the *Sunday Tasmanian* also had a strange experience while taking photographs of the place. After photographing the interior of Ward C, she checked her shots before leaving but found, to her dismay, that the camera's data card was completely blank.

And from the almost obligatory psychiatric hospital apparitions we shall journey to another, almost stereotypical site for hauntings, and as we have seen previously, a lighthouse can be a spooky as any building.

The Goose Island Lighthouse sits on Goose Island, a small rocky outcrop in Bass Strait to the north of the Tasmanian coast and west of Flinders Island. Built in 1846 by convict labour, the tower is constructed of masonry rubble and was originally known as the Goose Island Road Station since its construction was undertaken by the Department of Roads.

Due to its remote location, discipline was an ongoing problem, and in 1852, one of the lighthouse assistants was believed to have swum out to a ship sheltering by the island and asked the captain take him to Adelaide. Conditions on the island were also tough due to the early lighthouse keepers having to live in dilapidated workman's huts, although these were later upgraded and a new headkeeper's cottage constructed.

Interestingly, in 1857, the lighthouse was attacked by bushrangers with the *Melbourne Argus* reporting that: "The cutter *Lucy* reports that Goose Island Lighthouse was plundered by three bushrangers on 31st March, in a square-sterned boat. Left the island steering northwest, supposed bound for the Promontory. No further details have been found."

Later, in 1922, two assistant keepers were attempting to row their long boat back to the lighthouse jetty after fetching the mail from a ship and were caught in a strong current that dragged the boat out to sea. Despite a search that found the boat and the mailbag, the bodies were not discovered for several months. They were returned and subsequently buried in the small cemetery on the island. Also buried in the cemetery is a six-year-old boy, the son of one of the keepers who drowned while playing in the island's rock pools, getting caught by the incoming tide.

However, as fascinating as this is, it is a little known ghost story that we are interested in. Kathleen Stanley, in her book *Guiding Lights—Tasmania's Lighthouses and Lighthousemen*, described the following:

> Sometime in the 1920s, the lightkeeper taking the middle watch at Goose Island laid down *The Complete Works of William Shakespeare* and looked absently at the little dog sleeping near the door of the light room. The animal stirred uneasily and the hair on its back rose as it got to its feet and ran to the edge of the top landing, barking furiously. The man heard the outside door of the tower open and close and then the inner one. He heard footsteps on the iron stairs and wondered. If there were trouble on the station either of the other two men could have called him up on the whistle pipe, which connected the lighthouse to the attendants' houses. Well, he would soon know the score—the footsteps had reached half way up; he would go to the top of the stairs, quieten the dog and shout down to whomever it was. But as he stepped on to the landing the dog's bark subsided to a growl and the sound of the footsteps began to recede. In a moment, the doors opened and closed again and all was quiet. Puzzled, the lighthouse keeper returned to his upright chair and his book. His relief was soon due and would, no doubt, explain. But on being questioned, the relief denied all knowledge of the visit as did the Head Keeper the next morning. Somewhat humorously, he suggested that the man on the middle watch had nearly met a ghost. And there the matter rested. Until the next occasion.

Although humorously dismissed by the lighthouse keeper, several other keepers have reported the same experience, suggesting that, just possibly, this lighthouse, like the Albany Lighthouse, Green Cape, and the Rottnest Island Light Station, among others, is haunted.

Tasmania is an island sometimes thought cut adrift from mainland Australia and, therefore, somewhat behind the times. Although this is obviously not the case, especially in today's world of instant communication and technology, what of other, smaller islands, for instance, those that make up Australia's external territories?

CHAPTER NINE

External Territories

Of Haunted Convicts Isles

The Australian External Territories are a group of non-self-governing dependencies of Australia and, apart from Antarctica, they are made up entirely of innumerable small reefs, cays, and atolls, and several remote and diverse islands in the Pacific and Indian Oceans including Norfolk Island, the Coral Sea Islands, Ashmore and Cartier Islands, the Cocos Islands, Christmas Island, and Lord Howe Island.

And of these small, almost forgotten island paradises, Norfolk Island appears to hold a reputation for being the most haunted. Indeed, according to Richard Davies, author of the *Ghost Guide to Australia*, it is the most haunted place in Australia with more ghosts per square kilometres than any other state or territory.

Discovered by Captain James Cook in 1774, Norfolk Island was originally settled by East Polynesians. Later, it was colonised by Great Britain as a convict colony and a place "of the extremist punishment, short of death" for the worst convicts from New South Wales and Van Diemen's Land (Tasmania) until it was abandoned in 1855.

Norfolk Island, for all its island paradise looks, was a horrific place where torture, lashings, murders, rapes, and cruelty were commonplace. With such a violent past, it is no surprise that today the island is seen by many as one of the world's most haunted islands.

Located between Australia, New Zealand, and New Caledonia, the island sits roughly 1,400 kilometres east of mainland Australia. In 1856, permanent civilian residence on the island began when it was settled from Pitcairn, and in 1901, it became a part of the Commonwealth of Australia. As well, it is inextricably linked to one of the most famous naval mutinies of all time involving the HMS *Bounty* and Fletcher Christian.

The descendants of the mutiny had lived on Pitcairn Island with their Tahitian wives since 1789, but with a population nearing 200, the tiny island could no longer support the community. As a result, nearly 200 people made the five-week journey to Norfolk Island, arriving in June 1856.

Nan Smith, an author, who has lived on the island for over fifty years once had a frightening experience with what she believes to be a ghost. In 1948, when she was a teenager, she was asleep in her bed when, around midnight, she awoke to find a young woman in a long white dress with blonde hair parted in the middle who looked "desperately sad. She gave off a sort of an aura that made you feel very sad. I was so frightened or so terrified I couldn't move I couldn't even call out. I remember just staring at her for as long as I could until I had to blink, and then she just gradually faded away."

Since that first sighting, Smith has seen the young woman on many occasions; however, she has never moved and has never spoken and appears to be quite harmless. However, another entity that appears in another bedroom was anything but and she described it as something evil "emanating from that corner there seemed to be a great force like a blast. And it blew the door into the hall closed with a great bang. I couldn't understand what caused it. But it was there and it was horrifying (and) one of the nastiest things I have ever felt."

Warwick Moss, host of *The Extraordinary Norfolk Island Ghosts* and who we have previously spoken about in relation to the Devil's Pool on Babinda Creek in Queensland, believes the place to be haunted and managed to interview Horsch Anderson, who was in charge of Norfolk Island restoration projects at Kingston, the site of the old convict settlement.

On the program Anderson recalled that when they were restoring the barracks they came across a convict seat or settee, and managed to trace it to the 99th Regiment who were stationed on the island in the 1800s. The seat was stored in a locked room in the Royal engineers office in the middle of the old convict settlement. Every night it was checked and locked, and yet, every morning the seat had been moved even though there was absolutely no way anyone could have entered the room. Later, a psychic who visited the place suggested that it was the spirit of a teenage girl who was raped and then buried alive by the officers at the time. The activity ceased after the psychic's visit.

Likewise, Shane Quintal, who worked in the Norfolk cemetery recalled one morning as he was checking inscriptions on gravestones when he heard a voice say: "Oh, excuse me." Looking around he noticed a couple of women farther up the road and figured that it must have been them. Not thinking much about this slightly odd encounter, he moved to another gravestone and noted that: "While I was down there, I heard this 'oh excuse me,' you know it was quite stern. I said, 'Can you hold on a sec.' It was 'oh excuse me.' I looked around and there was no one in the cemetery."

Interestingly, the voices were those of two separate females and the graves that Quintal had been checking were both marked Quintal, his ancestors. Had he somehow upset his forebears who were now questioning what he was doing?

Quality Row, in Kingston, the island's capital, is the town's principal thoroughfare, a long, straight road of the island's oldest residential buildings, and also has a reputation for ghosts and hauntings. Shadowy entities have been seen there for over a century, and residents and visitors alike have reported disembodied footsteps, unearthly screams, poltergeist-like behaviour, and unexplained cold spots.

A resident of Quality Row, Maev Hitch, explained how she was sitting by the fire one night when she sensed something: "It was as if a hand touched me and pushed my face around, right around. It wasn't a painful feeling, but it was a fear, a heavy feeling." Later that night, she saw an apparition, a large luminous figure somewhat like a cobweb, "about eight feet long, across the doorway, right across the doorway. It wasn't like a spider's web or a web you see indoors. It was very, very thick." Apparently, it hovered there for ten seconds, then disappeared, and with it, so did the sense of dread.

Halfway along Quality Row is Government House, a stately old building that seems to reinforce the authority it once held on this small island. It too is believed to be a veritable hotbed of paranormal behaviour, so much so that, in the late 1800s, the wife of one of the administrators living in the building became so distraught at repeated poltergeist-like behaviour that she called a Catholic priest to exorcise the entity. However, according to Tim the Yowie Man in his book *Haunted and Mysterious Australia*, the exorcism wasn't too successful as the encounters simply continued.

As well, at Number 8 Quality Row, Michal Stephens, the official secretary from 2003 until 2006, experienced a number of strange happenings, which included "footsteps and thumps on the floorboards in the main house every couple of months," and that it was "very unnerving in the annex at particular times. One night I felt air rush past my face as if someone was walking past, then a small flag above my desk shook, despite the fact that the windows were closed and it was a still night."

Oddly enough for a place like Norfolk Island, there is a legend of a phantom hitchhiker—something we have seen exists pretty much all over the world, including Lake George in New South Wales. However, unlike the usual hitchhiker stories, this one involves a feeling that someone else is in the car with the driver, and only disappears when the vehicle reaches a certain point, Middlegate, in the centre of the island. No one has any idea who this phantom passenger could be.

Locals believe spirits of the dead still roam the island, and the island's most famous resident, Colleen McCullough, a former sceptic, has no doubt the place is haunted. As she recalled on a television interview: "I had never seen or ever thought to see a ghost. When I came to Norfolk Island I discovered that all the Pitcairners believe in ghosts."

McCullough, the celebrated author of *The Thornbirds* and numerous other novels, is known as a no-nonsense sort of person who is not afraid to speak her mind, which makes her experiences all the more interesting, especially when she encountered a visitor she could feel but not see: "Somebody sat on the end of my bed. I was immersed in what I was doing and somebody sort of went plonk on the bed and I looked up and was thinking 'oh shit, what's going on' and there was nobody there." And she added: "The only thing he ever did until I married was sit on the end of the bed." Interestingly, after McCullough married, the entity disappeared, so she believes it was a man, a gentleman at that.

241

Six months after her wedding, McCullough was standing in her kitchen at 3:00 a.m. making a sandwich when "someone squeezed past me behind and when they squeezed past me they put their hands around my waist or on my waist and my feeling was warm and spontaneous, but there was nobody there."

Later, in the early hours of morning, she noticed that the lights in her studio were on and upon going to inspect it, noticed in shadows a man in a red shirt. Thinking it was a prowler, McCullough lunged at the figure, which moved back into the shadows. McCullough recalled that she "realised that he didn't move the way a person moves," and when she looked around, there was nobody there.

Apart from that, she also believes that a poltergeist resides in one specific room of her house, the Conservatory, and when there is a camera man there to take her photograph, interferes with the flashes on their cameras.

But it should not be a surprise that this tiny, remote settlement is so haunted given the names of so many places on the island, names such as Ghost Corner, Bloody Bridge, Slaughter Bay, and Gallows Gate. Indeed, just reading these names gives an idea of what the place must have been like.

But from one island to another, this time to the stunningly beautiful Lord Howe Island, a volcanic remnant in the Tasman Sea between Australia and New Zealand roughly 600 kilometres east of Port Macquarie and about 900 kilometres from Norfolk Island. The island itself is only small and harbours a tiny population, although it does have an airstrip.

Dani Rourke, who runs Pinetree Lodge with her husband, believes the resort is haunted by the ghost of an old whaler, Captain Thomas Nichols, who also happens to be her great-great-grandfather.

Although there was never a whaling station on Lord Howe Island, during the 1840s and 1850s, it was a popular stop for whaling ships due to its abundance of fresh water and food. Captain Nichols apparently arrived on Lord Howe in 1862, where he met the sixteen-year-old Mary Andrews, one of the first children born on the island. Soon after, accompanied by Mary's mother, they sailed to Norfolk Island to be married. Later, the couple returned to Lord Howe Island and over the next twenty years had ten children.

Captain Nichols is buried in the Pinetrees Cemetery, which is close to the Pinetrees staff accommodation, an old building with four bedrooms and an outside toilet known as "Anchorage." It is believed to be haunted by the ghost of the captain, and staff and visitors have often reported mysterious knocks on the windows during the night, footsteps, spooky laughter, doors being flung open by an icy breeze, and once a young girl was awoken by the frightening sensation of an invisible entity trying to suffocate her.

Although "Anchorage" was demolished in 2010 and new accommodation was built, the ghost of Captain Nicholls still appears, with one of the chefs once reporting that he walked out of his room one morning to find a strange arrangement of sticks in the shape of arrows that pointed to the cemetery. As no one had placed the sticks there, it was assumed that Nichols was still around.

Apart from this, he seems to enjoy flicking lights on and off and starting coffee machines when no one is around. Among the guests, there have also been a few frightened teenagers insisting that they sleep in the same room as their parents.

Rourke's only firsthand experience with the ghost of Captain Nicholls was just before she was married and, after a few drinks, had gone with some friends to Pinetrees for dinner. As they were the last to leave, they locked up; however, the folding doors on the Boatshed are old and the tracks don't work very well. The group managed to close and lock the doors when they began to shake violently as if someone was on the other side. They shouted out to whoever it was telling them to come around to a side door but received no reply. Then they heard footsteps on the deck and a loud knocking. Now completely puzzled, Rourke opened a side door only to find that there was no one there.

Another ghostly legend coming from this beautiful but tragic island is that of Black Billy, a black American who lived on the island in the mid-1800s and who disappeared without a trace while pig hunting with a friend by the name of Williams.

Pigs were a problem on the island, although they did provide a good food source, so Black Billy and Williams decided to go pig hunting. Williams later returned but there was no sign of Black Billy, with Williams explaining that they had become separated in the bush. Although foul play was suspected, nothing could be proven, and Williams soon left the island.

Since that day, the ghost of Black Billy has appeared on numerous occasions, generally at a place called Far Flats. Indeed, in the early 1900s, a group of people were camped at the flats one night when, just as the fire was dying out, a man in a dark coat walked out of the gloom, bent down, and lit a pipe. One of the group yelled out to the figure, but it ignored him and simply vanished.

Meanwhile, across the continent, nearly 6,000 kilometres to the northwest of Lord Howe Island is Christmas Island, a small, isolated island in the Indian Ocean, which is a remarkable 2,600 kilometres from Perth and over 2,700 kilometres from Darwin. It is, by anyone's standards, seriously remote.

Named Christmas Island because it was discovered on Christmas Day 1643, it has a population of just over 2,000 people mainly of Chinese-Australian descent and is known for its unique flora and fauna due to geographic isolation and minimal human disturbance, including red crabs who march across the island every year. It is also considered haunted, especially by the Chinese-Australian population who believe that, due to its remote location, many people who have died on the island have done so without any later blessing from their loved ones or family and so remain in some sort of limbo, a shady half world between life and death.

The Hungry Ghost Festival, which is held every fourteenth day of the seventh lunar month is held to appease the ghosts unleashed from hell. This celebration by the Chinese population, descendants of coolies, is made to keep the spirits of ancestors content and reluctant to enter homes, and the population will stay indoors at night, fearful the gates of hell are open for those who venture out.

Interestingly, in 2012, a member of a seventy-two strong contingent of Australian Federal Police on the island swore to colleagues he had seen the apparition of a "lady in white" floating among the Islamic and Chinese graves bordering a main road out of the island's township. And while this may have been laughed at by other AFP members, many have reported the same vision.

Indeed, at the Christian Cemetery people have reported seeing the ghost of a woman with European features wearing a long flowing white dress from around the 1920s or 1930s. It is thought that she is the wife of a former phosphate minor, and her spirit is said to sometimes wander along the road that runs by the cemetery as if waiting for someone.

Tim the Yowie Man, in his book *Haunted and Mysterious Australia* tells the tale of a bus driver who, in the early '90s "actually stopped for a lady thinking she wanted a lift to a nearby hotel. He opened the automatic door and let her board the otherwise empty bus. He drove straight to the hotel, but when he pulled up to let her off, she had vanished into thin air."

This story very much parallels a story we previously examined, this time in Kalamunda where the legend states that a bus driver travelling down Kalamunda Road towards Great Eastern Highway stopped to pick up an elderly lady who was waiting at the bus stop outside the cemetery. She got on and sat in the front row of seats and for a couple of minutes and spoke to the driver. The conversation then stopped and the bus driver thought nothing of it and continued to drive. However, the next time he looked behind him, the woman had disappeared.

As such we must ask, is this simply an urban legend, very much similar to the tales of ghostly hitchhikers that haunt lonely rural roads, or is this the same apparition seen by the policeman floating among the Islamic and Chinese graves on the island? And who is to say as it has the hallmarks of both.

Whatever the case, it seems that Australia's External Territories, much like the mainland, is just as haunted as any place in the world and, given the convict history of most of these places, this is far from surprising.

A Final Word from the Author

As I previously suggested when examining the Babinda Creek mystery, I have made a conscious effort to stay away from Indigenous reports of ghostly activities, mainly as a sign of respect and because I cannot claim to have anything but a rudimentary understanding of these societal norms and beliefs. Having said this, I acknowledge that there exists a great wealth and diversity of Indigenous traditional culture that contains many elements of the supernatural and paranormal. However, this is not for me to examine.

I should also apologise for any words I may have used that could be deemed offensive in any way. In general, one finds, when researching old Australian folklore, that terms and phrases we may find offensive today were commonplace then and to not use these terms and phrases would be to take away from the very essence of the story. As such terms like "Chinaman," "Coolie,"' or "Blackfellow"—or whatever have remained in the text—whereas I would not use them in any other context.

As well, although I do believe in ghosts and paranormal activity in general, I am sceptical about most reports and truly feel that most supernatural or paranormal experiences can be logically explained. Having said that, in this book I have simply presented the stories as I have heard or read them, and so one needs to take it with a grain of salt, even though it has been written in good faith.

One must also remember that, when in pursuit of ghosts and so-called denizens of the night, that many of the places described are in fact private property and to intrude upon this is trespassing. True, there are many public buildings mentioned as well as hotels, museums, and pubs, and these can be easily visited. Having said this, just because a place is mentioned in this book does not necessarily mean that the people mentioned believe in ghosts or even want to discuss the subject. As such, one needs to be sensitive in these matters.

And, as anything to do with ghosts is fraught, especially when trying to describe exactly what they are and why they exist, I shall leave you instead with this thought by Paul F. Eno from his book *Faces at the Window*:

> There are an infinite number of universes existing side by side and through which our consciousnesses constantly pass. In these universes, all possibilities exist. You are alive in some, long dead in others, and never existed in still others. Many of our "ghosts" could indeed be visions of people going about their business in a parallel universe or another time—or both."

JG Montgomery

Acknowledgements

Thanks to the following for contributing to this book; Kirsten Willcox, Tim the Yowie Man, Steve Salliard, Kate Garkut, Nic Montgomery, Michael Montgomery, Dan Backhouse, Elyse Herrald-Woods, Stuart McCallum, Marianne Hope, Fiona Levings, and Mark Hallam.

Also a huge vote of thanks to Dinah Roseberry for her direction and editing and to Simon Mead who assisted with the title.

Bibliography and Further Reading

Adoranti, K. & David R. "A Glimpse into Haunted Buildings in Suburban Melbourne." *Herald Sun*, 30 October 2014.

Andrews, J. "Black Rock House Hosts Ghost Tours." *Herald Sun*, 3 June 2014.

Aldersey, J. "Inside Fortuna Villa." *Bendigo Advertiser*, 26 February 2015.

Argoon, A. "The Ghost of Mark 'Chopper' Read is Haunting Pentridge Prison." *Herald Sun*, 26 June 2014.

"Australia's top 10 haunted haunts." *Australian Woman's Weekly,* 27 October 2010.

Banks, K. "Ghost Busters Go High Tech in Pub." *Queensland Times*, 10 August 2012.

Beatty, B. *A Treasury of Australian Folk Tales and Traditions.* Sydney: Uri Smith, 1960.

Bell, G. *Historic Pubs Around Sydney.* Sydney: Ginninderra Press, 2007.

Beniot, L. "Ghost Hunter Sees the Light After Dying Twice." *Morning Bulletin*, 27 July 2103.

"Brisbane City Hall 'Haunted by Ghosts'." *Courier Mail*, 23 November 2008.

Budd, D. "Haunted Richmond Bridge in Tasmania." *Examiner*, 5 August 2012.

Carey, A. "*The Iconic Annandale Abbey Is in the Midst of a Makeover to Restore Its Former Glory.*" *Daily Telegraph*, 22 October 2013.

Caines, K. "Spirit Investigators Take Residents on Haunted Tour of Campbelltown to Seek Ghost of Fred Fisher." *Macarthur Chronicles*, October 2014.

Calligeros, M., D. Sankey, and A. Wight. "Police Find Body of Man Drowned at Devil's Pool." *Brisbane Times,* 2 December 2008.

Campion, V. "Picton Haunted Hunters Are Ghost Busted." *Daily Telegraph*, 5 January 2011.

Carrodus, H. and L. Sharp. "Ghost Hunters and Unexplained Activities." *Bendigo Advertiser*, 30 August 2014.

Carswell, A. "US Ghostbuster Tells of the 'Most Disturbing Thing I've Ever Seen' and It Was Down Under.*" Daily Telegraph*, 2 February 2014.

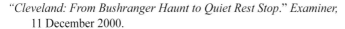

"Cleveland: From Bushranger Haunt to Quiet Rest Stop." Examiner,
11 December 2000.

Connellan, M. "Historic Hero of Waterloo Pub at the Rocks Celebrates 170th
Birthday." *Daily Telegraph*, 31 August 2013.

"Cue." Sydney Morning Herald, 8 February 2004.

Dadson, M. "There's Definitely Something Here." *Examiner*, 21 June 2013.

Dale, A. *"Children's 'Ghosts' Haunt Picton Cemetery." Daily Telegraph*,
21 January 2010.

Dale, A. *"The Haunting of Picton—Terrifying Truth or Ghost Busted?" Daily
Telegraph*, 22 January 2010.

Dardanis, A. "History, a Ghost and 85 Years of Stories Haunt Brisbane Arcade."
Courier Mail, 29 March 2009.

Davis, R. *Great Australian Ghost Stories*. Sydney: Harper Collins, 2012.

Dean, S. "Mutilated Cats in the Kitchen, a Mother Wailing for her Lost Child and the
Ghosts of the Insane: A Chilling Tour of Australia's Spookiest Halloween Haunts."
Daily Mail, 31 October 2014.

Dobbin, M. "Hidden Places' Open Day." *Sydney Morning Herald*, 15 June 2009.

Dovey, C. "No TV, No Internet . . . No Worries on Lord Howe Island." *Courier Mail*,
22 June 2014.

Eno, P. F. *Faces at the Window*. RI: New River Press, 1998.

Fairley, J. and S. Welfare. *Arthur C Clarke's Mysterious World*. UK: Book Club
Associates, 1981.

Felix, R. *What Is a Ghost?* Derbyshire: Felix Films Ltd., 2009.

Fodor, N. *On the Trail of the Poltergeist.* NY: Citadel Press, 1958.

Gillies, F. "The Magic Touch in Inner Sydney." *Daily Telegraph,* 24 May 2009.

Grace, L. "It's Halloween, So Here Are Some of South Australia's Scariest Places."
Advertiser, 31 October 2013.

Grace, L. "South Australia's X-Files: Part 4—Kapunda's Haunted History; the Stuart
Pearce Mystery." *Advertiser*, date unknown.

Goldman, J. *The X-Files Book of the Unexplained*. London: It Books, 1995.

Gould, J. "Ambos Fear Ghost of Old Chief." *Queensland Times,* 12 April 2012.

Green, A. *Ghosts of Today*. London: Kaye & Ward, 1980.

Guiley, R. E. *Harper's Encyclopedia of Mystical & Paranormal Experience.*
San Francisco: Harper, 1991.

Hamilton, J. "Can Man Calls Time on Police." *Herald Sun*, 27 June 2011.

Hauck, W. D. *The International Directory of Haunted Places: Ghostly Abodes, Sacred
Sites and Other Supernatural Locations*. New York: Penguin Books, 2000.

"Haunting: Australia' in Barossa and Kapunda." Barossa Herald, 13 March 2014.

Henderson, F. "Australia's Most Haunted Hotel." *Courier*, 9 August 2103.

Hoffman, T. "Larundel's $500m Transformation from Psychiatric Hospital to Modern
Residential Hub." *Herald Sun,* 16 September 2014.

"Horny Ghost Called Kevin Spooks Wife." *Daily Telegraph*, 30 September 2010.

Howard-Wright, M. *Eyewitness. Australian Ghosts*. Western Australian: Artlook, 1980.

House, A. "*Australia's Most Haunted Hotels*." *Daily Telegraph*, 27 October 2014.

Hudson, S. "Western Australia's New Norcia a Self-Sufficient Monastic Town Which Opens Its Heart to All." *Weekly Times*, 22 April 2014.

Huett, S. *Only in Tasmania*. Deloraine: Striped Wolf Publishing, 2012.

Jones, G. "*Ghosts Roaming Haunted Parliament House*." *Daily Telegraph*, 18 August 2009.

Lawless, A. "Fright Night Bites Deep in WA." *Sunday Times Perth Now*, 31 October 2013.

Lee, S. "'Ghost' of Mark 'Chopper' Read Abuses Group of Lawyers Touring Pentridge Prison, Screaming 'Get Out, Get Out' from His Old Cell." *Daily Mail*, 27 June 2014.

Lynch, R. " 'Bluestone Betty' Haunts Cemetery." *Queensland Times*, 24 December 2011.

Machen, M. "Veil Lifted on Chalmers Church's Renaissance." *Examiner*, 17 October 2014.

Martain, T. "*Locked Inside Ward C WILLOW COURT*." *Sunday Tasmanian*, 22 June 2008.

Masanauskas, J. "Bodies to Stay in Queen Victoria Market Plan." *Herald Sun*, 2 February 2013.

Mather, A. "Saturday Soapbox: Much to Learn from Tassie's Ghosts." *Mercury*, 27 December 2014.

McColgan, John. *Southern Highlands Story*. Glebe: Fast Books, 1995.

McCulloch J., and A. Simmons. *Ghosts of Port Arthur* (Revised Edition) Tasmania: AD Simmons, 1995.

Michael S. "Ghost Hunters Capture Eerie Image of Young Girl Kneeling on the Floor of an Asylum." *Daily Mail* (Australia), 16 March 2015.

Michell J. and B. Rickard. *Unexplained Phenomena*. London: Rough Guides Ltd., 2000.

Mills M. "Haunting Australia's Ghost Hunters Make Spooky Connections at Old Geelong Gaol." *Geelong Advertiser*, 20 February 2015.

Montgomery, J. G. *A Case for Ghosts*. Adelaide: Ginninderra Press, 2012.

Montgomery, J. G. *WYRD*. Devon: CFZ Publications, 2014.

Mooney, J. "Mischievous Spirit in WA Ghost Story?" *WA News*, 10 May 2013.

Nash, J. "Child Killer Ernest Austin Still Haunts Notorious Aussie Jail More Than a Century Later." *Herald Sun*, 30 May 2104.

Neal, M. and J. McLaren. "Ghost Files: Elephant Bridge Hotel." *Standard*, 16 October 2008.

NT News. "Forget Mulder and Scully—The *NT News*' top 8 Spooky X-Files Stories." 16 July 2104.

O'Malley, N. *"Historic Berrima Jail Has Finally Served Its Time."* *Sydney Morning Herald*, 22 October 2011.

Orr, A. "More Than Ghosts in This Haunted House." *WA News,* 13 May 2013.

Pedler, C. "Your Guides to Ghosts: Video, Photos." *Bendigo Advertiser*, 2 August 2014.

Petrinec, M. "Things That Go Bump in the Night." *Morning Bulletin*, 4 November 2005.

Pinkney, J. *Haunted: The Book of Australia's Ghosts*. Rowville: Five Mile Press, 2005.

Pinkney, J. *The Ultimate Book of Unsolved Mysteries*. Rowville: Five Mile Press, 2009.

"Raising the Spectre." *The Age*, 31 October 2010.

Randell, A. *"Is the Ghost of the House In?"* *Examiner*, 16 July 2005.

Reed, A. W. *Myths and Legends of Australia*. Sydney: AH & AW Reed, 1965.

Richardson, Lance. "A Spook in the House." *Traveller*, December 2010.

Righi, B. *Ghosts, Apparitions and Poltergeists. An Exploration of the Supernatural through History*. Woodbury: Llewellyn Publications, 2008.

Scanlon, M. "Fright Night." *Newcastle Herald*, 8 October 2011.

Scanlon, M. "Dark Tales from the Big House on the Hill." *Newcastle Herald,* 2 October 2004.

Seal, G. *Great Australian Stories. Legends, Yarns and Tall Stories*. Australia: Allen & Unwin, 2009.

"Secrets of the Past Finally Unlocked at Aradale Mental Hospital." *Wimmera Mail-Times*, 30 April 2009.

Smyth, T. *"Whistling Past the Courthouse."* *Sydney Morning Herald*, 10 July 2005.

Sparvell, R. "The Five Spookiest Places in Perth to Spend Halloween." *WA News*, 30 October 2014.

Spence, J. and A. *The Ghost Handbook*. London: Macmillan, 1998.

Speight, J. "Maitland Gaol—Most Haunted Site." *Newcastle Herald*, 18 January 2013.

Stead-Churchill, L. "Houses with Spirit." *bmag*, 20 October 2013.

Sweeney, K. "More Feature: Into the Dark." *Bendigo Advertiser*, 13 June 2011.

Tabori, P. *Harry Price—Ghost Hunter*. London: Sphere Books, 1974.

Tam, A. "Who Wants to See a Ghost Tonight? On the Hunt for Paranormal Activity at the Quarantine Station." *Daily Telegraph,* 5 August 2014.

Tatnell, P. "Sydney Ghost Hunter Offers to Investigate Kevin the Randy Poltergeist." *Sydney Morning Herald,* 30 September 2010.

Tim the Yowie Man. *Haunted and Mysterious Australia*. Sydney: New Holland, 2006.

Tim the Yowie Man. *In the Spirit of Banjo*. Canberra: Pendragon Publishing, 2014.

Tim the Yowie Man. *"Wild Green Cape Captivates."* *Sydney Morning Herald*, 9 March 2014.

Tim the Yowie Man. *"Hall Gang Re-enactment in Collector for 150th Anniversary."* *Canberra Times*, 16 January 2015.

Tim the Yowie Man. "Is Burnima Near Canberra the Most Haunted House in Australia?" *Canberra Times*, 30 October 2015.

Thackwray, L. "If It's Not Their Child . . . Then Whose Is It? Woman Claims Mysterious 'Ghost Baby' Photobombed Family Portrait." *Daily Mail,* 11 March 2015.

"The Devil's Pool Legend: Why It Has Claimed So Many Lives." *Brisbane Times,* 1 December 2008.

Thompson, C and K. Saarikko. *Macabre Canberra*. (First Edition). Canberra: self-published, 2008.

Thompson, S. "Supernatural History of Menangle House on Show with Ghost Tours." *Daily Telegraph* 7, June 2014.

Thomson, B. "Bendigo Fortuna's New Life Begins as Paul Banks Settles Property." *Bendigo Advertiser*, 27 June 2013.

"Toodyay and Northam shine." *Echo News*, 3 January 2014.

Toy, M. "Melbourne's Creepiest Ghost Stories and Spookiest Locations Revealed." *Herald Sun,* 28 October 2014.

Toy, M. "Victorian Psychiatric Patients' Grim Fate in Hellish 1800s Hospitals." *Herald Sun*, 10 December 2014.

Toy, M. "It Happened to a Mate of a Mate of Mine: Our City's Myths Tested." *Herald Sun*, 17 July 2014.

Tucker, A. "Port Dock Hotel Co-owner Shares His Stories of 13 Years at Todd St. Port Adelaide." *Advertiser*, 13 December 2012.

Underwood, P. *Nights in Haunted Houses*. London: Headline, 1994.

Walsh, L. "Best of Sunday: Ghost Stories." *Advertiser*, 2 January 2011.

Wearne, P. "Leederville Pub Shuts for Revamp." *West Australian*, 30 January 2014.

Webb, C. "Old Melbourne Gaol Gives Up Ghosts of Children Past." *Sydney Morning Herald*, 23 December 2009.

Weier, B. "Ipswich a Haven for Ghosts." *Queensland Times,* 12 May 2010.

Wellfare, J. "Alone in the Dark." *Air Force,* the official newspaper of the Royal Australian Air Force. Vol. 47, April 2005.

Wilson, I. *In Search of Ghosts*. London: Headline, 1995.

Wright, T. "The Ghost Ships That Creep Across the Blue." *Sydney Morning Herald*, 3 July 2012.

Websites

http://archiver.rootsweb.ancestry.com
http://blog.library.ipswich.qld.gov.au
http://bmag.com.au/your-brisbane
http://darkerbrisbane.weebly.com
http://eidolonparanormal.blogspot.com.au
http://exhibitions.slv.vic.gov.au
http://forums.atomicmpc.com.au
http://hauntedcue.blogspot.com.au
http://hauntedtoodyay.blogspot.com.au
http://hauntsofbrisbane.blogspot.com.au

http://john.curtin.edu.au/folklore
http://karinamachado.com
http://news.bbc.co.uk
http://oakabella.blogspot.com.au
http://paranormal.about.com
http://rggs.qld.edu.au
http://soulsearchers.spheresoflight.com.au
http://sydneyforeveryone.com.au
http://tasmaniaforeveryone.com
http://thehistorygirl.blogspot.com.au
http://theparanormal.ca
http://the-riotact.com
http://wadjemup.blogspot.com.au
http://waterfallgully.com.au
http://weirdaustralia.com
http://what-when-how.com/haunted-places
https://findery.com/MadameSpooky
www.abc.net.au
www.adelaidegaolheritage.com.au
www.aussieghosts.com
www.aussieghosts.com
www.aww.com.au
www.bendigotourism.com
www.blackrockhouse.org.au
www.britannica.com
www.castleofspirits.com
www.chapelhill.homeip.net
www.coachandhorseshotel.com
www.coomaexpress.com.au
www.dailytelegraph.com.au
www.davesact.com
www.diggerhistory.info
www.eidolonparanormal.net
www.environment.sa.gov.au/adelaidegaol
www.ghosthuntersofaustralia.com.au
www.ghoststories.com.au
www.ghoststudy.com

www.ghostweb.com
www.haunted.com.au
www.hauntedaustralia.com
www.heraldsun.com.au
www.historicalbany.com.au
www.ipswich.qld.gov.au
www.jackwongsue.com
www.kalamundahotel.com.au
www.lighthouses.org.au/
www.lonelyplanet.com
www.macdonnellranges.com
www.montecristo.com.au
www.nationaltrust.org.au
www.nationaltrust.org.au/tas
www.news.com.au
www.paranormal.com.au
www.paranormalaustralia.com
www.paranormalfieldinvestigators.com
www.quarantinestation.com.au
www.redbubble.com
www.rottnestisland.com
www.royalhotelharrisville.com.au
www.smh.com.au
www.theweeklyreview.com.au/geelong
www.thisishorror.co.uk
www.traveller.com.au
www.travellingtype.com
www.trueghosttales.com
www.urbanghostsmedia.com
www.wanowandthen.com
www.weekendnotes.com
www.westsydneyparanormal.org
www.wikipedia.org

Every effort has been made to ensure all source material is listed. However, it is possible that I have missed some references, and if this is so, then I apologise to the original author or publication.

Places Index

JG Montgomery is a forty-something-year-old public servant. He was born in Cornwall in the United Kingdom, the son of an Australian Air Force officer, and has lived in an amazing number of places as well as attended an incredible amount of schools.

He is a bass player, guitarist, vocalist, and song writer in a mod pop band and has served in both the Australian Army Reserve and Australian Air Force. He has university degrees in cultural heritage and teaching and was once a cricket coach. He is also a decorated state emergency service volunteer.

Haunted Australia: Ghosts of the Great Southern Land is his sixth book. He is also the author of *A Case for Ghosts* (Ginninderra Press, 2012), the illustrated children's book *The Oomee Mau Mau* (Willow Moon, 2012), *WYRD-A Journey into the Beliefs and Philosophies of the Known and Unknown* (CFZ Press, 2014), *Meditations in Orange* (Pendragon Publishing & Design, 2014) and *Summer to Summer* (Pendragon Publishing & Design, 2016).

JG also contributed and edited poetry in *Capital Reflections* (Pendragon Publishing & Design, 2014)

He lives in Canberra, Australia, with his partner Kirsten, two cats, a short black dog, six ducks, and a lot of goldfish.